I have campaigned for over fifteen years for the government to curb aspects of the operation of Sharia courts in this country. I am deeply concerned by the knowledge that many women and girls in this country are suffering from gender discrimination often associated with polygamy and domestic violence.

We are fortunate to live in a democracy which enshrines the principle of equality before the law and is committed to the promotion of gender equality. Yet, I have sat with oppressed and abused women from communities which allow discrimination, here in this country, and wept with them as they told their stories. Tim Dieppe and Christian Concern have supported my work in this area for many years and they continue to highlight the many concerning issues that we see, of which aspects of the treatment of women in Sharia courts are but one example.

I welcome this book in which Tim helpfully informs us about the increasing influence of Islamism in this country. The vast majority of Muslims are peace-loving and law-abiding citizens of this country. Many, however, are also victims of those who would seek to enforce Sharia law on their communities, and even across the nation. Anyone concerned about the future of this nation and about preserving the Christian freedoms that our forefathers passed down to us should read this important book.

The Right Honourable The Baroness Cox of Queensbury

As Christians, we desire to foster compassionate, gospel-focused relationships with people of all faiths. Therefore, we must recognise that God's common grace means that each culture has commendable aspects. However, we must also hold each religion and ideology up to the light of Scripture. By fairly representing and analysing the core teachings of Islam, Tim has provided valuable resources in these articles that are accurate, balanced, and well-informed, and will equip the reader to better understand the key doctrines of Islam.

Graham Nicholls, *Director of Affinity*

The growth of Islam in the UK raises tremendous cultural, political, and spiritual challenges. In *The Challenge of Islam*, Tim Dieppe tackles all three issues — helping Christians to then respond with conviction, truth, and compassion. With Islam, arguably the greatest missional challenge — and opportunity — facing the UK church in the decade(s) to come, this book is a superb resource, both for church leaders and for Christians who have Muslim friends, neighbours, or classmates.

Dr Andy Bannister, *Director of Solas, Author of: 'Do Christians and Muslims Worship the Same God?'*

This book written by Tim Dieppe is a wake-up call, well written and detailing the truth about Islam. It demonstrates the disturbing fact that the Church is asleep and even encouraging and nurturing the very monster which will destroy it. Islam embodies the spirit of Antichrist prophesied in the Bible that threatens the whole world. Many Christians are deceived into thinking, as the Pope said in his prayer video released in January 2016, that all religions lead to the same God. The god Mahommed chose to subjugate the nations he fought and conquered, was one of many Egyptian gods worshipped at that time, and one whose symbol is still today the crescent moon. Our God is the 'Creator of Heaven and earth', whose symbol is an empty cross, who demonstrated His love for us by sending His Son to die to save us from our sins including the worship of Allah and all other false gods. This book must urgently be read by politicians as well as Christians.

Rev. David Hathaway DD, *International Evangelist*

From Sharia-compliant banking to antisemitism and threats to free speech, Islam now represents a major challenge to the historic common law tradition and social order of British society. Years of warning about the imminent dangers of Islamisation in the West have gone largely unheeded by the political class, bringing us to a moment of crisis and a potential tipping point. Tim Dieppe has had his finger on the pulse of these changes and exigencies for many years, researching, writing and speaking fearlessly on the subject as a modern cultural prophet. In this important volume, he applies his intellectual acumen to the very real threat to our historic way of life in these islands if Islamisation is left unchecked. We ignore his warning at our peril. A must read for anyone serious about the preservation of our hard-won liberties.

Rev. Dr Joseph Boot, *Founder and President of the Ezra Institute*

THE CHALLENGE OF ISLAM
Understanding and responding to Islam's increasing influence in the UK

THE CHALLENGE OF ISLAM
Understanding and responding to Islam's increasing influence in the UK

Tim Dieppe

Wilberforce Publications
London

Copyright © 2025 Tim Dieppe

The moral right of the authors under the
Copyright, Designs and Patents Act 1988 has been asserted.

All rights reserved.

Published in Great Britain in 2025 by
Wilberforce Publications Limited
70 Wimpole Street, London W1G 8AX

Wilberforce Publications Limited is a wholly owned subsidiary of Christian Concern. No part of this publication may be reproduced or transmitted in any form or by any means, electronic or mechanical, including photocopy, recording or any information storage and retrieval system, without prior permission in writing from the publisher.

Unless otherwise noted, all Scripture quotations are from The ESV® Bible (The Holy Bible, English Standard Version®), © 2001 by Crossway, a publishing ministry of Good News Publishers. Used by permission. All rights reserved.
https://www.esv.org/resources/esv-global-study-bible/copyright-page/

ISBN 978-1-9161211-8-8

Printed in Great Britain by Imprint Digital, Exeter

"The fact that in Mohammedan law every woman must belong to some man as his absolute property – either as a child, a wife, or a concubine – must delay the final extinction of slavery until the faith of Islam has ceased to be a great power among men. Thousands become the brave and loyal soldiers of the faith: all know how to die but the influence of the religion paralyses the social development of those who follow it. No stronger retrograde force exists in the world. Far from being moribund, Mohammedanism is a militant and proselytizing faith. It has already spread throughout Central Africa, raising fearless warriors at every step; and were it not that Christianity is sheltered in the strong arms of science, the science against which it had vainly struggled, the civilisation of modern Europe might fall, as fell the civilisation of ancient Rome."

Winston Churchill, *The River War, 1899*

"Millions of modern people ... have forgotten all about Islam. They have never come in contact with it. They take for granted that it is decaying, and that, anyway, it is just a foreign religion which will not concern them. It is, as a fact, the most formidable and persistent enemy which our civilization has had, and may at any moment become as large a menace in the future as it has been in the past...

...The final fruit of this tenacity, the second period of Islamic power, may be delayed: but I doubt whether it can be permanently postponed."

Hilaire Belloc, *The Great Heresies, 1938*

Contents

Foreword xiii

Introduction 1

1. The Challenge of Islam in the UK 3
2. From *fatwa* to Fear 23
3. Sacrificing Girls to Political Correctness 39
4. Islam, Dawkins, and Free Speech 45
5. Islamophobia: Threat to Free Speech 55
6. Open Letter: APPG Islamophobia
   Definition Threatens Civil Liberties 95
7. What's wrong with Islamic finance? 101
8. What's wrong with Multiculturalism? 115
9. Is Islam a Religion of Peace? 129
10. Is Islam Antisemitic? 141
11. Did Paul claim the Athenians worshipped Yahweh? 191
12. Solutions for a Segregated Society 203

Foreword

Every so often a book is written which helps the lay person get 'up-to-speed' with something which is important, yet puzzling to the majority of us, and one such book has finally come on the market, *The Challenge of Islam,* by Tim Dieppe.

Islam is no longer a religion which is "over there" in the Middle East or Asia, but very much now here in the West, especially in Europe, a continent which has seen the growth of Islam expand exponentially in this century alone, not only taking everyone by surprise, but creating a sense of alarm as it seeks to dominate and even replace long-standing European institutions and cultures, while simultaneously imposing a strong censorship against anyone who might dare to confront what it is doing publicly, and how it goes about it.

Tim Dieppe has not only been watching what has been happening but has also been personally engaging with Muslims primarily in the UK – the one country where Islam has had its greatest successes in pushing its agenda upon the indigenous population. In the last eight years, between 2016 and 2024, he wrote nine to ten articulate articles concerning some of the European Muslims' most aggressive actions, with solutions concerning how Europeans should deal with them. This book takes those articles and puts them into one tome, so that the reader can have the latest and most egregious controversies compiled in one place.

He starts with a 2019 article he wrote concerning the 1988-1989 Salman Rushdie affair, suggesting that thirty years on we in the West, because of this controversy, have moved from 'Fatwa' to fear due to the consequences of anyone who criticises Islam being called "Islamophobic". His solution is to move from fear, back to faith again.

In 2018 Tim tackled the subject of sex-grooming gangs, which were primarily made up of Pakistani Muslim men, who raped, beat and sometimes killed thousands of mostly white English girls in Britain for over forty years, while the police, schoolteachers and even social workers who knew what was happening failed to stop any of it, for fear of being called "racist".

In 2017 Tim delved into the problem of free speech and Islam, zeroing in on Muslims' attack against Dr Richard Dawkins, a famous atheist, because of his public criticism of Islam, and followed it up with a radio debate with a Muslim called Ajmal Masroor on this topic. In this debate, Tim was challenged to show one reference where Muhammad had called for those who mocked him to be killed. Tim provided several in the Hadith, the Tafsir, and in Islamic Law.

In 2024 Tim penned a follow-up article looking at the problem many have when trying to define the term "Islamophobia", and suggested that to try to do so would be a threat to 'free speech'. To support his thesis he employed two examples, one in politics and the other in academia, where those who have tried to talk about Islam have been libelled and even suspended. A better term might possibly be "anti-Muslim hatred", since this does not include legitimate criticism of Islam as an ideology. Tim concluded his follow-up article with a historical overview of where this debate has been heading.

Earlier, in 2018, Tim was a signatory to an open letter signed by forty leading experts, who felt that defining "Islamophobia" was detrimental due to its consequences for freedom of speech.

Also in 2018, Tim, who has a background in working in finance, tackled the sticky problem of Islamic Finance (also known as "Sharia-Compliant Finance"). In this article he suggested that the government and mainstream financial institutions should not promote it, pointing out that Islamic Financing is a modern, even radical interpretation of the Qur'an, that it is promoted by Islamic extremists, that the belief that one is removing interest is deceptive, that it was employed to create a separate and even rival financial system to that which we have in the West, that it is illiberal, undemocratic and discriminatory, that, due to its secrecy it is open to money laundering and fraud, and that, due to its complexity and transaction costs it especially disadvantages Muslims; so much so that, ironically, it is not even supported by most Muslims.

Later in 2018 Tim looked at the desire in the UK for "Multiculturalism", suggesting that it is a failure because it neglects to acknowledge that there are no neutral nor relative cultures, and that at the root of multiculturalism is a hatred of Christianity. His solution is to confront multiculturalism and bring people back to Christianity.

In that same year, Tim asked whether Islam was a religion of peace. He looked at the word "Islam" itself and concluded that it does not mean peace (as most Muslims would like us to believe). He then looked at what the term "Jihad" actually means, what the Qur'an says about it, how Muhammad modelled it, and how religious scholars in all four schools of law actually supported it. He concluded with a quick historical overview of how the violence of Jihad was used throughout the history of Islam.

More recently, in 2024, Tim engaged in a debate with Reza Aslan concerning whether Islam is antisemitic. To support his case Tim went to the very authorities on Islam, the Qur'an, as well as the Hadith, the Sira, and the Tafsir, and finished with writings and statements from modern Muslim scholars and politicians, to find support for antisemitism, concluding that Islam "as defined by its texts, is quite antisemitic".

In 2019 Tim penned a short article asking whether Paul claimed that the Athenians in Acts 17 worshipped Yahweh. This was a side discussion to the larger debate at that time concerning whether Allah and Yahweh were the same god. Tim concluded that indeed they weren't.

Ironically, Tim, at the very beginning of these sets of articles, way back in 2016, prophetically penned what he considered were the solutions to these varied difficulties with Islam, entitled "Solutions for a Segregated Society". In this final article he proposed ten solutions to help Muslims integrate into British Society: 1) curb

Shariah courts 2) enforce registration of religious marriages 3) ban the face veil in public 4) tighten up marriage visa rules 5) hold police accountable for treating everyone equally 6) stop promoting Islamic finance 7) Identify Britain as a Christian country based on Biblical precepts 8) defend free speech 9) ban foreign funding of Islam in the UK and 10) reduce levels of immigration.

Now if only the 'powers-that-be' had heeded Tim's ten excellent proposals back in 2016, and had implemented them, the problem of Islamic integration would not have occurred. What's more, there would have been no need for him to have even written these amazingly astute articles, nor the necessity to compile them into a book.

Nonetheless, they didn't listen, and consequently they didn't implement any of the above. That is why this book had to be written and why it is so important, especially for anyone who is interested in Islam in the West, yet has not understood what has happened, or doesn't have the time to try to do so, making this a "MUST READ" book. I therefore highly recommend that everyone get a copy for their library, and buy others as a great gift for a friend, especially a Muslim friend.

Dr Jay Smith, *Director of the 'Master of Arts in Apologetics and Polemics of Islam' (MAPI) at the Veritas International University*

Introduction

Back in 2003, highly respected Bible teacher David Pawson wrote *The Challenge of Islam to Christians*.[1] In this book, Pawson related how and why he controversially prophesied in 2002 that Islam would take over Great Britain. He hoped he was wrong but believed that he was right. Pawson was careful to say that even if he was on the right lines, his prophecy was not inevitable. God is always ready to relent of his judgment if his people repent.

I too hoped that Pawson was wrong. But I respected his warning and benefitted from reading his book. It would have been very interesting to hear Pawson's thoughts and reflections more than twenty years later, but sadly, he died in 2020. Nothing has happened in the intervening time, however, that would cause anyone persuaded by his prophecy to doubt its truth. Pawson was writing before the 7-7 attacks in London in 2005. He was writing before the grooming gang scandals ever came to light. He was writing before Lee Rigby's murder in 2013, before the Westminster attack in 2017, and before the Manchester Arena and London Bridge attacks, also in 2017, before Sir David Amess MP's murder in 2021, and before any political party had considered formulating a definition for Islamophobia.

In the 2001 census shortly before the publication of Pawson's book, the Muslim population of Britain was 1.6m or 2.8%. According to the latest census in 2021, the Muslim population is now 3.9m or 6.5% of the population. Islam is the fastest growing religion in the country, and its influence has massively increased in the twenty years since Pawson made his prediction.

---

[1] Pawson, David. (2003), *The Challenge of Islam to Christians* (London: Hodder & Stoughton).

I hope that Pawson was wrong, but whether he was right or wrong about Islam actually taking over the country, he was certainly right that Islam poses a challenge. It is a challenge that requires bold and courageous responses from faithful Christians. Part of that response will include confident witnessing and evangelism to Muslims. This is why I co-authored with Beth Peltola the book *Questions to Ask Your Muslim Friends*.[2] We long to see our Muslim friends becoming Christians and we are encouraged that this is indeed happening in churches up and down the country.

In *The Challenge of Islam* I have sought to highlight the influence that Islam now has in the UK, particularly in the first chapter from which the book takes its title. The other chapters seek to inform Christians further about the nature and influence of Islam in various areas of our culture. Each of these chapters has been published online before in a variety of outlets as noted at the start of each chapter. They are collected here in book form for easy reading and reference and because they fit together, serving to highlight the challenge of Islam in the UK today.

I hope that this book helps Christians understand the challenge of Islam and to equip them to respond to this challenge. At its root, this is a battle for the soul of the nation. It is a battle we cannot afford to lose.

---

[2] Peltola, Beth, and Tim Dieppe (2022), *Questions to Ask Your Muslim Friends: A Closer Look at Islamic Beliefs and Texts* (London: Wilberforce Publications).

1

THE CHALLENGE OF ISLAM IN THE UK

There is no doubt that Islam poses a challenge to Christians living in the UK. It is growing in influence and has political as well as religious ambitions. Islam is already threatening our democracy[1] and changing our culture.

Many Christians have been focused on the challenge of secularism, but we need to wake up to what I believe is the even more serious and pressing challenge of Islam. Just how influential is Islam in the UK? What do Muslims believe? What is attractive about Islam? And how, as Christians, should we respond to all this?

The Influence of Islam

Former Home Secretary Suella Braverman didn't hold back in an op-ed in February 2023:

> "The truth is that the Islamists, the extremists and the anti-Semites are in charge now. They have bullied the Labour Party, they have bullied our institutions, and now they have bullied our country into submission."

> "This is a crisis. And the fightback must start now, with urgency, if we are to preserve the liberties we cherish and the privileges this country affords us all. If we are to have any chance of saving our country from the mob."[2]

---

[1] https://christianconcern.com/comment/chaos-in-parliament-as-islamic-protests-cause-security-concerns/

[2] https://www.telegraph.co.uk/news/2024/02/22/islamists-are-bullying-britain-into-submission/

She was commenting following security concerns in parliament which led the Speaker of the House of Commons to break with parliamentary convention amidst extraordinary scenes in parliament.[3] In 2021, Sir David Amess MP was stabbed to death by a Muslim who was unashamed of his Islamic motives in court.[4] Alo Harbi Ali told the court:

"If you encourage someone to an act of Jihad it is a good thing."

Harbi Ali also stated plainly: "I killed him in the cause of Muslims and for the sake of Allah." Back in 2010, Stephen Timms MP was stabbed by a Muslim woman with Islamic motives. He was fortunate to survive the attack. Earlier this year, Mike Freer MP announced that he would step down as an MP at the next election because of serious threats to his personal safety. He mentioned attacks by Muslims Against Crusades.[5]

After the recent debates on Gaza in the House of Commons, a journalist reported that an MP had told him he had, "weighed up his own physical safety when deciding how to vote.".[6] How many other MPs may have done the same? Islam is now influencing our democracy, but not with benign intentions or means.

But is Suella right? Are the Islamists in charge now? Let's take a more detailed look at the influence of Islam in the UK to assess where we are and what can be done about it.

The fastest growing religion in the UK

At the last census in 2021, there were 3.9 million Muslims in the UK, or 6.5% of the population.[7] This has risen quite rapidly from only 105,000 in 1960.[8] The previous census in 2011 showed a Muslim population of 2.7 million. Islam was therefore the fastest growing

---

[3] https://christianconcern.com/comment/chaos-in-parliament-as-islamic-protests-cause-security-concerns/
[4] https://christianconcern.com/comment/sir-david-amess-victim-of-islamic-terrorism/
[5] https://www.mikefreer.com/news/statement-next-general-election
[6] https://twitter.com/DPJHodges/status/1760593429556334793
[7] https://www.ons.gov.uk/peoplepopulationandcommunity/culturalidentity/religion/bulletins/religionenglandandwales/census2021
[8] http://www.ijesd.org/papers/29-D438.pdf

religion in the UK over the ten-year period from 2011-2021, showing growth of some 44%. Pew Research estimated that by 2050, 17% of the population will be based on moderate migration.[9]

The average age (median) of Christians in England and Wales is 51-years.[10] This compares with an average age of 27-years for Muslims, and an average age of 40-years for the population as a whole. Already in 2015, 8.1% of all school age children were Muslim.[11] The name Muhammad, when allowing for spelling variants, has been the top boys' name for babies in Britain for six years running.[12]

Surveys reveal lack of integration
The Policy Exchange report: "Unsettled Belonging: A survey of Britain's Muslim communities", published in 2016, claimed to be the most extensive research of British Muslims ever conducted.[13] The report found that 53% of Muslims were born outside the UK, while 93% had parents born outside the UK. This demonstrates that much of the growth is occurring through immigration.

The survey found that 96% of British Muslims believe that the 9/11 attacks were not carried out by Al Qaeda.[14] The vast majority believe that there is some other explanation, and this is commonly understood in Muslim communities.

According to the report, 43% of Muslims supported the introduction of Sharia law broadly defined. 53% preferred to send their children to a school with strong 'Muslim values'. 44% said

---

[9] https://www.pewresearch.org/religion/2017/11/29/europes-growing-muslim-population/
[10] https://www.ons.gov.uk/peoplepopulationandcommunity/culturalidentity/religion/articles/religionbyageandsexenglandandwales/census2021#religion-by-age
[11] http://www.mcb.org.uk/wp-content/uploads/2015/02/MCB-Muslims-in-Numbers-infographic-final.jpg
[12] https://www.ons.gov.uk/peoplepopulationandcommunity/birthsdeathsandmarriages/livebirths/datasets/babynamesenglandandwalesbabynamesstatisticsboys
[13] https://policyexchange.org.uk/publication/unsettled-belonging-a-survey-of-britains-muslim-communities/
[14] https://policyexchange.org.uk/publication/unsettled-belonging-a-survey-of-britains-muslim-communities/

that schools should be able to insist on 'a hijab or niqab' with the uniform, while 32% disagreed with this.

The ICM survey of 2015 found that 7% of Muslims support the objective to create an Islamic state.[15] Only 3% said that they support the way in which ISIS is establishing a caliphate. This is a small minority of British Muslims, but 3% of 4 million Muslims is around 120,000 people supporting violent means of establishing a caliphate. When it comes to free speech, the same survey found that 78% believed that no publication should have the right to publish pictures of Muhammad. This rose to 87% when talking about the right to publish pictures making fun of Muhammad. Muslims are thus very intolerant of criticism of their religion and do not support free speech in this respect.

The survey asked whether violence was justified in a number of given situations. As many as 24% sympathised with violence by organised groups to protect their religion. 18% sympathised with violence against those who mock Muhammad. Sympathy with terrorist actions for political protest was much lower at 4%. 31% agreed that it is acceptable for British Muslims to keep more than one wife, even though that is illegal in this country. 35% believed that Jewish people have too much power in Britain.

More recent polling carried out on behalf of the Henry Jackson Society in 2024 found that only 24% of British Muslims believed that Hamas committed murder and rape in Israel on October 7th 2023.[16] 29% of British Muslims had a positive view of Hamas, and this time 32% supported the introduction of Sharia law in the UK. 21% supported legalising polygamy and 57% supported compulsory Halal food in all schools and hospitals. 52% thought that it should be illegal to show any image of Muhammad.

---

[15] http://www.icmunlimited.com/wp-content/uploads/2016/04/Mulims-full-suite-data-plus-topline.pdf
[16] https://henryjacksonsociety.org/2024/04/08/only-one-in-four-british-muslims-believe-hamas-committed-murder-and-rape-in-israel-on-october-7th/

The Casey Review

The government commissioned Dame Louise Casey to review integration in society. Her report was published in December 2016.[17] She found that there was indeed a problem in terms of integration of religious minorities. In a striking statement, she said:

> "None of the 800 or more people that we met, nor any of the two hundred plus written submissions to the review, said there wasn't a problem to solve."[18]

In many ways it was encouraging that there is widespread recognition of the problem.

Casey articulated something of a cultural clash in some of our communities:

> "I also found... cultural and religious practices in communities that are not only holding some of our citizens back but run contrary to British values and sometimes our laws. Time and time again I found it was women and children who were the targets of these regressive practices. And too often, leaders and institutions were not doing enough to stand up against them and protect those who were vulnerable."[19]

She made clear that many institutions are too accommodating, out of fear of being labelled Islamophobic:

> "Too many public institutions, national and local, state and non-state, have gone so far to accommodate diversity and freedom of expression that they have ignored or even condoned regressive, divisive and harmful cultural and religious practices, for fear of being branded racist or Islamophobic.
>
> ... At its most serious, it might mean public sector leaders ignoring harm or denying abuse."[20]

---

[17] https://www.gov.uk/government/publications/the-casey-review-a-review-into-opportunity-and-integration
[18] Casey Review, p5
[19] Casey Review, p5
[20] Casey Review, p16

She highlighted Islam in particular, and said:

"We found a growing sense of grievance among sections of the Muslim population, and a stronger sense of identification with the plight of the 'Ummah', or global Muslim community."[21]

Sir Trevor Phillips, former head of the Equalities and Human Rights Commission, said in 2016 that "the integration of Muslims will probably be the hardest task we have ever faced."[22] This is a remarkably strong statement, and all the more significant coming as it does from the man who claims to have commissioned the report that first introduced the term 'Islamophobia' to Britain 20 years ago.

The problem is exacerbated by the concentration of Muslims in certain urban areas. The 2021 census showed that major cities such as Bradford, Luton, and Birmingham have Muslim populations of over 30%, compared with 6.5% for the overall population of the nation.[23] An organisation called Muslim Vote compiled a list of parliamentary constituencies in 2024 where the Muslim vote is at least 10%.[24] They found 14 constituencies which are over 30% Muslim, and 31 constituencies which are over 20% Muslim. The Casey Review said that "people of Muslim faith live in increasing and greater concentrations (relative to other minority ethnic and faith groups) in particular local electoral wards in certain areas in the north, the Midlands and London."[25] This creates segregated communities where some Muslims have little interaction with people from other communities, and where children attend Muslim-majority schools.

This leads to skewed perceptions of reality. The Casey review cited a survey of pupils at a non-faith secondary school which found that pupil estimates of the Asian population of Britain ranged from

---

[21] Casey Review, p13
[22] https://www.thetimes.co.uk/article/my-sons-living-hell-j72t7fppc
[23] http://www.ons.gov.uk/ons/rel/census/2011-census/key-statistics-for-local-authorities-in-england-and-wales/rft-table-ks209ew.xls
[24] https://themuslimvote.co.uk/who-should-i-vote-for
[25] Casey Review, p23

50% to 90% (the actual figure was 7%).[26] This was most likely in an area with a high concentration of Muslims in the population.

Cultural influence

During a 2023 panel discussing "Muslims in the West", a British Islamic scholar and jurist (chair of the Fatwa Committee for the Islamic Council of Europe) said that the situation of Muslims living in the UK was a lot better than it was 20 years ago.[27] He said:

> "Our brothers and sisters, if you go outside you think that you are in a second Afghanistan, but you are in Londonistan. So it is really amazing, overwhelming. Don't ever, my brothers and sisters, look at yourselves as a subjugated minority. We are the leaders of humanity. We should look at ourselves as we have something to offer."

Certainly, the influence of Islam has increased over the last few decades. Islam has a disproportionate influence on our culture, given that it represents only 6.5% of the population. Numerous mainstream supermarkets and restaurant chains sell halal meat, often without labelling it as such.[28] The UK carries out more halal slaughter than the rest of Europe. London hosts an Islamic shopping festival.[29] A London Eid festival claims to attract 350,000 people.[30] Is there any Christian festival that can compare? Mainstream retailers such as Marks and Spencer sell Islamic clothing such as hijabs,[31] even while women risk their lives by protesting against the hijab in countries such as Iran.

Muslim commentator Ed Hussain wrote a book in 2021 about his travels to major mosques across the UK. His book,

---

[26] Casey Review, p49
[27] https://www.memri.org/tv/british-islamic-scholar-jurist-haitham-al-haddad-muslims-west-afghanistan-londonistan-not-subjugated-minority-leader-humanity
[28] https://www.independent.co.uk/voices/if-we-can-t-ban-halal-meat-we-should-at-least-let-people-know-when-they-re-buying-it-a7178481.html
[29] https://www.muslimshoppingfest.com/
[30] https://www.londoneid.com/
[31] https://www.marksandspencer.com/hijab/p/clp22522579

Among the Mosques, is a disturbing read.³² Hussain finds that in some places there are areas that are considered no-go for 'whites'. Not a single white face is to be seen in such areas. He finds Islamic monocultural areas which demonstrate the abject failure of multiculturalism. Major retailers have deserted such areas, where there are also no pubs. He also found that fundamentalist literature of the kind banned in Saudi Arabia is on sale in virtually every Islamic bookshop he found. Hussain warns:

> "What will happen when Birmingham or Bradford have a Muslim majority and organised caliphists hold the balance of power? Does the city begin by banning alcohol sales, using council funds to remove statues offensive to monotheism, enforcing new school uniforms for girls that exclude short skirts, banning nightclubs and gay bars, or making Fridays a local holiday for communal prayers?
>
> "Caliphism and clericalism are sequestering an entire community away from meaningful contact with mainstream Britain. The cordon sanitaire around many minds will become solidified unless we change course."

As far as religious influence goes, this is most symbolically demonstrated with the fact that many church buildings have been converted to mosques. Indeed, the mosque attended by the Manchester Arena attacker was previously a Methodist church. More shockingly, the Muslim call to prayer was chanted in Gloucester Cathedral in 2017,³³ and in St Mary's Cathedral, Glasgow, the Qur'an was recited during a Communion service.³⁴

Education

Education is a key battleground for the future generations of our nation. In education, exam boards have rescheduled exams to

---

[32] https://christianconcern.com/resource/islamic-monocultures-the-fruit-of-multiculturalism/

[33] http://www.express.co.uk/news/uk/756360/islamic-call-to-prayer-historic-british-gloucester-cathedral-outrage

[34] https://www.christiantoday.com/article/bishop.michael.nazir.ali.condemns.koran.reading.at.anglican.cathedral.epiphany.service/103716.htm

avoid clashing with Ramadan.[35] Islamic schools have been found to contain extremist material.[36] One teacher in a mostly Muslim school related how some of her pupils tried to convince her that Afghanistan was much nicer now with the Taliban in control. When she asked a class of 13-year-olds to raise their hands if they hated Britain, thirty hands immediately shot up with absolute certainty. She said: "Most of the lads I teach think women should have fewer rights than men. They spend citizenship lessons arguing that wives should not work."[37] There have been several examples of successful protests leading to increased Islamisation of schools. St Stephen's school in Newham was named best primary school in England in 2017. In 2018 the school faced a targeted campaign after it banned girls under the age of 8-years from wearing the hijab in school.[38] The school asked for government support, pointing out that standard Islamic teaching does not require the hijab until puberty. However, the school was forced to reverse its decision after the government refused to intervene. It emerged that there are some 150 schools around the country which make it compulsory for children to wear hijabs.

In 2019, Muslims parents withdrew their children from Parkfield Community School in Birmingham to protest against lessons promoting homosexuality and gender equality.[39] An estimated 600 pupils, or 80% of the school enrolment, were withdrawn. 98% of the school enrolment is Muslim. In 2023, over 300 Muslim children were kept out of a school in Manchester for three days in protest

---

[35] https://www.theguardian.com/education/2016/jan/06/popular-exams-in-uk-to-be-rescheduled-to-avoid-ramadan
[36] http://www.dailymail.co.uk/news/article-3911470/The-extremist-schools-t-close-Four-Muslim-colleges-ordered-shut-Government-use-courts-defy-ministers.html
[37] https://www.thetimes.co.uk/article/bd7f0f4d-74a3-473e-967a-b09d000a4b10?shareToken=524d43edb4fd360854575f49e799e0b2
[38] https://www.telegraph.co.uk/news/2018/02/14/ministers-politically-correct-enforce-hijab-policy-schools-former/
[39] https://www.dailymail.co.uk/news/article-6766643/Birmingham-Muslim-parents-withdraw-600-children-Parkfield-Community-School-LGBT-lessons.html

over "age inappropriate sex education teaching."[40] 200 parents wrote to the school to voice their complaints.

In 2021, a teacher at Batley Grammar School decided to teach a lesson about blasphemy and free speech. He illustrated the lesson by showing a cartoon of Muhammad.[41] Crowds gathered outside the school to protest, forcing the school to shut for two days in a row. The teacher was subsequently suspended and was forced to go into hiding for his own safety. He remains in hiding to this day. This is certainly the most effective lesson he ever taught. The whole school and the rest of the country learned that we do not have free speech when it comes to Islam. There is a de facto Islamic blasphemy law in place.

In 2023, following the Hamas attacks in Israel, the headteacher of Barclay Primary School banned students from wearing pro-Palestinian badges.[42] Protests from parents followed, forcing the school to close two days early at the end of term because ensuing threats made staff fear for their safety. A letter to parents from the school warned that it may have to "revert to online learning" if the safety of children and staff could not be guaranteed. Police officers were stationed at the school for a week, and private security had to be hired by the school.

The influential Michaela Community School is a secular school led by Katherine Birbalsingh, who is known as Britain's strictest head teacher. The school came top in the country on Progress 8 scores. Some Muslim pupils campaigned to have Muslim prayers in the playground.[43] Pupils were being pressured to support the prayers. The school responded by banning prayer rituals in the

---

[40] https://5pillarsuk.com/2023/06/26/hundreds-of-muslim-kids-kept-off-manchester-school-in-protest-at-sex-education-teaching/
[41] https://christianconcern.com/comment/teacher-requires-protection-for-showing-a-cartoon/
[42] https://www.mailonsunday.co.uk/news/article-12981279/Second-London-school-accused-Islamophobia-shut-amid-safety-fears-bomb-hoax-forced-close-following-prayer-ban-outrage.html
[43] https://www.telegraph.co.uk/news/2024/01/16/katharine-birbalsingh-taken-to-high-court-muslim-prayer-ban/

playground. This resulted in a campaign and threats, including a brick thrown through a teacher's window, and a bomb threat, which was taken seriously by police. A pupil brought a legal case against the school for banning prayer rituals, which the High Court rejected in April 2024.[44]

In 2023, four boys were suspended from a school in Wakefield after a copy of the Qur'an was allegedly damaged. The copy of the Qur'an was owned by one of the boys and was dropped on the floor after another boy knocked into the boy holding it, causing it to be slightly scuffed.[45] The boy who dropped the Qur'an, and his family, then received numerous threats of violence, including death threats. Astonishingly, the police got involved and recorded the dropping of the Qur'an as a 'non-crime hate incident'. This means that police are operating as if there is an Islamic blasphemy law in force. Can anyone imagine a similar response if a Bible were dropped by a school pupil?

Honour crimes and prisons

There were over 2,800 'honour-based' abuse offences recorded by police in 2021 – that's an average of eight per day.[46] Many more are undoubtedly unrecorded.

In 2016, a Glasgow shopkeeper was killed, effectively for being the wrong type of Muslim.[47] He had been granted asylum when he moved from Pakistan in 1998. It was expected that Scotland would be a safe place for him and his family. The Crown Prosecution Service has been accused by a whistleblower of being afraid to tackle honour crimes for fear of causing unrest in Asian communities.[48]

---

[44] https://christianconcern.com/comment/high-court-upholds-michaela-schools-ban-on-prayer-rituals/
[45] https://christianconcern.com/comment/wakefield-quran-desecration-claim-will-test-the-government/
[46] https://www.gov.uk/government/statistics/statistics-on-so-called-honour-based-abuse-offences-england-and-wales-2021-to-2022/statistics-on-so-called-honour-based-abuse-offences-england-and-wales-2021-to-2022#key-results
[47] http://www.telegraph.co.uk/news/2016/07/07/muslim-man-admits-murdering-shopkeeper-asad-shah-who-wished-belo/
[48] http://www.telegraph.co.uk/news/2016/11/07/cps-afraid-to-tackle-honour-crimes/

Some of these will be against Christian converts from Islam who can face serious threats from family members for rejecting Islam. In prisons, Muslims are disproportionately represented, being 18% of the prison population.[49] A government report found that prison Imams are routinely distributing extremist literature amongst prisoners.[50] There are also reports of prisoner-run 'sharia courts' operating in prisons, carrying out various types of corporal punishment.[51] The net result is that Muslim prisoners leave prison more radical than when they went in, with many others converting to Islam in prison.[52] The latest statistics show that 20% of Muslim prisoners are white which compares with 7.8% of the general Muslim population, an indicator of levels of conversions amongst the prison population.

Volunteer prison chaplain Paul Song was removed from the prison chaplaincy at HMP Brixton in 2017 by the more senior prison imam. Pastor Paul Song had nearly 20 years' experience working in the prison and running Alpha courses and Just10 courses with prisoners. The imam said that Pastor Song was 'too radical'. No complaints had been made by any prisoners, and some vocally supported him. With help from the Christian Legal Centre, Pastor Song was later reinstated as volunteer chaplain in 2018.[53] Pastor Song highlighted how Islamic extremists in the prison hijacked his Bible classes, loudly acclaiming the killers of Lee Rigby and claiming that his murder was justified. He described how Muslim gangs dominate the jail, intimidating prisoners into converting to Islam and even physically assaulting him over his Christian faith.[54]

---

[49] https://www.telegraph.co.uk/news/2024/03/19/one-five-muslim-prisoners-white-islamic-gangs-conversions/
[50] http://www.bbc.co.uk/news/uk-36419430
[51] http://www.bbc.co.uk/news/av/uk-36437686/sharia-courts-in-british-prisons
[52] https://www.standard.co.uk/news/london/the-jihadi-training-camp-right-in-the-heart-of-london-a3249941.html
[53] https://christianconcern.com/news/pastor-paul-song-wins-return-to-brixton-prison/
[54] https://www.dailymail.co.uk/news/article-6172025/A-chilling-account-Muslim-gangs-took-Brixton-prison-Christian-chaplain.html

In 2020, there was a terrorist attack inside HMP Whitemoor.[55] Two inmates with bladed weapons attacked and injured five prison staff, all of whom required treatment in hospital, one with serious injuries. The inmates were wearing fake suicide belts and using improvised weapons. Shouts of 'Allahu Akbar' were reportedly heard during the attack. One of the attackers had been convicted of preparing an act of terrorism in 2015. Another was serving time for a violent offence and had converted to Islam in prison.

Jihadists

British intelligence services have said that they have a watchlist of some 43,000 people whom they consider pose a potential terrorism threat. 90% of these are Muslim.[56] Some 850 British Muslims travelled to support or fight for jihadist groups in Syria or Iraq.[57] Another 600 were stopped on the way.[58] The mother of one of these fighters claimed that her son had been radicalised in just 17 days in London after attending sermons at local mosques.[59] It is not physically possible for the intelligence services to monitor all these people, given that MI5 employs only some 5,000 people.[60] It takes three teams of six people, and support staff, to monitor one person round the clock.[61]

The government's most recent report on countering terrorism, in 2023, makes clear that the primary domestic terrorist threat comes from Islamist terrorism, which accounts for approximately 67% of attacks since 2018, around 75% of MI5 caseload, and 64% of those in custody for terrorism-related offences.[62] There were around 800

---

[55] https://www.bbc.co.uk/news/uk-england-cambridgeshire-51062381
[56] https://www.dailymail.co.uk/news/article-8450211/MI5s-terror-watchlist-doubles-43-000-just-one-year.html
[57] http://www.bbc.co.uk/news/uk-32026985
[58] https://www.theguardian.com/world/2016/jan/15/foreign-secretary-600-uk-citizens-isis-syria-philip-hammond
[59] http://www.telegraph.co.uk/news/2016/05/23/jihadi-johns-fourth-beatle-unmasked-as-refugee-given-shelter-in/
[60] https://www.mi5.gov.uk/about-us
[61] http://www.bbc.co.uk/news/magazine-22718000
[62] https://assets.publishing.service.gov.uk/government/uploads/system/uploads/attachment_data/file/1186413/CONTEST_2023_English_updated.pdf

ongoing investigations by Counter Terrorism Police at any one time, and there were 169 arrests for terrorism-related activity in 2022. Since 2018, there have been nine terrorist attacks in the UK, and 39 late-stage terrorist attacks have been disrupted. The current terrorism threat level is 'Substantial', meaning that an attack is likely. It has emerged, meanwhile, that police were trained on 'Islamophobia' by radical group MEND which has defended jihadists and led prayers for "Palestinian victory."[63] Separately, Metropolitan Police were forced to cut ties with advisor Mohammed Kozbar after it emerged that he had 'liked' a post on X, formerly Twitter, in which the former head of extremist group Hizb ut-Tahrir had said he could no longer speak for the body.[64] He had also previously praised Hamas' founder as "the master martyr of the resistance." There are real concerns about infiltration into mainstream and government-linked organisations by Muslims with radical sympathies.

The head of the Armed Forces said in 2016 that jihadists were "hiding in plain sight" among migrants.[65] One foster mother was shocked to find that the supposed 12-year-old boy she fostered was actually a 21-year-old trained Jihadist, skilled with a rifle, and with both Taliban and child abuse material on his phone.[66]

Sharia law

It has been estimated that there are over 85 Sharia courts operating in the UK.[67] This has created a *de facto* parallel legal system for people in some communities. Women, in particular, may face tremendous family pressure to use Sharia courts, and may lack both the necessary English language skills and a proper understanding of their rights under British law to otherwise enjoy the protections

---

[63] https://www.thejc.com/news/uk/police-trained-on-islamophobia-by-jihadist-backers-ftd6r447
[64] https://www.telegraph.co.uk/politics/2024/02/24/met-cuts-ties-adviser-previously-praised-hamas-founder/
[65] http://www.telegraph.co.uk/news/2016/12/14/jihadists-hiding-plain-sight-among-migrants-head-armed-forces/
[66] http://www.dailymail.co.uk/news/article-3863392/Foster-mother-discovers-12-year-old-Afghan-refugee-orphan-cared-21-year-old-jihadi.html
[67] Denis MacEoin, *Sharia Law or 'One Law for All?'*, Civitas, June 2009, page 69

that would be afforded them through the English court system.[68] In addition to family pressure, refusal to settle a dispute in a Sharia forum could lead to threats and intimidation, being labelled as an unbeliever, or being ostracised from the community.[69] Machteld Zee has exposed how many of those promoting the operation of Sharia councils in the UK are actually fundamentalists who want to turn the UK into an Islamic state, imposing Sharia law on all citizens.[70] Sharia law is inherently discriminatory against both women and non-Muslims. In these courts, a woman's voice counts half as much as a man's voice. Some Sharia court judges have argued for child marriage, or say that "a husband should not be questioned why he hit his wife."[71]

In 2014, Britain became the first non-Islamic country to issue a sovereign Sharia bond. There are now around nine banks offering Sharia-compliant products in the UK.[72] In 2014, a government report stated that there were over 100,000 retail customers.[73] Elsewhere I have outlined the various problems with Islamic finance, which is based on a modern, radical interpretation of the Qur'an, and is promoted by fundamentalists.[74] The UK, nevertheless, remains committed to London becoming a centre for Islamic finance.

Beliefs of Muslims

Rather than discussing the five pillars of Islam, or the six articles of faith, which can easily be found elsewhere if you are not familiar with them, I wish to consider the worldview of those at the more fundamentalist end of the spectrum in the UK.

---

[68] Sharia Law in Britain: A Threat to One Law for All & Equal Rights, One Law for All, June 2010, p. 16.
[69] Baroness Caroline Cox, A Parallel World: Confronting the abuse of many Muslim women in Britain Today, Bow Group, 2015, p. 9.
[70] Machteld Zee, *Choosing Sharia? Multiculturalism, Islamic Fundamentalism & Sharia Councils*, Eleven International Publishing (2016), pp. 111-118
[71] Machteld Zee, Choosing Sharia? Multiculturalism, Islamic Fundamentalism & Sharia Councils, Eleven International Publishing (2016), p.118
[72] https://www.comparebanks.co.uk/banktype/sharia/
[73] https://assets.publishing.service.gov.uk/media/5a806aaeed915d74e622e547/2015047_Is_Fin_A5_AW_ENG_WEB.pdf
[74] http://www.christianconcern.com/islamicfinance

Problems in society

Britain is seen as failing morally and spiritually. Immorality is on public display in our culture, on TV, in films, and in the music industry. Socially, family breakdown is evident. Culturally, there is a loss of national identity. Economically there are many issues and criticisms that can be made. Spiritually, Christianity is seen as weak and in decline. Only 5-7% of the population regularly attend church. The critique is made by Muslims that our society is obviously failing in many ways, and we, as Christians, would agree.

Where we would differ would be in the diagnosis of the reasons for the failure of our society. The Islamic view would be that Christianity is to blame for the present failures of our society. Britain is understood to be basically a 'Christian culture'. But the Islamic view is that Christianity has failed to provide a moral foundation for our society; that Christians lack confidence in their beliefs and cannot define or defend their faith well; that Christianity is failing to attract people to church whereas Islam is growing rapidly in this country, with many converts from Christianity to Islam. Christians are seen as living no differently to unbelievers, lacking moral integrity, with similar levels of family breakdown. In any case, as Muslims see it, Christianity is false and based on a corrupted Scripture.

The attraction of Islam

The solution, therefore, is very clear to the Muslim mindset: Britain and British people should accept Islam as the foundation for society. It is useful to understand the attraction of Islam in this context.[75] Islam is viewed as a moral religion. Alcohol is not allowed, nor is adultery, stealing, or various other crimes. Women cover themselves up, rather than flaunt their sexuality. There are clear penalties for moral violations, both in this life and the next. Christianity, by contrast is seen as relatively immoral, especially when one compares Christian cultures with Islamic cultures. Islam is also a simple reli-

---

[75] For more on this see: Pawson, D. (2003). *The Challenge of Islam to Christians*. London: Hodder & Stoughton.

gion. It has a simple creed with a simple theology: one God. There are no complications like a Trinity, or an incarnation, or the atonement, or the Ascension. There is a clear morality: good deeds are weighed against bad. It is fatalistic. Islam, then, is easy. It is the easiest religion in the world to join (and the hardest to leave)! There are only five things to do. The five pillars of Islam. It is very clear whether you have done what is required or not. Islam is recent. It came after Christianity. It has built-in defences against Christianity. Being more recent implies in the minds of some people that it is better, newer, improved and more relevant compared with other religions.

Islam is also a masculine religion. It is a religion for men and by men. Islam attracts men. Christianity is often seen as effeminate, and weak. There are more women than men in most churches. Islam is understood to be a reverent religion. Muslims pray five times a day. Christians are thought to pray only on Sundays. Muslims kneel and bow down before God when praying. Church worship often lacks such obvious reverence. In a consumeristic society people will choose the religion that they prefer. Islam can appear to be better and more attractive than Christianity in all these ways.

How can the Church respond?
Islam poses a challenge to the church in the UK. It is growing rapidly and gaining influence throughout our society. So how can the church respond?

I would like to outline five pillars for responding to Islam.

First, Prayer: Islam is a spiritual entity. This is a spiritual battle. The Bible tells us that our struggle is not against flesh and blood (Eph 6:12). Prayer is key. We need to clearly understand that Muslims are redeemable whereas Islam is not, and pray accordingly. Islam works against Christianity and the gospel. All of our interactions and responses to Islam need to be grounded in prayer.

Second, Love: Jesus said that we should even love our enemies (Mt 5:44). Muslims are not our enemies, but Islam is an enemy of Christ. Our responses to Islam need to be motivated by love: love for Muslims and love for others. We cannot respond to anger and hatred in any way other than with love. We also need to show that we as a church will love and support those who, at great personal cost, are willing to leave Islam to follow Christ. This is why we at Christian Concern set up our Safe Haven[76] project to show exactly that kind of love to converts.

Third, we need to confront: It is a mistake to see confrontation as unloving. Jesus confronted the Pharisees in the most forthright manner (Mt 23). Paul confronted the Athenians with the futility of their idolatry (Acts 17:22-34). Paul even publicly confronted Peter over his compromising behaviour (Gal 2:11-14). Islam is an ideology that needs to be confronted. Paul said: "We demolish arguments and every pretension that sets itself up against the knowledge of God, and we take captive every thought to make it obedient to Christ" (2 Cor 10:5 NIV). Islam sets itself up against the knowledge of God. Its 'truth' claims need to be confidently confronted. The church needs to build up resources for Christians to help them confidently challenge and confront Islam in our society at every level – whether it is with friends and neighbours, or in the public square and in the media. We lovingly confront Muslims with the truth claims of Christianity and desire that they should experience the love of Christ. Beth Peltola and I wrote the book *Questions to Ask Your Muslim Friends* with this in mind.[77] It is intended to equip Christians to engage with their Muslim friends in conversations about their faith.

Fourth, expose: Paul said, "Have nothing to do with the fruitless deeds of darkness, but rather expose them" (Eph 5:11). There are aspects of Islam that need to be exposed. Islam is an intolerant religion. This does not mean that all Muslims are intolerant people. Rather, it means that the ideology presented in the Qur'an and in the example of Muhammad, is intolerant. It is also discriminatory against both women and non-Muslims. It advocates violence and

---

[76] https://www.safe-haven.org.uk/
[77] https://www.wilberforcepublications.co.uk/questions-to-ask-your-muslim-friends

cruel punishments. It seeks political power. These aspects need to be exposed. Christian Concern seeks to do this with various articles and resources on Islam and its influence.[78] Christians need to shine a light on things that are being done in the name of Islam, to expose their true nature.

Fifth, resist: The influence of Islam in our society needs to be resisted in law and in politics. Christians need to be actively involved in this kind of resistance. Amos said: "Hate evil, love good; maintain justice in the courts" (Amos 5:15). Christians should use our legal rights and freedoms to maintain and protect Christian freedoms. A great example of successful resistance was the campaign to stop the mega-mosque from being built in London for the 2012 Olympics. The original plans were for a building that could hold at least 40,000 worshippers, making it the largest place of worship in the whole of Europe.[79] The mosque was backed by Islamic group Tablighi Jamaat, which preaches a conservative and separationist version of Islam. The mosque was successfully resisted with a campaign led by Alan Craig and a small group of others, which also garnered support from the local moderate Muslim community.[80] Christian Concern supports Christian street preachers who are deemed to have offended people by insulting Islam, with a 100% success record in defending free speech so far. We have also defended Christians who have lost their jobs for witnessing to Muslims. Baroness Cox has valiantly sought to resist the influence of Sharia courts through parliamentary bills. This kind of resistance needs to grow and gain wide support in the Church as we seek to preserve our Christian freedoms.

Part of the challenge of Islam is that Islam is bold and unashamed in its approach. In this respect, it can put to shame those Christians who shy away from talking about their faith or proclaiming its relevance to society. In the end, the only effective response to radical

---

[78] https://christianconcern.com/ccissues/islam/
[79] http://www.telegraph.co.uk/comment/3632591/The-shadow-cast-by-a-mega-mosque.html
[80] https://www.nytimes.com/2007/11/04/world/europe/04megamosque.html

Islam is radical Christianity. If more of us were radical, bold and unashamed about our faith, confident in confronting and challenging Islam's claims, then many more Muslims would turn to Christ. As it is, there are reports of some churches baptising ex-Muslim believers on a regular basis. God appears to have chosen to use Islam to awaken the church. The question is, will we respond to this call?

2

FROM *FATWA* TO FEAR
30 YEARS ON FROM *THE SATANIC VERSES* AFFAIR

Note: This article was written in 2019 to mark 30 years since an Iranian *fatwa* was issued calling for the murder of author Salman Rushdie following the publication of his book *The Satanic Verses*. Thirty years later, I looked at the ongoing effects of the incident and how it has led to fear of insulting Islam.

Very sadly, in August 2022, Salman Rushdie was brutally and repeatedly stabbed while on stage, while about to give a public lecture in New York. Rushdie was fortunate to survive, but suffered damage to his liver and hands, and lost the sight of his right eye. His attacker subsequently explained what he thought of Rushdie: "He's someone who attacked Islam, he attacked their beliefs, the belief systems."[1]

The *fatwa*

On 14 February 1989, the following announcement was made on Radio Tehran:

> "We are from Allah and to Allah we shall return. I am informing all brave Muslims of the world that the author of The Satanic Verses, a text written, edited, and published against Islam, the Prophet of Islam, and the Qur'an, along with all the editors and publishers aware of its contents, are condemned to death.
>
> I call on all valiant Muslims wherever they may be in the world to kill them without delay, so that no one will dare insult the sacred

---

[1] https://news.sky.com/story/sir-salman-rushdies-alleged-attacker-hadi-matar-says-he-was-surprised-the-author-survived-12675424

beliefs of Muslims henceforth. And whoever is killed in this cause will be a martyr, Allah willing. Meanwhile if someone has access to the author of the book but is incapable of carrying out the execution, he should inform the people so that that he may be punished for his actions. May Allah's blessing be upon you all." — Rouhollah al-Mousavi al-Khomeini.

This was how the infamous *fatwa* was released. It immediately received international attention and was headline news right across the world. A foreign leader had issued a death sentence on a British citizen, no matter that he lived in Britain and had broken no British law. He had said that British Muslims had a duty to kill him. Author Salman Rushdie had to go into hiding with 24-hour police protection for over a decade.

This was a watershed moment for Britain in terms of the influence of Islam in the UK and the challenges that it posed. The repercussions are still being felt. In this article I will explore what happened 30 years ago, discuss the implications, the real Satanic verses, and the lasting repercussions on our culture today.

What is a *fatwa*?

The first time most British people ever heard of a *fatwa* was when this *fatwa* hit the headlines. A *fatwa* is an authoritative legal ruling issued by an appropriate Islamic authority – in this case, Ayatollah Khomeini. Khomeini was the leader of the 1979 Iranian revolution which overthrew the last Shah of Iran and set up the Islamic Republic of Iran. He became the Supreme Leader of the Islamic Republic as well as the primary spiritual leader for some 50 million Shia Muslims.

A month after the Khomeini *fatwa,* the Islamic Conference of Foreign Ministers met in Riyadh, with 46 Islamic countries represented, and pronounced the following in their communique:

> "The Conference declared that blasphemy could not be justified on the basis of freedom of thought or expression. It strongly condemned the blasphemous publication "Satanic Verses" whose author is regarded as an apostate. It appealed to all members of

the International community to ban the book and take necessary measures to protect the religious beliefs of others."[2]

Although this communique stopped short of expressly calling for Rushdie to be killed, in declaring the publication blasphemous and the author apostate, this was seen as supporting the verdict of Khomeini's *fatwa*, which pronounced Rushdie guilty of crimes deserving of the death penalty.

The Book

On 26 September 1988, *The Satanic Verses* by Salman Rushdie was published in the UK by Viking Penguin. Rushdie had won the prestigious Booker Prize for a previous novel and had earned a reputation as a highly regarded contemporary novelist who was unafraid to tackle controversial subjects.

The Satanic Verses is a novel, using magical realism and dream visions to tell a lengthy imaginative story. Some parts of the book are clearly based on aspects of the life of Muhammad. Muhammad is not mentioned by name, however, nor is Mecca or Sharia law. Instead there is a character called 'Mahound' who founds a religion of 'Submission' in a fantastical polytheistic city of 'Jahilia'. It is, nevertheless, as Kenan Malik explains, "a fictionalised, satirical account of the origins of Islam."[3] 'Mahound' is an ancient derogatory name for 'Muhammad'. 'Submission' is the literal meaning of 'Islam'. *'Jahiliyya'* is an Arabic word for 'ignorance', used by Muslims to describe the Arabic world prior to the revelation of the Qur'an to Muhammad.

In an interview broadcast on 14 February 1989 Rushdie was asked:

> "The controversy, in a sense, has been about your acting on the historic text of the Koran and playing with that. How much of that was based on historical fact?"

---

[2] https://ww1.oic-oci.org/english/conf/fm/18/18%20icfm-final-en.htm
[3] Kenan Malik, *From Fatwa to Jihad: The Rushdie Affair and Its Legacy* (London: Atlantic, 2009), xv

He replied:

"Almost entirely. Almost everything in those sections – the dream sequences – starts from an historical or quasi-historical basis, though one can't really speak with absolute certainty about that period of Mohammed's life." [4]

What are the Satanic verses?

According to numerous authoritative Islamic traditions, early in his career when Muhammad was struggling to attract followers, he gave a revelation which endorsed polytheism, which meant that more people joined him. These are verses he recited, which remain in the Qur'an:

"So have you considered al-Lat and al-'Uzza? And Manat, the third - the other one?" (Q 53:19-20)

Originally, this reference to three gods was followed by these verses which endorse them:

"These are the exalted cranes (intermediaries). Whose intercession is to be hoped for."

The angel Gabriel is said to have then corrected Muhammad, and these later verses were removed from the Qur'an and became known as the Satanic verses.[5]

This story provides the context for the following verse from the Qur'an:

"And We did not send before you any messenger or prophet except that when he spoke [or recited], Satan threw into it [some misunderstanding]. But Allah abolishes that which Satan throws in; then Allah makes precise His verses. And Allah is Knowing and Wise." (Q 22:52)

---

[4] Lisa Appignanesi and Sara Maitland, *The Rushdie File* (Syracuse University Press, 1990), 21-22

[5] A.M.I. Hishām, et al., *The life of Muhammad: a translation of Ishāq's Sīrat rasūl Allāh* (trans. A. Guillaume; Oxford: Oxford University Press, 1967), 165-166. Al-Tabari, *The History of al-Tabari Vol. VI: Muhammad at Mecca* (trans. W. M. Watt and M. V. McDonald; vol. 6: State University of New York Press, 1989), 107-112. For further discussion of the Satanic verses and other sources see: https://www.answering-islam.org/Green/satanic.htm

It is worth remembering here that the Qur'an is not even roughly in chronological order. It is also worth noting that some verses of the Qur'an (which Allah himself is said to have inspired, not Satan) are abrogated or superseded by later verses. This is made clear in the Qur'an, which teaches the concept of abrogation in verses such as this one:

> "We do not abrogate a verse or cause it to be forgotten except that We bring forth [one] better than it or similar to it. Do you not know that Allah is over all things competent?" (Q 2:106, cf. Q 16:101)

The point here is that Salman Rushdie did not invent the concept of 'Satanic verses', or of some verses which Muhammad recited, having been inspired by Satan. This is part of standard Islamic tradition, as is the idea that Allah has abrogated some of his own inspired verses. Rushdie used this idea to inform the provocative title of his book. Of course, this incident raises serious questions about the source of Muhammad's revelations and the trustworthiness of Allah.

The Reaction

The book was published on 26th September 1988. On 5th October, the Indian government announced that the book would be banned in India. This was quickly followed by Pakistan, Saudi Arabia, Egypt, Somalia, Bangladesh, Sudan, Malaysia, Indonesia, Qatar, and South Africa. Meanwhile, back in England, the book won the Whitbread "best novel" award in November and was shortlisted for the Booker Prize.

Salman Rushdie wrote an open letter to the Indian prime minister complaining about the ban and arguing for the importance of the right to freedom of expression.[6] This was responded to by Sayed Shahabuddin, an Indian MP. Some representative statements from his response are:

> "Yes, I have not read it, nor do I intend to. I do not have to wade through a filthy drain to know what filth is."

---

[6] Appignanesi and Maitland, *The Rushdie File*, 34-36

"No, your act is not unintentional or a careless slip of the pen. It was deliberate and consciously planned with devilish, forethought, with an eye to your market. Here in India our laws are very clear... Whoever with deliberate and malicious intention of outraging the religious feelings of any class of citizens of India ... shall be punished with imprisonment ... or with a fine ... or with both. I wish you were in India Mr Rushdie, to face the music."

"To sum up, your magnum opus is objectionable on three grounds: it is a crime against human decency; it is an insult to Islam; it is an offence under Indian law. And tell your British advisors that India shall not permit 'literary colonialism', nor what may be called religious pornography."[7]

Back in England Muslim outrage mounted, culminating in a demonstration in Bradford on January 14th, where copies of the book were ceremoniously burned, followed by 8,000 Muslims demonstrating at Hyde Park on 27 January. Amongst the placards were some reading: "*Islam – Our Religion Today, Your Religion Tomorrow.*"[8] Many others simply called for Rushdie to be killed.[9] A petition was submitted to Penguin Books asking for the book to be withdrawn and pulped, and for Penguin to apologise for publishing it. Penguin also received threats and hate mail. Penguin stood firm, although WH Smith withdrew the book from its stores.

The first deaths followed shortly afterwards with five killed in rioting in Islamabad, Pakistan, and then another killed and a hundred injured in Kashmir on 13 February 1989.

---

[7] Appignanesi and Maitland, *The Rushdie File*, 37-41
[8] Philip Jenkins, *God's Continent: Christianity, Islam, and Europe's Religious Crisis* (Oxford: Oxford University Press, 2007), 1
[9] Malik, K. *From Fatwa to Jihad: The Rushdie Affair and Its Legacy*, 185

Reactions After the *Fatwa*

Media in Tehran claimed that the book was published at the request of the British Intelligence Services as part of a deliberate attempt to confront Islam.[10] A reward of £1,500,000 was offered to kill Rushdie.[11]

Rushdie went into hiding, but said in an interview:

> "Frankly I wish I had written a more critical book, religion that claims it is able to behave like this, religious leaders who are able to behave like this, and then say this is a religion which must be above any kind of whisper of criticism, that doesn't add up."[12]

Robert Maxwell countered the reward for killing Rushdie with this:

> "I will offer $10m to the man or woman who will not kill, but civilise the barbarian Ayatollah, the test of which shall be that he shall publicly recite the Ten Commandments, with special reference to the sixth ('Thou shalt not kill') and the ninth ('Thou shalt not bear false witness against thy neighbour')."[13]

Iqbal Sacranie, of the UK Action Committee on Islamic Affairs said:

> "Death, perhaps, is a bit too easy for him ... his mind must be tormented for the rest of his life unless he asks for forgiveness to Almighty Allah."[14]

Sacranie went on to become the first secretary general of the Muslim Council of Britain, and Sir Iqbal Sacranie in 2005.

Sayed Abdul Quddus, joint secretary for the Council of Mosques in Bradford, said:

"I totally agree with what Ayatollah Khomeini has said in public. Every Muslim blames Salman Rushdie. If any Muslim will get a chance, he won't avoid it and he should not. Why not? He (Rushdie)

---

[10] Appignanesi and Maitland, *The Rushdie File*, 70-71
[11] Appignanesi and Maitland, *The Rushdie File*, 79
[12] The Guardian, 15 February 1989. https://www.theguardian.com/books/1989/feb/15/salmanrushdie
[13] Appignanesi and Maitland, *The Rushdie File*, 103-4
[14] The Guardian, 15 February 1989. https://www.theguardian.com/books/1989/feb/15/salmanrushdie

has tortured every Muslim. Why should people be brutally murdered and lose their lives and Salman Rushdie not pay."[15] West Yorkshire Police later confirmed that they would not be bringing charges of incitement to murder against Muslim leaders in Bradford. The CPS cited insufficient evidence and questions around whether such a prosecution would be in the public interest.[16] Anthony Burgess likened the threats against Rushdie to Jihad:

> "To order outraged sons of the prophet to kill him and the directors of Penguin Books on British soil is tantamount to a jihad. It is a declaration of war on the citizens of a free country and as such it is a political act. It has to be countered with equally forthright, if less murderous, declaration of defiance."[17]

After a few days, Rushdie issued an apology expressing regret for the distress caused by the publication.[18] Ayatollah Khomeini was not impressed:

> "Even if Salman Rushdie repents and becomes the most pious man of time, it is incumbent on every Muslim to employ everything he's got, his life, his wealth, to send him to hell."[19]

In October 1989, Kalim Siddiqui, founder of the Muslim Institute, addressed an audience in Manchester Town Hall, with TV cameras present. He told the audience that the *fatwa* was just, and that Rushdie should be killed. He asked the audience how many supported the death sentence for Rushdie. The majority raised their hands. He then asked how many would be willing to carry it out. Almost all of them kept their hands up. This electrifying scene was captured on camera and played on the evening news.[20] Nevertheless, Siddiqui was not prosecuted for incitement to murder.

---

[15] The Guardian, 15 February 1989. https://www.theguardian.com/books/1989/feb/15/salmanrushdie
[16] Appignanesi and Maitland, *The Rushdie File*, 104-5
[17] The Independent, 15 February 1989. Cited in: Appignanesi and Maitland, *The Rushdie File*, 79
[18] Appignanesi and Maitland, *The Rushdie File*, 97-98
[19] Appignanesi and Maitland, *The Rushdie File*, 99
[20] Malik, K., *From Fatwa to Jihad: The Rushdie Affair and Its Legacy*, 185 https://www.theguardian.com/commentisfree/2006/may/28/religion.islam

Archbishop supports extension of blasphemy laws

Home Secretary, Douglas Hurd, announced on 1 February 1989 that the government had no plans to change the blasphemy laws in response to Islamic demands.[21] The Archbishop of Canterbury, Robert Runcie, while condemning incitement to murder, also condemned the offence caused by the book. He added:

> "I firmly believe that offence to the religious beliefs of the followers of Islam or any other faith is quite as wrong as offence to the religious beliefs of Christians."[22]

In the context of demands for the blasphemy law to be extended to include blasphemy against Islam, this astonishing and appalling statement lent support to criminalising criticism of Muhammad. A Vatican official also condemned Salman Rushdie for blaspheming.[23] The Chief Rabbi, however, whilst stating that he thought the book should not have been published, made clear that he did not support any extension to the blasphemy laws.[24]

The International Response

Foreign Secretary, Sir Geoffrey Howe, was taken by surprise by the strength of opinion from EC foreign ministers who were keen to do more than merely issue a statement as he had done. The twelve countries of the EC recalled their ambassadors and suspended all high level visits between their countries and Iran.

In France, publication of *The Satanic Verses* was suspended for security reasons.[25] In Canada, imports of the book were stopped pending a review of the book for possible hate propaganda.[26] In the US several prominent bookstore chains, including Barnes & Noble, and independent bookstores pulled the book from their shelves.[27]

---

[21] Appignanesi and Maitland, *The Rushdie File*, xiii
[22] Appignanesi and Maitland, *The Rushdie File*, 101-102
[23] Appignanesi and Maitland, *The Rushdie File*, 116
[24] Appignanesi and Maitland, *The Rushdie File*, 197-99
[25] Appignanesi and Maitland, *The Rushdie File*, 130
[26] Appignanesi and Maitland, *The Rushdie File*, 144
[27] Appignanesi and Maitland, *The Rushdie File*, 147

Thousands of literary writers signed a statement expressing solidarity with Rushdie.[28] One anonymous person from Karachi wrote to say that Rushdie speaks for him and others like him who wish to recant from Islam but are unable to do so publicly in Islamic society on pain of death.[29]

Meanwhile, the UK government seemed keener to express sympathy with the offence caused to Muslims than to stand up for freedom of expression. Sir Geoffrey Howe explained to a meeting in Birmingham that there was nothing he could do about the book under British law; instead he discussed the obligation of immigrants to integrate.[30] He later criticised the book for being "extremely rude" about Britain.[31] Margaret Thatcher joined him in criticising the novel for the offence caused.[32] Labour party leader Neil Kinnock, by contrast, later revealed that he had met Rushdie in hiding and defended his right and that of his publishers to release a paperback edition. Roy Hattersley and a number of other senior Labour figures disagreed.[33] Commentators opined that it was not really appropriate for the government to make pronouncements on the quality of a novel.

More violence

An imam in Brussels who had made a lenient statement about Rushdie was shot dead on 30 March 1989.[34] On 9 April the ground floor of Collet's Penguin Bookshop in London was destroyed by a firebomb and a Dillons store was also attacked.

An anonymous official at Viking Penguin was interviewed for his perspective. He defended the publication, but said that the security costs all over the world would far outweigh any profits from sales of the book. He added:

[28] Appignanesi and Maitland, *The Rushdie File*, 109-112
[29] Appignanesi and Maitland, *The Rushdie File*, 221-22
[30] Appignanesi and Maitland, *The Rushdie File*, 108
[31] Appignanesi and Maitland, *The Rushdie File*, 115
[32] Appignanesi and Maitland, *The Rushdie File*, 114
[33] Appignanesi and Maitland, *The Rushdie File*, 129
[34] Appignanesi and Maitland, *The Rushdie File*, 126-7

"I don't know if Viking Penguin can stand this indefinitely. ... this is censorship by fear and intimidation."[35]

Between December 1988 and March 1989, Viking received 30,000 letters of protest and 16 bomb threats.[36] Penguin CEO, Peter Mayer, received death threats to himself and his family, and letters written in blood pushed under the door of his house.[37]

In July 1991, the Italian translator of *The Satanic Verses* was stabbed in his apartment in Milan by an Iranian. He survived the attack.[38] Nine days later the Japanese translator of the book, Hitoshi Igarashi, was found stabbed to death in his university office.[39] In 1989, the Islamic Centre in Japan had requested publishers not to translate or reproduce the novel, describing it as "anti-Islamic."

The aftermath

Salman Rushdie finally came out of hiding in 1998, after the Iranian government distanced itself from the Khomeini *fatwa*. The *fatwa* itself still stands though, and as recently as 2016, a bounty of $600,000 was offered by state-run Iranian media outlets for the death of Rushdie.[40] Rushdie was knighted for his services to literature in 2007. Since 2000 he has lived in the United States. In 2012, Rushdie published *Joseph Anton: A Memoir*, an account of his life under police protection, during which time he used the pseudonym, Joseph Anton.[41]

---

[35] Appignanesi and Maitland, *The Rushdie File*, 149
[36] Appignanesi and Maitland, *The Rushdie File*, 149
[37] Malik, K., *From Fatwa to Jihad: The Rushdie Affair and Its Legacy*, 12
[38] New York Times, 13 July 1991. http://movies2.nytimes.com/books/99/04/18/specials/rushdie-translator.html
[39] Washington Post, 13 July 1991. https://www.washingtonpost.com/archive/politics/1991/07/13/satanic-verses-translator-found-slain/6ee67d24-9b02-4eaf-994e-107ff814f64f/?utm_term=.5c7c52f58735
[40] The Independent, 21 February 2016. https://www.independent.co.uk/news/people/salman-rushdie-iranian-state-media-renew-fatwa-on-satanic-verses-author-with-600000-bounty-a6887141.html
[41] http://www.spiegel.de/international/world/salman-rushdie-speaks-about-his-time-in-hiding-and-his-new-book-a-857034.html

Twenty years later - *The Jewel of Medina*

Twenty years to the day after the publication of *The Satanic Verses*, on 26th September 2008, the London offices of publishers, Gibson Square, were firebombed.[42] Gibson Square was planning to publish a novel, *The Jewel of Medina*, about Muhammad's youngest wife Aisha.

Originally, Random House had intended to publish *The Jewel of Medina*, but it cancelled its plans after it received an email suggesting that it might inspire violent reactions from some Muslims. Random House put out a statement explaining that it had received:

> "from credible and unrelated sources, cautionary advice not only that the publication of this book might be offensive to some in the Muslim community, but also that it could incite acts of violence by a small, radical segment."[43]

Malik claims that all Random House had received was an email from an academic and a critical post on an online forum.[44] An actual *fatwa* and actual violence had not stopped Penguin from publishing *The Satanic Verses* twenty years earlier. Now the merest suggestion that it could inspire violence was enough to cancel publication of *The Jewel of Medina*. As Salman Rushdie said:

> "This is censorship by fear and it sets a very bad precedent indeed."[45]

Gibson Square Publishing then bought the rights and announced that it would publish *The Jewel of Medina* in the UK.[46] After the arson attack, publication was postponed in the UK. However, the book was published in the US, Germany, Denmark, Serbia and Italy with no repercussions. It was later published in the UK by Gibson Square Books in 2009.

---

[42] The Guardian, 28 September 2008. https://www.theguardian.com/uk/2008/sep/28/muhammad.book.attack
[43] http://www.randomhouse.com/rhpg/medinaletter.html
[44] Malik, K., *From Fatwa to Jihad: The Rushdie Affair and Its Legacy*, 195
[45] Malik, K., *From Fatwa to Jihad: The Rushdie Affair and Its Legacy*, 196
[46] http://news.bbc.co.uk/1/hi/entertainment/7597437.stm

The idea that Random House would cancel publication after the suggestion of possible inspiration of violence would have been unthinkable before the Rushdie *fatwa*. Furthermore, if Random House had gone ahead and ignored these suggestions, it is likely that nothing would have happened. Random House drew attention to the book with its cancellation. As Kenan Malik says, *"The fear of giving offence ... made it easier to take offence."*[47]

Repercussions today

Malik appropriately comments that, *"Rushdie's critics lost the battle, but won the war."*[48] They did not succeed in banning publication of *The Satanic Verses*, but they did succeed in establishing a principle in society that it is wrong to offend other religions and cultures. Even more significantly, they established a *de facto* assassin's veto, whereby the mere threat of violence means that something perceived as critical of Islam can be self-censored. The *fatwa* has become internalised, and we now live in a culture of self-censorship by fear.

The ICM survey in 2015 found that 78% of British Muslims believed that no publication should have the right to publish pictures of Muhammad. This rose to 87% when talking about the right to publish pictures making fun of Muhammad.[49] Further, 18% sympathised with people who take part in violence against those who mock Muhammad.

In 2017, two British newspapers published a correction notice: "We are happy to make clear that Islam as a religion does not support so-called 'honour killings'."[50] No matter that many Muslims would disagree with this, and that Ayatollah Khomeini and his supporters would certainly have disagreed. The death penalty for apostasy is a

---

[47] Malik, K., *From Fatwa to Jihad: The Rushdie Affair and Its Legacy*, 196
[48] The Guardian, 29 September 2018. https://www.theguardian.com/commentisfree/2018/sep/29/satanic-verses-sowed-seeds-of-rift-grown-ever-wider
[49] http://www.icmunlimited.com/wp-content/uploads/2016/04/Mulims-full-suite-data-plus-topline.pdf
[50] https://www.spiked-online.com/2017/01/18/policing-criticism-of-islam-the-new-star-chamber/#.WICLbxuLSUk

form of honour killing that is clearly part of Islamic teaching.[51] This means that the press regulator is now watching out for statements that are seen to be critical of Islam. This is a new form of censorship that would not have been imagined prior to the *fatwa*.

Last year, Canadian journalist Lauren Southern was refused entry into the UK. She had committed no crime. She had previously distributed posters with slogans about Allah such as "Allah is Gay" or "LGBT for Islam UK".[52] This was a response to an article which questioned whether Jesus was gay. Clearly the border forces believe that someone whom some may consider to have insulted Allah is a threat to society. Another person was refused entry into the UK because of his 'anti-Islamisation beliefs'.[53] We are now living in a culture that goes to quite some lengths to protect Islam from criticism, but not Christianity.

From *fatwa* to fear to …

30 years after the *fatwa*, fear of criticising Islam is part of our culture. No one wants to be labelled 'Islamophobic'. But it is actually those who are silenced by fear who are really 'Islamophobic'. We are all aware that some Muslims will turn to violence if they feel that Muhammad has been insulted, and that there are enough Muslims sympathising with this in the UK to create a culture of fear. Blasphemy laws have been abolished, but publishers and others are careful not to criticise Islam anyway. We have moved from *fatwa* to fear.

It is time to say enough to Islamic intimidation, threats and censorship. This is no way to run a free society. The police and the government should robustly defend free speech in every area of society and clamp down on threats of violence of any form. Rather than saying that all religions should be respected, they should defend criticism of religions. Christians and others should be able

---

[51] https://www.christianconcern.com/our-concerns/islam/ex-muslims-face-threats-and-violence-for-leaving-islam
[52] https://www.christianconcern.com/our-issues/islam/banning-critics-of-islam
[53] https://www.christianconcern.com/our-issues/islam/banning-critics-of-islam

to clearly expose the discriminatory nature of Islam and its links with terrorism and other activities without fear of prosecution or of violent threats. Sometimes the truth is offensive, but people have no right not to be offended. Journalists, politicians and others should be entirely free to say that Muhammad was a false prophet who taught and practiced immoral things. We need to move from fear to faith and boldly proclaim that Jesus Christ is the way, the truth and the life, and that no one comes to the Father except by Him. Having moved from *fatwa* to fear, it is time to move from fear to faith and freedom.

3

SACRIFICING GIRLS TO POLITICAL CORRECTNESS

Note: This article was written in 2018 following revelations of the 'worst ever' child grooming scandal in Telford, where hundreds of young girls were found to have been raped, beaten, sold for sex, and some even killed. Here I explain the strong Islamic connection with these crimes and their justification from Islamic teaching. I argue that thousands of young girls are being sacrificed on the altars of multiculturalism and political correctness. The abuse continues to this day.[1]

Britain's 'worst ever' child grooming scandal

The front-page headline of the *Sunday Mirror* on 11 March 2018 read "'Worst ever' child grooming scandal exposed: Hundreds of young girls raped, beaten, sold for sex and some even killed over 40 years, as authorities failed to act."[2]

The story is a somewhat familiar one, of white or Sikh British girls, some as young as 11-years-old, being drugged, raped and beaten by 'Asian' sex gangs over an extended period of time. In this context, 'Asian' is a euphemism for 'men of Muslim background, predominantly Pakistani'. It is familiar story because of the exposés of similar sex gangs in Rotherham, Rochdale, Oxfordshire, and various other places.

---

[1] https://christianconcern.com/comment/another-report-on-grooming-gangs-meanwhile-abuse-continues/
[2] https://www.mirror.co.uk/news/uk-news/britains-worst-ever-child-grooming-12165527

Fear of 'racism'

The Mirror carried out an 18-month investigation and found that as many as 1,000 children could have suffered at the hands of sex gangs since the 1980s. Victims say that the abuse of young girls is ongoing. The investigation found that social workers knew of the abuse in the 1990s, but police took a decade to launch a probe. Authorities failed to keep details of abusers from Asian communities for fear of being accused of 'racism'. Council staff viewed the abused children as 'prostitutes' instead of victims. In one case, police failed to investigate it five times, only investigating after an MP intervened.

Subsequently, an inquiry raised the number of victims of child sexual exploitation in Rotherham to 1,510.[3] The number of victims was previously estimated to be 1,400. This is in a community of 260,000: Telford's population is 170,000, and the scale of abuse there is feared to be the most brutal and long-running of all.

The Scapegoating of Rotherham

In his book about the grooming scandals,[4] Peter McLoughlin explains how Rotherham was the designated scapegoat for these rape gangs. The Jay Report was an 'Inquiry into Child Sexual Exploitation in Rotherham'.[5] The Casey Report also focused on Rotherham.[6] These investigations resulted in the entire council cabinet resigning and the government taking over. But Rotherham is not the only place where this has been occuring and where local government and other officials have been turning a blind eye in the name of political correctness. Why have there not been similar inquiries into child sexual exploitation in Bradford, Manchester, Oldham, Oxford, Rochdale, Bristol ... and Telford? If the councils

---

[3] https://www.bbc.co.uk/news/uk-england-south-yorkshire-43126804
[4] Peter McLoughlin, *Easy Meat: Inside Britain's Grooming Gang Scandal*, New English Review Press (2016).
[5] https://www.rotherham.gov.uk/downloads/file/1407/independent_inquiry_cse_in_rotherham
[6] https://www.gov.uk/government/publications/report-of-inspection-of-rotherham-metropolitan-borough-council

in these cities were held to the same standards, then they should all be resigning. Rotherham is a convenient scapegoat to distract from the full scale of the abuse elsewhere.

Predominantly Muslim convictions

Peter McLoughlin has compiled a list of all the grooming gang convictions since 1997.[7] To date, 275 of the 317 men convicted have Muslim names. This means 87% of the convicts are of Muslim heritage. Given that Muslims are only 5% of the population, this would mean that a Muslim man is some 127 times more likely to be convicted as being part of a grooming gang than a non-Muslim.

The Islamic Connection

The Casey Report makes clear that the child exploitation in Rotherham was carried out by men largely from the Pakistani Heritage Community.[8] They are mostly Muslims. Victims of these grooming gangs have frequently reported that they were given an Asian name and told to read the Qur'an, which demonstrates the extent of Islamic influence.[9]

Use of sex slaves by Islamists is now well known, whether it is by Boko Haram taking girls captive, or by ISIS fighters, or other Islamic groups. These groups justify their actions by reference to the Qur'an:

> "O Prophet, tell your wives and your daughters and the women of the believers to bring down over themselves [part] of their outer garments. That is more suitable that they will be known and not be abused." (Q 33:59)

Women and girls are to cover up if they do not intend to invite abuse. In this way, non-Muslim girls who do not cover up are seen to be inviting abuse.

---

[7] https://www.pmclauth.com/sentenced/grooming-gang-statistics/gangs-jailed [Accessed 2018]
[8] https://www.gov.uk/government/publications/report-of-inspection-of-rotherham-metropolitan-borough-council
[9] https://www.thetimes.co.uk/article/mothers-of-prevention-v6wn7b8vrjc

Slavery is also discussed in the Qur'an, and slave women are described as "those your right hands possess."

"And [also prohibited to you are all] married women except those your right hands possess." (Q 4:24)

This means that Muslim men are permitted to rape female slaves – even if they are married. This teaching is even clearer in the Hadith:

> "O Allah's Messenger! We get female captives as our share of booty, and we are interested in their prices, what is your opinion about coitus interruptus?" The Prophet said, "Do you really do that? It is better for you not to do it. No soul that which Allah has destined to exist, but will surely come into existence." (Bukhari 3:34:432)

Here, Muhammad's followers are concerned that the value of their female slaves might deteriorate if they became pregnant after being raped. Muhammad advises against using *coitus interruptus* to avoid pregnancy.

Multiculturalism to blame

I have recently written in more depth about multiculturalism and how it is based on the idea that all cultures are equal.[10] In the worst examples of the doctrine of multiculturalism being applied, those convicted of serious crimes are excused because of their culture. In one case in 2013, a Muslim man in Nottingham who raped an underage girl was spared a prison term after the judge heard that the man had been taught in an Islamic faith school that women are worthless.[11] Here Islamic values are being used by a judge to justify no prison sentence for child rape. This undermines the fundamental principle of one law for all.

What is even more problematic is that Islamic values are rarely mentioned as a factor in explaining these rape gangs. There is a conspiracy of silence even at the cost of more girls being raped. Until we recognise the strong Islamic cultural factors involved, we

---
[10] See chapter 7.
[11] https://www.telegraph.co.uk/news/uknews/crime/10060570/Oxford-grooming-gang-We-will-regret-ignoring-Asian-thugs-who-target-white-girls.html

will not be able to properly tackle this problem. Multiculturalism and political correctness continue to prevent us from protecting young girls.

Government denies Islamic connection

In 2018, Lord Pearson asked a question in the House of Lords about the Islamic connection with these rape gangs. Replying on behalf of the government, Lord Young said:

"There is nothing in the Koran that encourages the sort of activity the noble Lord has referred to. ... Islam, like all world religions, does not support, advocate or condone child sexual exploitation. Indeed, respect for women is inherent in its faith."[12]

This is classic multiculturalist nonsense according to which all religions are basically the same, and all are forces for good in the world. If only that were true! However, it is demonstrably false. Many Muslims would disagree with Lord Young. He should try reading the Qur'an for himself. I recommend starting with surah 4, to understand what the Qur'an says about women.

How many girls sacrificed?

How many girls have suffered at the hands of these rape gangs? We know it has been going on for over 40 years, and still more details keep coming out in more locations. Only last month I saw a formal letter from a school warning parents about an Asian man looking suspiciously at young girls on the way to and from school in Greater London.

Thousands of girls have been sacrificed on the altar of multiculturalism. Teachers, police officers, social workers, schools, local authorities, and others have turned a blind eye for fear of being called 'racist', even though criticising a culture or a religion is not strictly racism. Denial of the Islamic connection is a denial of truth

---

[12] https://hansard.parliament.uk/Lords/2018-03-13/debates/AA1542AD-0A4F-4A1B-B93E-695AADDA26C2/ChildSexualExploitationGroomingGangs#contribution-CAC4B4E1-D327-412E-9FE6-80C0A2D4F26E

and a denial that contributes to the perpetuation of these crimes. Multiculturalism and political correctness have a lot to answer for. How many more girls will be sacrificed to these ideologies?

4

ISLAM, DAWKINS, AND FREE SPEECH

Note: This article followed a radio discussion I had on BBC Radio Ulster in 2017 with Imam Ajmal Masroor about free speech. Richard Dawkins had just had an event cancelled in Berkley, California due to protests about his criticism of Islam. That cancellation raised the profile of the debate about Islam and free speech. Here I discuss how intolerant Islam is of criticism of Muhammad.

Radio discussion on free speech

In 2017, prominent atheist Richard Dawkins had an event cancelled[1] in Berkley, California due to what was described as his "abusive speech" against Islam. This raises important questions about free speech and our ability to criticise Islam. I was invited to discuss this on BBC Radio Ulster on Wednesday with Ajmal Masroor, who is a London-based Imam who regularly appears in the media to discuss Islam-related issues. In the course of the discussion, Ajmal claimed that he would renounce his faith if there was an example where Muhammad said that someone should be killed for insulting him. The full 22-minute recording of this interview is available online.[2] In what follows, I will transcribe parts of the interview and refer to the recording with timings in square brackets so that you can check for yourself what was said.

---

[1] https://www.independent.co.uk/news/people/richard-dawkins-islamophobic-berkeley-event-cancelled-islam-muslim-uc-university-california-a7860281.html
[2] https://soundcloud.com/christianconcern/tim-dieppe-comments-after-richard-dawkins-is-accused-of-abusive-speech-against-islam

Should Dawkins be shut down?

Dawkins has been outspoken in his criticism of Christianity as well as of Islam. As he himself said:

> "I am known as a frequent critic of Christianity and have never been de-platformed for that. Why do you give Islam a free pass? Why is it fine to criticise Christianity but not Islam?"[3]

I pointed this out in the interview [5:00] and argued that Christians respond to harsh and offensive criticisms by looking to debate and discuss the claims being made. Indeed, Christians have debated with Richard Dawkins about Christianity and he can clearly be seen to have lost those debates, particularly the one with John Lennox which can be viewed on YouTube.[4] By contrast, criticism of Islam is too often seen as Islamophobic, or hate speech, and silenced, as has happened to Richard Dawkins with the cancellation of his event in California.

Ajmal agreed that Richard Dawkins should not have been shut down [3:03]. He also agreed that people feel limited in their ability to criticise Islam [6:42], but he claimed that Islam encourages free speech.

Are all religions equal?

Ajmal argued that all religions are forces for good in the world [8:37]. I was asked whether I agreed with this or sympathised with Dawkins' view that Islam is evil.

I began by comparing Jesus and Muhammad:

> Me [9:12]: "I want to compare Jesus and Muhammad on these points. When Jesus was heavily criticised, insulted, beaten, tortured, nailed up to a cross, what did he say? He said, 'Father forgive them', for what they are doing. Whereas when Muhammad was insulted, he said they should be killed. That's the real difference

---

[3] https://www.independent.co.uk/news/people/richard-dawkins-islamophobic-berkeley-event-cancelled-islam-muslim-uc-university-california-a7860281.html
[4] https://www.youtube.com/watch?v=zF5bPI92-5o

here that you have. You have to compare Jesus and Muhammad in terms of what they did and what their actions are."

I then went on to discuss Dawkins' contentious statement about Islam [9:39]. I began by putting his remarks in context. Here is what Dawkins had said:

> "It's tempting to say all religions are bad, and I do say all religions are bad, but it's a worse temptation to say all religions are equally bad because they're not."
>
> "If you look at the actual impact that different religions have on the world it's quite apparent that at present the most evil religion in the world has to be Islam."
>
> "It's terribly important to modify that because of course that doesn't mean all Muslims are evil, very far from it. Individual Muslims suffer more from Islam than anyone else."[5]

Note that he qualifies this by looking at the *"actual impact"* and, as I pointed out, more people are being killed in the name of Islam today, including many Muslims, than by any other religion in the world. I therefore agree with Dawkins, and against Ajmal, that all religions are not equally good.

Ajmal promises to renounce his faith

Ajmal then took great exception to my statement that Muhammad asked for people who insulted him to be killed.

> Ajmal [10:00]: "The prophet Muhammad was mocked, stoned, and all sorts of horrible things were perpetrated against him by his people. He never asked a single person to be killed because they insulted him or mocked him, never."
>
> Me: "Yes he did."
>
> Ajmal: "If you do not know Islam, it is OK to say I don't know Islam. I know my faith very well. Where in the Qur'an or the sayings of the prophet does it say kill a person who has mocked me? Can you give me one example of a statement of the prophet, which

---

[5] https://www.telegraph.co.uk/science/2017/06/11/richard-dawkins-religious-education-crucial-british-schoolchildren/

is authentic and referenced where the Prophet said: 'Kill the person who has mocked me.'?"

Me: "It is in the Hadith."

Ajmal: "It is not in the Hadith, don't give us the name called Hadith. Which book, what reference, and what is the exact quote."

Ajmal knows that it is unreasonable to expect exact quotations and references off the top of my head in a live radio interview. He then promised to renounce his faith if I could find a reference for Muhammad asking for someone who insulted him to be killed.

Ajmal [11:03]: "I will give you my own guarantee, I will renounce my faith if you can show me that the Prophet said kill a person who has mocked me, kill a person who has insulted me."

I then promised to put up some references on social media straight after the interview.

Did Muhammad ask for anyone who insulted him to be killed?

I was able to do a quick Google search on my phone while listeners were calling in, and found some references to quote. I tweeted an online article[6] and quoted some of these references [19:00].

From the Qur'an:

> Indeed, those who abuse Allah and His Messenger–Allah has cursed them in this world and the Hereafter and prepared for them a humiliating punishment. (Q 33:57)

Note that this includes abuse of the Messenger, and that they are cursed in this world. The passage continues as follows, commanding Muhammad's wives to wear veils so that the insults will stop, and promising that the insulting liars will be "seized and massacred."

> O Prophet, tell your wives and your daughters and the women of the believers to bring down over themselves [part] of their outer garments. That is more suitable that they will be known and not

---

[6] https://www.thereligionofpeace.com/pages/quran/insulters-islam.aspx

be abused. And ever is Allah Forgiving and Merciful. (60) If the hypocrites and those in whose hearts is disease and those who spread rumours in al-Madinah do not cease, (61) We will surely incite you against them; then they will not remain your neighbours therein except for a little. Accursed wherever they are found, [being] seized and massacred completely. (Q 33:59-61)

Another passage promises a painful punishment for those who abuse the Prophet:

> And among them are those who abuse the Prophet and say, "He is an ear." Say, "[It is] an ear of goodness for you that believes in Allah and believes the believers and [is] a mercy to those who believe among you." And those who abuse the Messenger of Allah–for them is a painful punishment. (Q 9:61)

This passage continues:

> Do they not know that whoever opposes Allah and His Messenger– that for him is the fire of Hell, wherein he will abide eternally? That is the great disgrace. (64) The hypocrites are apprehensive lest a surah be revealed about them, informing them of what is in their hearts. Say, "Mock [as you wish]; indeed, Allah will expose that which you fear." (65) And if you ask them, they will surely say, "We were only conversing and playing." Say, "Is it Allah and His verses and His Messenger that you were mocking?" (Q 9:63-65)

Note how those who have insulted or mocked Muhammad are described as "hypocrites." Later on, this passage continues:

> O Prophet, fight against the disbelievers and the hypocrites and be harsh upon them. And their refuge is Hell, and wretched is the destination. (Q 9:73)

From the Hadith:

Here is one story in which Muhammad asks for someone who insulted him to be killed.

> Allah's Apostle said, "Who is willing to kill Ka'b bin Al-Ashraf who has hurt Allah and His Apostle?" Thereupon Muhammad bin Maslama got up saying, "O Allah's Apostle! Would you like that I kill him?" The Prophet said, "Yes," (Sahih Bukhari 59.369)

The same incident is recounted in another Hadith:

> "Who will kill Ka'b b. Ashraf? He has maligned Allah, the Exalted, and His Messenger. Muhammad b. Maslama said: Messenger of Allah, do you wish that I should kill him? He said: Yes." (Sahih Muslim 1801)

In another incident, a man who mocked Muhammad by pouring the abdominal contents of a camel on Muhammad's back was killed along with others who joined in the mockery:

> Once the Prophet was offering prayers at the Ka'ba. Abu Jahl was sitting with some of his companions. One of them said to the others, "Who amongst you will bring the abdominal contents (intestines, etc.) of a camel of Bani so and so and put it on the back of Muhammad, when he prostrates?" The most unfortunate of them got up and brought it. He waited till the Prophet prostrated and then placed it on his back between his shoulders. I was watching but could not do any thing. I wish I had some people with me to hold out against them. They started laughing and falling on one another. Allah's Apostle was in prostration and he did not lift his head up till Fatima (Prophet's daughter) came and threw that (camel's abdominal contents) away from his back. He raised his head and said thrice, "O Allah! Punish Quraish." So it was hard for Abu Jahl and his companions when the Prophet invoked Allah against them as they had a conviction that the prayers and invocations were accepted in this city (Mecca). The Prophet said, "O Allah! Punish Abu Jahl, 'Utba bin Rabi'a, Shaiba bin Rabi'a, Al-Walid bin 'Utba, Umaiya bin Khalaf, and 'Uqba bin Al Mu'it (and he mentioned the seventh whose name I cannot recall). By Allah in Whose Hands my life is, I saw the dead bodies of those persons who were counted by Allah's Apostle in the Qalib (one of the wells) of Badr. (Sahih Bukhari 4.241)

Here is another story in which Muhammad endorses the killing of a slave who slandered him.

> A blind man had a slave-mother who used to abuse the Prophet and disparage him. He forbade her but she did not stop. He rebuked her but she did not give up her habit. One night she began to slander the Prophet and abuse him. So he took a dagger, placed it on her belly, pressed it, and killed her. A child who came between her legs was smeared with the blood that was there. When the morning came, the

Prophet was informed about it. He assembled the people and said: I adjure by Allah the man who has done this action and I adjure him by my right to him that he should stand up. Jumping over the necks of the people and trembling the man stood up. He sat before the Prophet and said: Messenger of Allah! I am her master; she used to abuse you and disparage you. I forbade her, but she did not stop, and I rebuked her, but she did not abandon her habit. I have two sons like pearls from her, and she was my companion. Last night she began to abuse and disparage you. So I took a dagger, put it on her belly and pressed it till I killed her. Thereupon the Prophet said: Oh be witness, no retaliation is payable for her blood. (Sahih Abi Dawud 4361)

Here is a further story in which Muhammad endorses killing someone who insulted him.

A Jewess used to abuse the Prophet and disparage him. A man strangled her till she died. The Messenger of Allah declared that no recompense was payable for her blood. (Sahih Abi Dawud 4362)

There are many more examples if we also include stories from the biography of Ibn Ishaq. A list of killings ordered or supported by Muhammad is available online.[7] Many of these were carried out for insulting Muhammad.

What does Sharia law say about insulting the prophet?

Based on the passages above, the consensus of Sharia law is that the punishment for insulting Muhammad is death. Several *fatwas* online make this clear. One says:

> The scholars are unanimously agreed that a Muslim who insults the Prophet (peace and blessings of Allaah be upon him) becomes a kaafir and an apostate who is to be executed.[8]

---

[7] https://wikiislam.net/wiki/List_of_Killings_Ordered_or_Supported_by_Muhammad
[8] https://www.muftisays.com/blog/Seifeddine-M/3016_17-09-2012/ruling-on-one-who-insults-the-prophet-peace-and-blessings-be-upon-him.html

There are some occasions when Muhammad chose to forgive people who insulted him. This same ruling argues:

> The Prophet (peace and blessings of Allaah be upon him) sometimes chose to forgive those who had insulted him, and sometimes he ordered that they should be executed, if that served a greater purpose. But now his forgiveness is impossible because he is dead, so the execution of the one who insults him remains the right of Allaah, His Messenger and the believers, and the one who deserves to be executed cannot be let off, so the punishment must be carried out.[9]

Another ruling also states that repentance would not avoid the death penalty:

> If the one who defamed him repents openly and is sincere, that will benefit him before Allaah, although his repentance does not waive the punishment for defaming the Prophet (peace and blessings of Allaah be upon him), which is execution.[10]

The classic manual of Sharia law, *The Reliance of the Traveller*, makes clear that apostasy carries the death penalty:

> When a person who has reached puberty and is sane voluntarily apostatizes from Islam, he deserves to be killed' (p. 595, o8.1).

The manual includes a list of *"Acts that Entail Leaving Islam."* These include: *"Reviling Allah or his Messenger."* (p597-98, o8.7).

Thus, insulting Muhammad is regarded as an act of apostasy which therefore carries the death penalty.

In 2017, a man in Pakistan was sentenced to death for allegedly insulting Muhammad on Facebook.[11] This is said to be the first ever death sentence involving social media.

---

[9] https://www.muftisays.com/blog/Seifeddine-M/3016_17-09-2012/ruling-on-one-who-insults-the-prophet-peace-and-blessings-be-upon-him.html

[10] https://islamqa.info/en/answers/14305/it-is-essential-to-respond-to-those-who-defame-the-prophet-peace-and-blessings-of-allaah-be-upon-him

[11] https://www.telegraph.co.uk/news/2017/06/12/man-sentenced-death-pakistan-insulting-prophet-muhammad-facebook/

Will Ajmal renounce his faith?

I have quoted several examples of Muhammad saying that someone who insulted him should be killed. These examples are the basis for Sharia law carrying the death penalty for insulting Muhammad. Ajmal said [21:06]: "No single person was ever put to death for insulting God or the Messenger." This is plain false.

Ajmal clearly said that he would renounce his faith if Muhammad can be shown to have said that a person who had insulted him should be killed. He challenged me to provide a single example, and I have provided several. He should therefore renounce his faith.

Later, Ajmal appeared to try to backtrack on his claim.

> In the Qur'an, where does it say, 'anyone who insults Allah, God, and his Messenger should be killed?' It doesn't say that. [20:12]

I agreed that those words do not appear in that form in the Qur'an, but that is not the point. Earlier, he had broadened his challenge to the Hadith, and to just a single example, and promised to renounce his faith if one could be found.

Ajmal should become a Christian

I sympathise with Ajmal. It is embarrassing for Muslims that Muhammad was extremely intolerant of criticism, and that criticism of Muhammad carries the death penalty. As I said in the interview, this was not the case with Jesus who cried out for forgiveness for his tormentors. Ajmal obviously prefers Christian ethics to Muslim ethics. He should follow Jesus rather than Muhammad. He should make good on his promise, renounce his faith, and accept Christianity.

5

ISLAMOPHOBIA: THREAT TO FREE SPEECH

Note: This essay was originally published in March 2024 as a briefing by the Free Speech Union entitled: *Banning Islamophobia: Blasphemy by the Backdoor.*[1] The briefing contained a foreword by Professor Richard Dawkins which is also reproduced here.

Foreword by Richard Dawkins

A phobia is an irrational fear; as in claustrophobia, agoraphobia or arachnophobia, all conditions deserving of sympathy. But fear can be rational too. An infantryman in a First World War trench would have every reason to fear going over the top. To accuse him of phobia would be uncharitable, to say the least. An Australian suspected of arachnophobia might point out that spiders with a dangerous bite are not rare. In Britain there's much less to fear from spiders, so my fear of them could fairly be called arachnophobia. Is there a group of people who, like Australians in the case of spiders, have good reason to fear Islam? If such a group exists, I suggest it would be found among Muslims themselves.

A gay Muslim living in an Islamic country might have reasonable misgivings. There are nine Muslim countries in which consensual homosexuality carries the death penalty. A Muslim woman in Iran might reasonably fear being arrested by the Morality Police for showing a tendril of hair. In Pakistan or Britain she might fear violent reprisals from her father, uncles or brothers if she's suspected of consorting with an unsuitable man. In Somalia, a girl might

---

[1] https://freespeechunion.org/banning-islamophobia-blasphemy-law-by-the-backdoor/

reasonably fear older female relatives who intend to hold her down and take a razorblade to her clitoris. Not phobia, just justifiable fear. In Saudi Arabia, an unmarried adulterer might reasonably fear the prescribed 100 lashes, while a married adulterer can expect the death penalty.

In Britain, phobia is hardly the right word for any fear Salman Rushdie might feel. Sir Iqbal Sacranie, the former Secretary General of the Muslim Council of Britain, said, "Death, perhaps, is a bit too easy for him. His mind must be tormented for the rest of his life unless he asks for forgiveness to Almighty Allah." A Muslim who is losing his faith would have good reason to fear the penalty for apostasy, which is death. When I taxed Sir Iqbal with this on television, he said, "It's very rarely enforced." That's good to hear, but a would-be apostate doesn't have to be phobic to still feel a reasonable fear.

The All Party Parliamentary Group's (APPG's) definition of Islamophobia begins with the statement that it is a form of racism. Tim Dieppe makes the obvious point that Islam is not a race, and he very well develops the inconsistencies that this remarkable solecism leads to. I'd make one further observation. A religion is something you can convert to, or opt out of. Your race isn't like that. You can't convert to a race or leave it. (That's if race is a meaningful concept at all. The point is controversial, but presumably the authors of the APPG report on Islamophobia think it is or they couldn't talk about racism.) The fact that you can't leave your race means that, if Islam is indeed a race, apostasy is literally impossible. Yet apostasy has to be possible in Islam or it couldn't be punishable by death. So the statement that Islamophobia is a form of racism is more than just incorrect. It contradicts a fundamental, and incidentally obnoxious, tenet of Islam.

In this brief Introduction I have not considered the issue of freedom of speech. Tim Dieppe covers it so well that I have nothing to add. Except this final thought. If 'Islamophobia' becomes punishable by law, will it be illegal to even state as a matter of fact that a woman in some Islamic countries can be stoned to death for the crime of speaking to a man other than her husband? Will I be arrested for stating the undenied fact that apostasy carries the death penalty? If so, bring it on. I look forward to defending myself in court.

Executive Summary

This essay argues that any attempt to define 'Islamophobia' poses a threat to freedom of speech. In particular, a definition that has been widely adopted by political parties and other organisations defines 'Islamophobia' so broadly that free speech is clearly inhibited. It has been proposed that the government also adopt this definition. Attempts to define Islamophobia should be dropped, including and especially by the government, political parties and local authorities. As Kemi Badenoch recently pointed out,[2] the Labour Party's adoption of this definition risks creating a "blasphemy law via the back door".

People in a free society must be free to criticise, question and even ridicule any belief or practice, including religious beliefs. The promotion of the concept of 'Islamophobia' risks silencing or censoring criticism of one religion above others. Acknowledging this is not tantamount to supporting irrational prejudice against Muslims.

A November 2018 report by the APPG on British Muslims, urged the government to adopt a legal definition of Islamophobia:

> Islamophobia is rooted in racism and is a type of racism that targets expressions of Muslimness or perceived Muslimness.

This definition was rapidly taken up by institutions including the Labour Party, the Liberal Democrats, the SNP, the Scottish Conservatives, Plaid Cymru, and the Scottish Greens. Members of these parties who fall foul of the definition risk being sanctioned: indeed, this is already happening. Others who have endorsed the definition include 52 local councils in England (15.6% of the total), five Welsh councils (22.7%), eight local authorities in Scotland (24%), as well as over 30 MPs and dozens of academics. The suspension of

---

[2] https://twitter.com/KemiBadenoch/status/1761856858220798395?s=20

Sir Trevor Phillips from the Labour Party in 2020-21 demonstrates how formal acceptance of the APPG definition by political parties serves to restrict freedom of speech. The suspension involved a confidential 11-page indictment and a meeting behind closed doors, which Phillips was barred from attending.

The APPG report claims that its aim is not "to curtail free speech or criticism of Islam as a religion", but its proposals nonetheless pose a threat to free speech. Indeed, the report implies that some criticisms of Islam might be out of bounds altogether:

> ...the recourse [to] a *supposed* right to criticise Islam results in nothing more than another subtle form of anti-Muslim racism... [our italics]

The report aims to broaden the definition of racism to include 'cultural racism', thereby inhibiting discussion of cultural practices. It also threatens the teaching of history: Islamophobia, we're told, includes "claims of Muslims spreading Islam by the sword or subjugating minority groups under their rule", which could, for instance, rule out criticising the actions of Boko Haram or Hamas. Even accusing Muslim majority states of exaggerating a genocide makes you an Islamophobe, meaning anyone who questions the Hamas government's description of Israel's military operation in Gaza as a 'genocide' is, according to the APPG's definition, Islamophobic. Finally, it is a threat to freedom of the press, in that journalists reporting on Islam-related stories are frequently accused of 'Islamophobia' and pressured to avoid covering Islamic aspects of news stories.

Defining 'Islamophobia' too broadly is a threat to free speech for non-Muslims and Muslims alike. The APPG definition in particular is not fit for purpose and should be dropped by those who have adopted it. In a free society, we must be free to debate and criticise any and all beliefs.

Introduction

This essay argues that allegations of 'Islamophobia' increasingly pose a threat to freedom of speech. In particular, a definition that has been widely adopted by political parties and other organisations defines 'Islamophobia' so broadly that it clearly inhibits free speech among their members. This is demonstrated by its use in practice as well as in theory. Proponents argue that the government should also formally adopt this definition.

People in a free society must be able to criticise each other's beliefs and practices. This necessarily includes religious beliefs and practices. The beliefs and practices of all religions and worldviews should be open to public scrutiny and people should be free to question, criticise, ridicule or joke about them. But the widespread acceptance of too broad a definition of 'Islamophobia' risks silencing or censoring criticism of Islam. It is therefore a threat to free speech.

There are people who harbour irrational prejudice against Muslims. In criticising a particular definition of 'Islamophobia' I'm not defending this prejudice. Muslim people are entitled to equal opportunities, equal treatment, and equal rights.

However, criticism of Islam is not the same as criticism of Muslims. Part of the purpose of this essay is to make clear that the two should be differentiated. Striking a believer, for example, is a crime; debating her beliefs is a right. Confusing the two risks shutting down debate and stifling free speech.

The government, and society as a whole, should be wary of attempts to define 'Islamophobia' in general, and adopting the APPG definition in particular. Free speech is already being curtailed by these attempts, and further adoption of such definitions is likely to further curtail free speech. Attempts to define 'Islamophobia' should be abandoned and replaced by the phrase 'anti-Muslim hatred'. I'm not arguing that 'anti-Muslim hatred' should be proscribed by law but merely pointing out that as a concept, it would be sufficient to describe the speech that those who use the term 'Islamophobia' object to. The Network of Sikh Organisations made the same point in its submission to the Home Affairs Islamophobia inquiry:

> We are of the view that 'anti-Muslim' hatred, (like 'anti-Sikh' or 'anti-Hindu') is much clearer language to describe hate

crime specifically against the Muslim community. We previously expressed this in written evidence to the APPG on British Muslims inquiry into a working definition of Islamophobia/ anti-Muslim hatred.[3]

This essay calls on the government not to adopt a formal definition of 'Islamophobia', and on political parties, local authorities and other groups to abandon the proposed APPG definition. The stakes are high. No religion should obtain a privileged position in society by preventing open criticism of its beliefs or practices. This is harmful to the functioning of a free and democratic society.

The origins of the term

French philosopher Pascal Bruckner points out that the term 'Islamophobia' was first used by colonial officials in the 19th century.[4] French official Andrée Quellien, writing in 1910, denounced both 'Islamophobia' and 'Islamophilia', and called for an objective view of Islam and Islamic practices. Another French official, Maurice Delafosse also criticised both 'Islamophobia' and 'Islamophilia'.

Bruckner argues that after the Iranian revolution of 1980, the term 'Islamophobia' "underwent a mutation that weaponized it".[5] Bruckner describes this as a "lexical rejuvenation" which aims at stigmatising criticism of Islam. French sources cite Ayatollah Khomeini describing Iranian women who rejected wearing the veil as being 'Islamophobic'.[6]

In the UK, Dr Zaki Badawi and Fuad Nahdi both claimed to have coined the term 'Islamophobia' in testimony to a House of Lords Select Committee.[7] The first known use of the word in print in the UK was by Tariq Modood in a book review published in *The Independent* on 16th December 1991, in which he discussed the view that *The Satanic Verses* was "a deliberate, mercenary act

---

[3] https://nsouk.co.uk/response-to-home-affairs-committee-islamophobia-inquiry/
[4] Paul Bruckner. 'An Imaginary Racism: Islamophobia and Guilt.' Wiley. 2018, pp.2-5.
[5] Ibid., 3.
[6] https://www.opendemocracy.net/en/5050/unpacking-idea-of-islamophobia-0/
[7] https://publications.parliament.uk/pa/ld200203/ldselect/ldrelof/95/2102307.htm

of Islamophobia."[8] Modood indicated that his own view was that "while Islamophobia is certainly at work, the real sickness is militant irreverence". It is instructive to note that in this case what is 'Islamophobic' is the content of a novel which does not actually formally reference Islam, though it can be taken as a satirical account of the origins of Islam.[9]

The term 'Islamophobia' gained significant profile and attention with the publication in 1997 of a report by the Runnymede Trust. Sir Trevor Phillips was then the chairman of the Runnymede Trust (the term has subsequently been used against him, as we discuss below). In his Foreword to the Runnymede report, Professor Gordon Conway wrote of a previous consultation paper published earlier in 1997, explaining:

> We did not coin the term Islamophobia. It was already in use among sections of the Muslim community as a term describing the prejudice and discrimination which they experience in their everyday lives. For some of us on the Commission it was a new term, a rather ugly term, and we were not sure how it would be received.[10]

There was also an important admission:

> The term is not, admittedly, ideal. Critics of it consider that its use panders to what they call political correctness, that it stifles legitimate criticism of Islam, and that it demonises and stigmatises anyone who wishes to engage in such criticism.

Indeed, the recent proposed definition of 'Islamophobia' has evolved in exactly the way the critics predicted. It is interesting to note how, even then, an attempted definition subtly conflated fear and criticism of Islam with fear of all or most Muslims. This is precisely the type of conflation which we encounter in current attempts to define the term. The Runnymede report bluntly stated: The term Islamophobia refers to unfounded hostility towards Islam.

---

[8] http://www.insted.co.uk/anti-muslim-racism.pdf
[9] See Chapter 5 of this book.
[10] https://www.runnymedetrust.org/publications/islamophobia-a-challenge-for-us-all

This summary definition clearly references Islam the religion, not Muslims the people. Presumably, then, to avoid being Islamophobic, one would need to have some foundation for hostility towards Islam, although the implication is that such blanket hostility would always be 'unfounded'. Even at this stage, then, there was an implication that you needed to agree or sympathise with Islamic teaching – or at least not criticise it – to avoid falling foul of the term.

But we are jumping ahead of ourselves. It is time to look at the APPG definition.

Islamophobia Defined

In November 2018, the All Party Parliamentary Group (APPG) on British Muslims released a report called *Islamophobia Defined*,[11] urging the government to adopt a legal definition of Islamophobia.

The proposed definition from the APPG is as follows:

> Islamophobia is rooted in racism and is a type of racism that targets expressions of Muslimness or perceived Muslimness.

In the Foreword to the report, Anna Soubry and Wes Streeting, co-chairs of the APPG on British Muslims, write:

> We hope our working definition will be adopted by Government, statutory agencies, civil society organisations and principally, British Muslim communities who have been central to this enterprise and whose valuable contributions have significantly shaped our thinking on this subject.

The report claims that "the aim of establishing a working definition of Islamophobia has neither been motivated by, nor is intended to curtail, free speech or criticism of Islam as a religion". It further states:

> Criticism of religion is a fundamental right in an open society and is enshrined in our commitment to freedom of speech.

---

[11] https://static1.squarespace.com/static/599c3d2febbd1a90cffdd8a9/t/5bfd1ea3352f531a6170ceee/1543315109493/Islamophobia+Defined.pdf

This is encouraging, but when we delve into the vagueness and ambiguity of the definition and the examples cited in the report, the commitment to free speech seems to disappear.

Adoption of the Definition

The APPG definition was rapidly adopted by many institutions. So broadly was it taken up, in fact, that it seems many people were waiting for someone to propose a definition which they could swiftly adopt. Of greatest concern is the formal adoption of it by political parties. Labour, the Liberal Democrats, the Green Party, the Scottish National Party, the Scottish Conservatives, Plaid Cymru, and the Scottish Greens have all formally adopted the definition. This means that members of any of these parties who say something which could fall foul of the definition risk being sanctioned. As we shall see, this has already started to happen.

A dedicated website lists the various parliamentarians, groups and academics that have endorsed the definition.[12] The website also lists over 30 MPs who have endorsed the definition as well as dozens of academics and Islamic organisations. Freedom of Information requests carried out by Hardeep Singh for a Civitas report found that 52 councils in England have adopted the APPG definition (15.6% of the total).[13] Additionally, many Welsh councils have adopted it (22.7%), as have eight Scottish local authorities (24%). Councillors in these areas, or indeed council workers, could face sanctions for saying something that falls foul of the definition.

Perhaps most notably, the dedicated website for the definition originally featured a *fatwa* on the necessity of endorsing the definition of Islamophobia. The *fatwa* cites Islamic texts to justify supporting the definition. It states:

> According to the principles of the higher objectives of the Sharia, 'the crux of the matter is the signified, not the signifier' (al- *'ibrat* bi-l-musammayāt lā bi-l-asmā'); in other words, we should not be

---

[12] https://islamophobia-definition.com/#endorsements
[13] https://www.civitas.org.uk/publications/islamophobia-revisited/

arguing over technical details relating to the definition but rather concern ourselves with the essence, i.e., what service the definition might do for the Ummah.[14]

The 'Ummah' is the global Muslim community. The *fatwa* also appears to imply that Muslims should not argue over technical details but consider whether the definition will serve the Ummah. This *fatwa* concludes that the proposed definition will indeed serve the Ummah, therefore implying an obligation on Muslims to support it.

Threats to Free Speech

There are various problems with this definition, which is already curbing free speech in some contexts. It is worth examining the issues in some detail.

'Islam' is not defined

There is no attempt to define 'Islam' or 'Muslimness' in the APPG report. The report is a 70-page discussion about defining 'Islamophobia' which makes no attempt to state what 'Islam' actually is. Therefore, we do not know what it is that people are accused of being 'phobic' of. This makes the definition of 'Islamophobia' vulnerable to people who may want to define 'Islam' in a particular way. For example, some Muslims would regard it as 'Islamophobic' to claim that Islam discriminates against women, whereas others would not disagree with this claim. Similarly, many Muslims would say it is 'Islamophobic' to claim that Islam teaches about violent jihad, whereas others would openly state that this is what it teaches. There are many widely differing interpretations of Islam. Is criticism of any or every interpretation equally 'Islamophobic'? Who decides precisely what is or is not 'Islamic'? If the meaning of 'Islam' is open-ended then it evades public scrutiny and accountability, and means one cannot know in advance what will be considered 'Islamophobic'.

---

[14] https://islamophobia-definition.com/wp-content/uploads/2019/03/Islamophobia-Fatwa_.pdf

Conflation of the religion with the people

It is one thing to criticise a religion or the beliefs and practices of a religion and another to discriminate against adherents of that religion. The definition of 'Islamophobia' immediately conflates the religion of Islam with Muslim people and makes this into an issue of 'Muslimness'. However, if the concern of the report is really Muslims as people, then it would be better to make that clear. It may have been more useful for the report to discuss the term 'Muslimophobia', which would at least make clear that it did not seek to prohibit criticism of a religion but rather, irrational discrimination against Muslims. This could also be described as 'anti-Muslim discrimination'. Using the word 'Islamophobia' will inevitably result in people concluding that they cannot criticise Islam without being accused of being 'Islamophobic'. We should aim to avoid this conflation by using a different term.

'Perceived Muslimness' is too vague

The definition of 'Islamophobia' hinges on 'Muslimness'. Just what 'Muslimness' means is left undefined, perhaps deliberately. In fact, the definition is actually rooted in 'perceived Muslimness', which is entirely subjective. It is not even clear who is doing the perceiving. Is it the victim or the perpetrator? For the definition to hinge entirely on subjective perception in this way is unacceptable. This means there is no way of knowing in advance whether something will be deemed 'Islamophobic' or not. What matters is whether someone *perceives* it to be so.

For example, a Freedom of Information request in 2017 found that as many as 25% of 'Islamophobic hate crimes' recorded by the Metropolitan Police were committed against non-Muslims or people of unknown faith.[15] Some of the victims were Hindus, atheists, Christians, Sikhs and even Jews. Does this make sense?

---

[15] https://www.spectator.co.uk/article/the-spectator-s-notes-16-march-2017/

Can one be Islamophobic towards a non-Muslim? If the definition hinges on perception, then presumably the answer is yes. Is 'perception' determined by appearance? If so, then one could only be Islamophobic towards someone who *looks* like a Muslim. But not all Muslims wear distinctive clothing. Both 'Islam' and 'Muslimness' are left undefined, but the use of this term as endorsed by the report certainly extends beyond appearance.

Furthermore, hardline groups sometimes define 'Muslimness' quite narrowly. Dame Sara Khan, head of the Commission for Countering Extremism, has written:

> A narrow understanding of 'Muslimness' leaves behind those Muslims who, because of how they choose to live their lives or practise their religion, don't have a 'Muslimness' that other Muslims find acceptable.[16]

Does this mean that a Muslim who decides not to wear a *hijab* is being Islamophobic, as the Ayatollah Khomeini maintained? What about someone who abandons the religion and converts to Christianity or atheism? Is that an Islamophobic act? Rooting the definition in perception could allow these actions to be described as 'Islamophobic'.

However, other interpretations of the definition would make it impossible for a Muslim to be Islamophobic. Is that how such a definition should work? Sara Khan comments on attempts by some Muslims to police the behaviour of others:

> In our own country, the abuse, vilification and hostility towards Ahmadiyyah Muslims by other Muslims is a case in point. Other Muslims boycott Ahmadiyyah businesses and restaurants, bully Ahmadiyyah children at school, and distribute leaflets calling for their death. If this abuse was experienced by Muslims at the hands of non-Muslims, it would be perceived as anti-Muslim hatred; why should it be any different just because the perpetrators are Muslims themselves?

---

[16] https://www.huffingtonpost.co.uk/entry/islamophobia-extremism-hate-crime-racism_uk_5c0566e8e4b066b5cfa475a3

She further writes, "An inclusive attempt to define Islamophobia must address this." But this kind of behaviour is studiously ignored in the report and anti-Muslim actions by other Muslims are not addressed.

Islam is not a race

The definition starts by saying: "Islamophobia is rooted in racism." The aim is clearly for 'Islamophobia' to be seen as a type of racism. But Islam is not a race. It is a religion. People from all kinds of ethnic backgrounds are Muslims. Muslims do not see themselves as anything like a separate race. This is clearly a wrongheaded way to define 'Islamophobia'.

Even if Islam were a 'racial' religion, restricted to a particular ethnic group, criticism of the beliefs and practices of this religion should still be allowed in a free and open society. Defining 'Islamophobia' as a "type of racism" is clearly an attempt to stigmatise any criticism of Islamic beliefs or practices as racist.

Freedom to criticise and even ridicule religious beliefs and practices is protected by a hard-won amendment to the Public Order Act 1986. Section 29J, known as the Waddington Amendment, reads as follows:

> Protection of freedom of expression
>
> Nothing in this Part shall be read or given effect in a way which prohibits or restricts discussion, criticism or expressions of antipathy, dislike, ridicule, insult or abuse of particular religions or the beliefs or practices of their adherents, or of any other belief system or the beliefs or practices of its adherents, or proselytising or urging adherents of a different religion or belief system to cease practising their religion or belief system.[17]

This is very strong protection for free speech in relation to religious belief. People can be persuaded to change their religion and there should be strong protections in law for people who wish to persuade others to change their religion, or indeed to abandon religious belief altogether.

---

[17] https://www.legislation.gov.uk/ukpga/1986/64/section/29J

The attempt to redefine 'Islamophobia' as a type of racism may be a deliberate attempt to restrict free speech when it comes to criticism of Islam, because racist speech is not covered by the Waddington Amendment.

Cultural racism

In fact, the authors of the report wish to extend the concept of racism to include 'cultural racism'. The report explains:

> The concept of racialisation thus situates Islamophobia within anti-racism discourse which is not however just informed by biological race, but by a culture – broadly defined – that is perceived to be inferior to and by the dominant one. (p39)

So, racism becomes not merely biological, but cultural. The implication is that if 'Islamic culture' is in any way perceived to be inferior to British culture, then that is by definition Islamophobic. By this definition, discussing how Islamic culture might give fewer rights to women, and how that might be inferior to a culture which provides women with more rights, would be Islamophobic. Opposing the mandatory wearing of the hijab or polygamous marriage on the grounds that they are bad for women could be classed as Islamophobic. Once we sign up to the concept of 'cultural racism', with 'Islamophobia' being defined in this way, we risk losing the freedom to criticise Islamic culture altogether. In theory, a member of a political party or organisation that has signed up to this definition could be disciplined for Islamophobia if they said that UK law is preferable to Sharia law.

Threat to History

A list of examples of Islamophobia in the report includes: "claims of Muslims spreading Islam by the sword or subjugating minority groups under their rule" (p.57). Again, this would, by implication, make it Islamophobic to talk about some of the actions of ISIS or Hamas or other fundamentalist groups or indeed the history of Muslim conquests and Islamic imperialism.

Historian Tom Holland has written a great deal about Islamic history. He wrote in a tweet:

> The definition of Islamophobia the Government is being asked to approve is one that threatens to criminalise "claims of Muslims spreading Islam by the sword or subjugating minority groups under their rule". But most Muslims, for most of history, would have been fine with these claims.[18]

In a further tweet he explained:

> The definition of Islam we are being given is of a liberalised, westernised Islam – but Islamic civilisation is not to be defined solely by liberal, Western standards. Military conquest and the subjugation of minority groups have absolutely been features of Islamic imperialism.[19]

And:

> We risk the ludicrous situation of being able to write without fear of prosecution about the Christian tradition of crusading or antisemitism, but not the Islamic tradition of jihad or the jizya.[20]

So, this definition of Islamophobia would silence historians or deem them Islamophobic if they write about the history of Islamic conquests. This is unacceptable in a free society.

The Network of Sikh Organisations has pointed out that discussion of foundational historical events for Sikhism would be deemed Islamophobic under this definition.[21] The Ninth Guru of Sikhism, Tegh Bahadur, was executed by Mughal authorities when he stood up for the freedom of religion of Hindu priests who were being converted to Islam by force. Merely relating this story could be deemed Islamophobic. The organisation points out that many gurdwaras have pictures of *shaheeds* or martyrs hanging on their walls which

---

[18] https://twitter.com/holland_tom/status/1128756384537956352
[19] https://twitter.com/holland_tom/status/1128757203740000256
[20] https://twitter.com/holland_tom/status/1128758289070739457
[21] https://nsouk.co.uk/2019/01/

could also be deemed Islamophobic.[22] This would mean one religion penalising another religion for talking accurately about its history. It is not only historical events, but the reporting of current affairs that can be caught up in this way. Another example provided in the report is: "Accusing Muslims as a group, or Muslim majority states, of inventing or exaggerating Islamophobia, ethnic cleansing or genocide perpetrated against Muslims." (p56). This makes it Islamophobic to accuse Hamas, for example, of exaggerating claims of genocide by Israel in Gaza. Islamic claims of 'genocide' are unassailable on pain of being deemed Islamophobic.

The language of 'phobia' is unhelpful

Strictly speaking, a 'phobia' is an irrational fear. In this sense 'Islamophobia' would mean an irrational fear of Islam. However, the 'phobia' suffix is now used as a catch-all to stigmatise legitimate criticisms of beliefs and behaviours. These include homophobia, transphobia and Islamophobia. Thus, all opposition to same-sex marriage can be characterised as an irrational fear of homosexuality – or homophobic –rather than a sincere religious conviction that marriage should be between a man and a woman. Likewise, expressing the view that some people may experience medical regret after gender reassignment surgery can be characterised as rooted in an irrational fear of transgender people – or transphobic. The effect of such 'phobia' terms is to silence legitimate debate.

Where does this end? Some people are promoting the term 'Christophobia' in order to join in the competition for victim status. But if every ideology gets its own 'phobia', would it not be impossible to legitimately criticise any? We could have Toryphobia, Capitalistophobia, Socialistophobia, Atheistophobia, Sikhophobia, Hinduphobia, Communistophobia, Environmentalistophobia, Libertarianophobia... President Putin has taken to accusing 'Western elites' of encouraging 'Russophobia' which exemplifies

---

[22] https://nsouk.co.uk/why-all-sikhs-should-oppose-the-controversial-definition-of-islamophobia/

the use of 'phobia' language to discredit people one disagrees with without actually engaging with the arguments.[23] In the discussion by Moray Council about adopting the APPG definition of Islamophobia, some members complained that they had experienced 'Anglophobia' whilst living in Scotland. Adoption of a definition of 'Anglophobia' was discussed.[24] Do we really want people competing for victim status in this way, with everyone seeking to shut down criticism of their own beliefs as being 'phobic'?

Muslims and members of other religions and political groups should not be afraid to be confronted with objections and criticisms. Likewise, if society does not want to encourage competition for victimhood and the silencing of legitimate debate, then it should not condone the labelling of criticisms as 'phobias'. By adopting a formal definition of 'Islamophobia', organisations and political parties are encouraging this stigmatisation and silencing of debate. If we accept 'Islamophobia', why not all the other phobias listed above?

Muslims themselves have spoken out against this. Khalid Mahmood MP was the first Muslim MP to be elected to Parliament. In a debate in the House of Commons, he said:

> I have been on the receiving end of hate mail and actions from both the far right and from the Islamist community. ... I will take no lessons from anybody who tells me that I am Islamophobic or that I am too much of a Muslim.
>
> We are proud Muslims, and we should start to move away from a victim mentality and be positive about who we are.[25]

In the same debate, John Hayes MP quoted Muslim scholar, Professor Mohammed Abdel-Haq:

---

[23] https://www.independent.co.uk/tv/news/russia-vladimir-putin-victory-day-speech-b2335372.html
[24] https://www.civitas.org.uk/content/files/Islamophobia-Revisited.pdf
[25] https://www.theyworkforyou.com/debates/?id=2019-05-16b.411.0&s=Khalid+Mahmood#g419.5

Most Muslims in this country see the preoccupation with Islamophobia, which is increasingly peddled by guilt-ridden white liberals and self-appointed Muslim campaigners, as far from being in their interests, an initiative that is likely to separate, segregate and stigmatise them and their families.[26]

Is the APPG report itself Islamophobic?

Amongst the list of examples of Islamophobia in the APPG report is this one:

> Accusing Muslim citizens of being more loyal to the 'Ummah' (transnational Muslim community) or to their countries of origin, or to the alleged priorities of Muslims worldwide, than to the interests of their own nations. (p.56)

This is interesting in the light of the *fatwa* above, which argues that Muslims should support the definition of Islamophobia precisely because it serves the Ummah. Even to report this *fatwa* could be Islamophobic according to this definition.

This would also mean that the Casey Review would be Islamophobic for reporting that:

> We found a growing sense of grievance among sections of the Muslim population, and a stronger sense of identification with the plight of the 'Ummah', or global Muslim community.[27]

Reporting of information like this could be censored as Islamophobic under this definition. No research or report by any organisation which has adopted this definition could safely speculate about loyalty to the Ummah.

Another example of Islamophobia in the report is characterising "Muslims as being 'sex groomers'" (p.57). Of course, the overwhelming majority of Muslims have nothing to do with grooming gangs but the perpetrators of these gangs have been described as "by and large... Muslim men of Pakistani heritage". In fact, this

---

[26] https://www.theyworkforyou.com/debates/?id=2019-05-16b.411.0#g416.3
[27] https://assets.publishing.service.gov.uk/government/uploads/system/uploads/attachment_data/file/575973/The_Casey_Review_Report.pdf

may be why the government resisted publishing its review into the characteristics of grooming gangs – for fear of being branded 'Islamophobic'.[28]

Other government reports that could be challenged on the grounds of alleged 'Islamophobia' would include Peter Clarke's investigation into the 'Trojan Horse' affair in Birmingham schools[29] and Eric Pickles' report into electoral fraud in Tower Hamlets.[30] Ofsted's attempts to promote shared values could also be challenged. This is aside from counter-terrorism reports and operations discussed below.

Threat to press freedom

Several journalists have been accused of being Islamophobic for reporting on Islam-related stories. These include *The Times* journalists Dominic Kennedy[31] and Andrew Norfolk,[32] both of whom wrote about the grooming gang scandal. Already journalists are very careful in what they say about Islamist terrorism. If the APPG definition were accepted, then reporting of issues such as these would be seriously hindered. Journalists might not even be able to mention the religion of Muslim perpetrators or discuss possible religious motivations for their crimes. There could be no public debate about whether mosques should be allowed to broadcast the call to prayer, for example, as any dissent would be deemed 'Islamophobic'.

The Muslim Council of Britain (MCB) already seeks to censor press articles that it alleges are Islamophobic. Miqdaad Versi, assistant secretary general of the MCB, regularly complains about alleged 'Islamophobia' in the UK media. He has issued numerous

---

[28] https://www.independent.co.uk/news/uk/home-news/grooming-gangs-review-petition-home-office-characteristics-research-debate-a9388746.html
[29] https://assets.publishing.service.gov.uk/government/uploads/system/uploads/attachment_data/file/340526/HC_576_accessible_-.pdf
[30] https://www.gov.uk/government/news/sir-eric-pickles-publishes-report-into-tackling-electoral-fraud
[31] https://www.mend.org.uk/wp-content/uploads/2017/04/MENDs-response-to-kennedy-allegations.pdf
[32] https://5pillarsuk.com/2019/06/27/report-unmasks-anti-muslim-reporting-by-times-journalist-andrew-norfolk/

complaints to the Independent Press Standards Organisation (IPSO) and frequently obtains corrections or apologies. In one case he succeeded in getting the *Sun* and the *Mail* to issue a correction stating: "We are happy to make clear that Islam as a religion does not support so-called honour killings."[33] Many Muslims would beg to differ and could cite scripture in defence of this practice. The journalist Will Heaven cites a national newspaper editor as confirming that he frequently corrects stories when Versi complains about them, simply to put a stop to the deluge of emails which will follow if no correction is published.[34] Separately, Heaven argues that there is a degree of self-censorship going on because of the 'chilling effect' of these complaints.[35]

It is no surprise that the MCB, with Versi taking the lead, has been one of the most vocal organisations campaigning for formal adoption of the APPG definition of Islamophobia[36] (and recently calling for an investigation into the Conservative Party's "structural Islamophobia").[37] If this definition were formally accepted in law, or by press associations or IPSO, this would lead to further censorship of media reporting on Islam-related issues. Press freedom to report honestly and openly about Islamic stories would be lost.

Fear of 'Islamophobia' hindering justice
The Casey Review highlighted another problem:

> Too many public institutions, national and local, state and non-state, have gone so far to accommodate diversity and freedom of expression that they have ignored or even condoned regressive, divisive and harmful cultural and religious practices, for fear of being branded racist or Islamophobic...

---

[33] https://www.spiked-online.com/2017/01/18/policing-criticism-of-islam-the-new-star-chamber/#.WICLbxuLSUk
[34] https://www.newenglishreview.org/revealed-the-press-regulators-leaked-guidelines-on-islamophobia/
[35] https://www.spectator.co.uk/article/the-tricks-and-tactics-of-miqdaad-versi/
[36] https://www.newstatesman.com/politics/2019/05/government-has-caved-ideologues-opposed-appg-definition-islamophobia
[37] https://mcb.org.uk/extremism-in-the-conservative-party-muslim-council-of-britain-writes-to-conservative-chair-asking-for-action-against-islamophobia/

At its most serious, it might mean public sector leaders ignoring harm or denying abuse.

Already then, even before there was a formal definition of 'Islamophobia', public institutions appear to have been afraid of this label and were turning a blind eye to injustice as a result. People have been afraid to say, or act on, what they really think, even at the risk of perpetuating injustice and harm. This situation would become worse should public institutions adopt a formal definition.

Undermining counter-terrorism operations

Richard Walton, former Head of Counter-Terrorism Command of the Metropolitan Police, has warned that adopting the APPG's definition of 'Islamophobia' would "over time cripple the UK's successful counter-terrorism strategy and counter-terrorism operations". He said:

> The APPG definition would thwart the prosecution of individuals for possession of extremist material and dissemination of terrorist publications; even prosecution for membership of (and encouragement of support for) proscribed terrorist groups. Imagine how Anjem Choudary might have used the label 'Islamophobic' in his defence.[38]

Lord Carlile, former Independent Reviewer of Terrorism Legislation, also warned of the legal problems that would arise from the government adopting this definition.

> Successful and accepted counter-terrorism measures would run the risk of being declared unlawful. The Prevent strand of counter-terrorism policy, which would be thrown into turmoil by the APPG, provokes a refrain of clichéd criticism, but that is rarely evidence based: Prevent demonstrates statistically and evidentially a high net profit of success, which would be lost. The APPG definition would lead to Judicial Review litigation that would hold

---

[38] https://conservativehome.com/2019/04/29/this-islamophobia-definition-would-if-adopted-by-ministers-pose-problems-for-national-security/

back the evolution of better counter-terrorism law and practice hand in hand with strengthened religious tolerance.[39]

A Policy Exchange report, co-authored by Richard Walton and Tom Wilson, warns:

> In essence, therefore, the proposed definition risks diminishing freedom of speech and impairing our ability, as a society, to debate the causes of Islamist extremism. Inadvertently, it could work against open and far reaching debate on Islamist and other threats, and effectively introduce a blasphemy law which could result in police interventions and arrests by officers for alleged Islamophobic ('racist') words and behaviour.[40]

The report cautions that legal adoption of the definition would result in the police, the Crown Prosecution Service, the judiciary, and Her Majesty's Prison and Probation Service, all being branded 'institutionally Islamophobic'. Indeed, the concept of 'institutional Islamophobia' is discussed at length in the APPG report. The vagueness of the definition would make this allegation impossible to defend against. If we are serious about tackling terrorism, we need to be able to have frank and open conversations about the causes and ideologies involved. Defining 'Islamophobia' in the way suggested by the APPG is a serious impediment to such conversations.

Silencing criticism of Islam

The APPG report makes explicit that some criticisms of Mohammed or of Islam should be out of bounds.

> As such, the recourse to the notion of free speech and a supposed right to criticise Islam results in nothing more than another subtle form of anti-Muslim racism, whereby the criticism humiliates, marginalises, and stigmatises Muslims. One, real life example of this concerns the issue of 'grooming gangs'. (p35)

Notice how the report refers to "a supposed right to criticise Islam", as if that right doesn't really exist. The report continues:

---

[39] https://policyexchange.org.uk/publication/islamophobia-crippling-counter-terrorism/
[40] https://policyexchange.org.uk/publication/islamophobia-crippling-counter-terrorism/

Participants reported being told that 'Mohammed is a paedophile', for instance. This comment does not, in a strictly grammatical sense, have the victim themselves as subject, but is rather an example of the 'criticism of Islam' as it is actually articulated and experienced. Yet, clearly, it is aimed at (and can achieve) harm to individual Muslims, and is not rooted in any meaningful theological debate but rather in a racist attempt to 'other' Muslims in general, associating them with the crime our society sees as most abhorrent of all. (p35)

What is being referred to here, as the report acknowledges, is actually criticism of Mohammed, not of Muslims. Indeed, some might argue that this *is* a valid theological debate because this is a criticism of Mohammed that is based on Islamic traditions. Various Islamic Hadith and histories narrate that Mohammed married Aisha when she was six years old and consummated the marriage when she was nine.[41] Would these Hadith and histories themselves be branded Islamophobic, insofar as they lend support to those making the supposedly Islamophobic allegation against the religion's founder?

It appears therefore that the authors of the report, while paying lip service to free speech, do want to silence criticism of Islam, considering such criticism 'Islamophobic' even when it is rooted in Islamic teaching. Legalisation of this definition comes dangerously close to bringing into effect an Islamic blasphemy law.

Allegations of Islamophobia abound

There is no attempt in the APPG report to determine in what circumstances, if any, accusations of Islamophobia would be invalid. If this definition had the force of law, then it is difficult to see how an accusation of Islamophobia could be disproven.

The APPG report claims, without any evidence, that "Muslim students who fail to secure entry offers from Russell Group universities" are victims of Islamophobia. This kind of claim evidences a tendency to blame any experienced difficulties on Islamophobia.

---

[41] https://www.answering-islam.org/Shamoun/prepubescent.htm

The list of those who have been accused of being Islamophobic is long and illustrious. It includes former Prime Ministers Theresa May,[42] Tony Blair,[43] and Boris Johnson.[44] Her Majesty's Chief Inspector of Education, Amanda Spielman, was accused of being Islamophobic for supporting a head teacher of a London primary school which banned the hijab for girls under the age of eight.[45] Sarah Champion, MP for Rotherham, was accused of being Islamophobic for warning that politicians should not be afraid to discuss the high number of sexual exploitation and grooming cases against men of Pakistani heritage in the UK.[46] For this, she lost her position in the Shadow Cabinet at the time. Maajid Nawaz, co-founder of Quilliam, who identifies as a Muslim, is often accused of Islamophobia for speaking out against Islamic extremism.[47] Even Muslims who endorse the APPG definition of Islamophobia are not exempt from accusations of being Islamophobic: Mayor of London Sadiq Khan, who identifies as a Muslim and has endorsed the definition, has also been accused of being Islamophobic.[48]

Opposition to the definition

The view that the APPG definition of Islamophobia threatens freedom of speech has united diverse groups. In May 2019, an open letter was sent to the then Home Secretary Sajid Javid warning the government against adopting the definition.[49] The letter was signed by over 40 experts from a range of religious backgrounds

---

[42] https://www.independent.co.uk/voices/as-a-british-muslim-i-m-terrified-that-theresa-may-winner-of-2015-s-islamophobe-of-the-year-is-my-new-prime-minister-a7133981.html
[43] https://sourcenews.scot/dossier-islamophobia-in-the-labour-party/
[44] https://www.theguardian.com/commentisfree/2020/jan/05/boris-johnson-islamophobia-sinister-level-muslims
[45] https://www.independent.co.uk/news/education/education-news/ofsted-hijab-ban-islamophobia-schools-amanda-spielman-national-education-union-neu-a8283786.html
[46] https://www.telegraph.co.uk/news/2017/08/17/sarah-champion-used-scapegoat-warning-cultural-link-child-sex/
[47] https://splinternews.com/what-we-mean-and-don-t-mean-by-islamophobia-1793858569
[48] https://www.ihrc.org.uk/event-report-islamophobia-awards-2018/
[49] https://archive.christianconcern.com/sites/default/files/Islamophobia_Open_Letter_To_Home_Secretary.pdf

representing Sikhs, Christians, atheists and others. Signatories included Professor Richard Dawkins, Bishop Michael Nazir-Ali, Peter Tatchell, Lord Singh of Wimbledon, Stephen Evans of the National Secular Society, Emma Webb of Civitas, Baroness Cox of Queensbury, Mohammed Amin MBE, Ade Omooba MBE, and myself on behalf of Christian Concern. The list includes names and organisations that are rarely found together. Stephen Evans, CEO of the National Secular Society, wrote:

> It's not often that we at the National Secular Society agree with Christian Concern! So when we do, it's always worth sitting up and taking notice.[50]

The open letter argued that the definition "is being taken on without an adequate scrutiny or proper consideration of its negative consequences for freedom of expression, and academic or journalistic freedom". It continued:

> We are concerned that allegations of Islamophobia will be, indeed already are used to effectively shield Islamic beliefs and even extremists from criticism, and that formalising this definition will result in it being employed effectively as something of a backdoor blasphemy law... we are concerned that the definition will be used to shut down legitimate criticism and investigation... No religion should be given special protection against criticism.[51]

Many other journalists and media commentators also criticised the definition. This effort was successful in that the government did not formally adopt the APPG definition but instead, announced that it would appoint two expert advisors to lead a new study to propose another definition.[52] Much later, in 2022 under a new Prime Minister, and in recognition of the various concerns expressed, the

---

[50] https://www.premierchristianity.com/home/silencing-criticism-of-islam-isnt-the-way-to-tackle-anti-muslim-hate/2793.article
[51] https://archive.christianconcern.com/sites/default/files/Islamophobia_Open_Letter_To_Home_Secretary.pdf
[52] https://www.gov.uk/government/news/new-process-set-out-to-establish-a-working-definition-of-islamophobia

government dropped plans to come up with an official definition of Islamophobia.[53]

The government's Islamophobia advisor

In July 2019, the government announced the appointment of Imam Qari Asim as an advisor to lead the work on proposing a definition of Islamophobia.[54] This appointment was made on the last full day in office of Theresa May's administration. Qari Asim has been a vocal critic of Boris Johnson, and it is likely that Theresa May and others in her administration were aware of this when they rushed his appointment through before leaving office. His appointment looked like a deliberate parting shot at the incoming prime minister, landing him with an appointee who would be difficult to replace.

A 2018 article by Boris Johnson that described women wearing the burka as looking like "letter boxes" or "bank robbers" actually argued *against* banning the burka.[55] Nonetheless, Qari Asim argued that Johnson's comments "fanned the flames of Islamophobia" and "legitimised the hatred that exists towards Muslim women".[56] For Asim, then, such comments, even made in jest, are unacceptable. Asim also tweeted a *Guardian* article in 2018 saying: "Boris Johnson's white privilege: imagine he was a black woman."[57]

In 2019, it was reported that Asim had expressed support for Pakistani radical cleric Khadim Rizvi.[58] Rizvi supported the death penalty for Asia Bibi who was falsely accused of insulting Mohammad. Asim posted a statement on his Facebook page in 2017 in solidarity with the cleric whose organisation was behind protests

---

[53] https://www.independent.co.uk/news/uk/home-news/islamophobia-definition-conservative-government-michael-gove-b2213075.html
[54] https://www.gov.uk/government/news/independent-expert-appointed-to-tackle-islamophobia
[55] https://www.telegraph.co.uk/news/2018/08/05/denmark-has-got-wrong-yes-burka-oppressive-ridiculous-still/
[56] https://www.lbc.co.uk/radio/presenters/tom-swarbrick/boris-johnson-legitimised-hatred-towards-muslims/
[57] https://x.com/QariAsim/status/970306190663213057
[58] https://premierchristian.news/en/news/article/govt-advisor-publicly-supported-cleric-who-wants-asia-bibi-dead

in Islamabad, which were marred by violence. In response to the news report, Asim took the post down and claimed that he had not intended to endorse Rizvi. Asim had previously signed a letter calling on the government to offer asylum to Asia Bibi.[59]

Asim has argued that all depictions of Muhammad are "haram" – meaning 'forbidden' – in Islam.[60] This would include medieval images which have been described as masterpieces. This is a strict interpretation of Islamic law which not all Muslims would agree with. In 2018 Qari Asim gave a talk at a workshop organised by The Centre for Muslim-Christian Studies on 'Law of the Land and Islam'. I was present at the event. The PowerPoint slides and an audio recording of his talk are available online.[61]

In his talk, Asim argued that Muslims should obey the law of the land *most of the time*. But he also made clear how he would like the law to accommodate Islamic ideas. For example, he would like to see polygamy legalised and inheritance to favour male heirs in line with Sharia principles. He also supports Islamic finance, including a ban on interest being charged.[62]

Asim then went on to discuss areas of current law that "really challenge Muslims". He highlighted 'same-sex marriage', the absence of blasphemy laws and the honour of the prophet. In relation to blasphemy and the honour of the prophet, Asim claimed that "Muslims cherish freedom of speech", but then went on to argue:

> As we can have exceptions to the freedom of speech on the basis of some words or actions being offensive or distasteful, then if this is something that is distasteful to Muslims, or they find it offensive... then whether we can have that exception or not.[63]

I understood this to mean that he would like exceptions to free speech protections to include any criticism of Muhammad. In the Q&A session I pressed him on whether it would make a difference

---

[59] https://www.bbc.co.uk/news/uk-46193439
[60] https://www.bbc.co.uk/news/magazine-30814555
[61] https://www.cmcsoxford.org.uk/research/public-life/law-workshops
[62] See chapter 10.
[63] https://www.cmcsoxford.org.uk/s/1-Rivers-presentation.mp3

if the criticism of Muhammad was actually based on fact (e.g. that he had led military campaigns or that he had discriminated against women). His reply was evasive.

The appointment of Asim to advise the government on a definition of Islamophobia was concerning for those who value free speech. The *Sunday Times* reported that Qari Asim had faced calls to step down because of these comments. Sir Trevor Phillips is quoted as saying:

> "Mr Asim seems to want British Muslims to be less British than others. I would urge Qari Asim to distance himself from the views he has aired or reconsider his role on the panel."[64]

Bob Seely MP said: "There are serious questions about Asim's suitability to lead a government inquiry."

Qari Asim responded with a statement claiming that his views on freedom of speech were misrepresented and taken out of context. Readers can access the audio of his talk for themselves. In his statement, Asim argues that he greatly values free speech:

> The purpose of the definition of anti-Muslim prejudice will be to defend free speech, while challenging hate speech.[65]

This contrasts strongly with the equivocal position he set out in his talk. Asim was not charged with defining "anti-Muslim prejudice". That is a phrase which clearly differentiates Muslim people from Islamic beliefs. He was instead charged with defining 'Islamophobia', yet his response deliberately avoided using that term. Had he suggested that "anti-Muslim prejudice" was a clear and sufficient definition then that would have been welcome – and there would be no need for him to come up with a new one – but he did not say that.

Asim stated that the purpose of the definition was to "defend free speech, while challenging hate speech". But 'hate speech' is notoriously difficult to define.

---

[64] https://www.thetimes.co.uk/article/tory-inquiry-imam-in-free-speech-row-vwg9w3m9m
[65] https://makkahmosque.co.uk/qari-asim-free-speech-and-challenging-hatred/

Asim's statement did not specifically say that people should be allowed to say things that some Muslims may find "offensive or distasteful". He did say that "offence is part of living in a free society", and that "it is inevitable that sometimes people will be offended by the free speech of others". But he appears to have carefully avoided saying that statements that might offend Muslims should be allowed. He also refrained from saying that criticism of Muhammed should be allowed. Therefore, despite his claim to strongly value free speech, his position on it remains equivocal.

In 2022, Asim backed calls for banning the film *The Lady of Heaven*, about Muhammad's daughter.[66] At this the government formally withdrew his appointment with a letter which said:

> Your recent support for a campaign to limit free expression – a campaign which has itself encouraged communal tensions – means it is no longer appropriate for you to continue your work with government in roles designed to promote community harmony.
>
> You have encouraged an ongoing campaign to prevent cinemas screening the film *Lady of Heaven*, a clear effort to restrict artistic expression, and the campaign you have supported has led to street protests which have fomented religious hatred.[67]

The government was right to rescind his appointment, but the fact that he was appointed to this role in the first place, given his views, remains a matter of concern.

The case of Sir Trevor Phillips

In March 2020, Sir Trevor Phillips, the former head of the Equalities and Human Rights Commission, was suspended from the Labour Party over allegations of Islamophobia.[68] This was in spite of the fact that Phillips had lobbied for the Racial and Religious

---

[66] https://www.bbc.co.uk/news/uk-england-leeds-61771695
[67] https://assets.publishing.service.gov.uk/government/uploads/system/uploads/attachment_data/file/1081996/DLUHC_to_Imam_Qari_Asim_-_11062022.pdf
[68] https://www.thetimes.co.uk/article/labour-suspends-race-pioneer-trevor-phillips-over-islamophobia-claims-m7qzzqz8d

Hatred Act 2006, which was the first law giving practical protection to Muslims.

The suspension of Phillips from the Labour Party demonstrates how formal acceptance of the APPG definition by political parties serves to restrict free speech. Those who raise valid questions about Islamic beliefs and practices are found guilty of Islamophobia – no matter what their prior track record.

Policy Exchange released a report which contains the full 11-page indictment that the Labour Party sent to Phillips.[69] He was not told who had made the allegations and was instructed to keep the matter entirely confidential. The letter made clear that a decision on the matter would be made behind closed doors in a meeting to which Phillips was not invited.

The allegations consisted of a series of well-known statements that Phillips had made in the media over the previous four years. The following is a typical example:

> He told a meeting at the Policy Exchange think tank in Westminster on Monday that Muslims "see the world differently from the rest of us".

But if Muslims do not see the world differently from others then why are they Muslims? One could equally say that "Christians see the world differently from the rest of us" without being guilty of hatred or prejudice. These are simply true statements. People with a particular worldview inevitably view the world through that perspective which is necessarily different to the view of those who do not accept that worldview. If it is Islamophobic to say Muslims see the world differently, then could it be Islamophobic to say that Muslims believe Muhammad is a prophet of Allah?

Other examples of Phillips' alleged Islamophobia are:

> "But the most sensitive cause of conflict in recent years has been the collision between majority norms and the behaviours of some Muslim groups. In particular, the exposure of systematic and

---

[69] https://policyexchange.org.uk/publication/the-trial-the-strange-case-of-trevor-phillips/

longstanding abuse by men, mostly of Pakistani Muslim origin, in the North of England."

And similarly:

"authorities in towns such as Rotherham and Rochdale remain reluctant to associate the child grooming scandals with social norms within the largely Pakistani Muslim neighbourhoods in which they took place."

These are statements of fact. The then Home Secretary, Sajid Javid, said in October 2018:

"It is a statement of fact – a fact which both saddens and angers me – that most of the men in recent high-profile gang convictions have had Pakistani heritage."[70]

Free speech is being seriously curtailed if we cannot make factual statements like these.

Sarah Champion, Labour MP for Rotherham, said that the country "has a problem with British Pakistani men raping and exploiting white girls".[71] Once again, a statement of fact, for which she lost her position in the shadow cabinet.[72]

Another of Phillips' alleged offences was citing survey findings that portrayed the Muslim community in an unfavourable light. For example:

"A third of UK Muslims would like their children educated separately from non-Muslims. A quarter disagreed with the statement that "acts of violence against anyone publishing images of the Prophet could never be justified"; and a quarter were sympathetic to the 'motives' of the Charlie Hebdo killers. These facts should presage a society in a turmoil of preparation for change; and a political and media elite engaged in serious debate as to how we meet this challenge to our fundamental values."

---

[70] https://www.spectator.co.uk/article/full-text-sajid-javid-s-conservative-conference-speech/
[71] https://www.thetimes.co.uk/article/mp-sarah-champion-faced-fury-for-sex-gangs-article-in-the-sun-9xrm3d3hv
[72] https://www.telegraph.co.uk/news/2017/08/16/sarah-champion-quits-jeremy-corbyns-shadow-cabinet-warning-pakistani/

This is a quotation from a Civitas report published in 2015 referencing a poll that year by the firm Survation, for the BBC.[73] Phillips was accused of Islamophobia merely for citing the findings of a survey. Is it Islamophobic to cite facts when they don't cast the Muslim community in a particularly favourable light? Is it Islamophobic to suggest that such facts give rise to questions that need to be debated and discussed in society? Is it Islamophobic to call for a debate at all – let alone to hold or participate in one?

Phillips wrote: "In essence, I am accused of heresy, and I am threatened with excommunication."[74] He was right, and we can anticipate more excommunications if the APPG definition continues to be accepted and adopted.

To his credit, Khalid Mahmood, Labour MP for Birmingham Perry Bar, and the longest-serving Muslim Member of Parliament as well as a member of the APPG on British Muslims, spoke out in defence of Phillips:

> "I'm afraid this whole episode has provided final proof – were any necessary – that the APPG definition of 'Islamophobia' is simply not fit for purpose... If anything good is to come out of this sad – and frankly embarrassing – episode for my party, it is that it can hopefully serve as a wake-up call to those who believe that the APPG definition of Islamophobia represents any kind of basis for progress. It does not. We need now to accept that reality and move on."[75]

In July 2021, Phillips was quietly readmitted to the Labour Party. This was welcome news, but it remains concerning that he was suspended in the first place.[76]

Sir Trevor Phillips' case is instructive because it shows where adoption of the APPG definition can lead. Freedom of speech has already been eroded within the political parties that have adopted

---

[73] https://www.civitas.org.uk/content/files/Race-and-Faith.pdf
[74] https://policyexchange.org.uk/publication/the-trial-the-strange-case-of-trevor-phillips/
[75] https://policyexchange.org.uk/publication/the-trial-the-strange-case-of-trevor-phillips/
[76] https://www.theguardian.com/uk-news/2021/jul/06/labour-lifts-trevor-phillips-suspension-for-alleged-islamophobia

the definition because members of those parties risk expulsion just for stating facts on issues relating to Islam. During the Covid-19 pandemic there was discussion about whether it was appropriate to broadcast the Islamic call to prayer during lockdown, but a Labour politician raising any questions about this risked being accused of Islamophobia. Debate on the role of religious ideology in motivating terrorism and grooming offences is already stifled. For free speech to prevail, the APPG's definition must be scrapped.

Indeed, any attempt to define 'Islamophobia' will struggle to avoid conflating criticism of the ideology with discrimination against the people. On the face of it, the word means fear of Islam – not of Muslims. If we want to retain free speech and allow criticism of different ideologies and religions, then we should avoid any attempt to define 'Islamophobia'.

The case of Professor Steven Greer
Professor Steven Greer is a human rights scholar with an outstanding international reputation. He was formerly a Professor of Human Rights at Bristol Law School and is a fellow of the Academy of Social Sciences and of the Royal Society of Arts. For seventeen years he taught a module entitled Human Rights in Law, Politics and Society (HRLPS). The unit was audited annually and externally examined, earning unanimous praise by external examiners.[77] So consistently popular was the course that when the entire undergraduate law curriculum was reviewed in 2019-2020, HRLPS was one of the few units whose continued inclusion in the curriculum generated no discussion or query.

All this changed in October 2020, when the Bristol University Islamic Society (BRISOC) formally complained to the university that the 'Islam, China and the Far East' module of the HRLPS unit was "Islamophobi". Professor Greer was not informed of the existence of the complaint until 11th December, and it was not until

---

[77] Steven Greer. 'Falsely Accused of Islamophobia: My Struggle Against Academic Cancellation.' Academic Press. 2023.

15th February 2021 that he was officially informed of the full allegations against him. In January 2021, BRISOC had launched an online social media campaign with a petition calling for Professor Greer to apologise to all Muslim students and for the offending material to be removed from the module. The petition, which remains online, has garnered over 4,000 signatures, and demands a formal apology from the university.[78]

BRISOC's complaint outlined the allegations against Professor Greer.[79] He has responded to all of them in his book.[80] Some of the statements made in the course of the HRLPS unit and deemed "Islamophobic" by BRISOC include:

- "Women who wear the hijab are less likely to work outside home [sic] or be involved in higher education."
- "The Qur'an also permits the physical chastisement by a husband of his wife."
- "Islam spread rapidly through war, conquest, trade and conversion."
- "Islam was a progressive faith insofar as its open to all." [sic]
- "Several other well documented areas of friction in traditional political Islam with regards to human rights: position of women – divorce, custody of children, inequality in legal testimony (woman's testimony in Sharia court is worth half that of a man), position of non-Muslims and other minorities in Islamic states – only Muslims are full citizens."

Some of these statements are matters of historical record, while others are textually and theologically accurate according to the Qur'an. Quite why the statement that Islam is "a progressive faith" should be deemed "Islamophobic" remains a mystery.

---

[78] https://www.change.org/p/university-of-bristol-stop-islamophobia-at-bristol-university-scrapthemodule
[79] https://www.change.org/p/university-of-bristol-stop-islamophobia-at-bristol-university-scrapthemodule
[80] Ibid. p. 115-119.

BRISOC further complained that Professor Greer had defended the government's Prevent programme. This is true. Professor Greer has argued that the Prevent counter-terrorism programme is not discriminatory, racist, Islamophobic or anti-democratic, and that it does not systematically violate human rights.[81] BRISOC's position appears to be that to deny that Prevent is Islamophobic is, itself, Islamophobic. An equivalently absurd claim would be that anyone who opposes Prevent is a terrorist sympathiser. The accusation of Islamophobia has the effect of shutting down debate and dissent, and demonising those who support Prevent.

BRISOC's social media campaign breached confidentiality about the complaint and also spread false and malicious accusations against Professor Greer in an attempt to silence and discredit him. In the ensuing social media storm Professor Greer was compared to Samuel Paty, the French school teacher beheaded by an Islamist militant in October 2020, for discussing Charlie Hebdo cartoons in a class discussion about free speech and blasphemy. A suspicious incident outside Professor Greer's home in February prompted him and his wife to flee the family home, taking refuge elsewhere for some days on the advice of the police.

It was not until July 2021 that the University Assessor's inquiry concluded by comprehensively, unequivocally and unreservedly exonerating Professor Greer. While the Assessor's report remains confidential, Professor Greer relates that he was not criticised in any way. On the contrary, his expertise and cooperation with the inquiry were praised.[82]

However, far from promptly announcing Professor Greer's innocence and launching disciplinary action against BRISOC for making malicious and unfounded complaints against him, the university instead wrote to Professor Greer on 6th September notifying him that the 'Islam, China and Far East' unit would be changed. By way of explanation, the letter cited "the likelihood of recurrence

---

[81] Ibid. p. 131.
[82] Ibid. p. 72.

of complaints" and stated that "it is important that Muslim students in particular do not feel that their religion is being singled out or in any way 'othered' by class material".[83] This capitulation to BRISOC failed to acknowledge that Christianity, liberalism, communism, and Confucianism were all exposed to critique in the HRLPS course. Why was Islam singled out for special protection? Why wasn't BRISOC subject to scrutiny when it emerged that its complaints against Professor Greer were vexatious?

The stress generated by this damaging campaign, and the failure of Bristol University to support Professor Greer, led him to be signed off work by a doctor for some months.

On 8th October 2021, Bristol University finally released a "statement regarding complaint [sic] against Professor Steven Greer".[84] The statement confirmed that "after a rigorous examination of the facts and considering the views of both parties, we can confirm that the complaint has not been upheld and those involved have been informed of the outcome". However, it went on to say: "Although the complaint has not been upheld, we recognise BRISOC's concerns and the importance of airing differing views constructively." But this is disingenuous: BRISOC's social media campaign was far from 'constructive', and given that none of the complaints were upheld, what exactly did the university 'recognise' about BRISOC's allegations?

The statement also expressly denied "claims that the human rights module taught by Professor Greer has been cancelled". This is not the full picture: while the HRLPS unit remains on the curriculum, the 6 September letter to Professor Greer clearly stated that the material relating to Islam would be removed, just as BRISOC had demanded.

What often goes unremarked about this sorry episode is that Bristol University has formally adopted the APPG definition of Islamophobia. The adoption of this definition is mentioned in

---

[83] Ibid. p. 72.
[84] https://www.bristol.ac.uk/news/2021/october/complaint-outcome.html

BRISOC's petition and in a statement provided to the press by the university.[85] BRISOC's petition complains that:

> The recent adoption of the All Party Parliamentary Group (APPG) definition of Islamophobia has had no effect in practice and we feel it is now our representative responsibility to highlight how the APPG definition of Islamophobia seeks to protect no one and is wholly not fit for purpose in addressing our experiences of Islamophobia, coupled with the fact that according to the university implementation of policies to protect its students have to be "balanced" with "academic freedom".

BRISOC is complaining here that the APPG definition has failed to address their "experiences of Islamophobia". BRISOC feels that the adoption of the APPG definition has been a failure simply because Professor Greer has not been found guilty of it. It is just as well that Bristol University's Assessor did not have the APPG definition in mind when determining whether Professor Greer had been Islamophobic. Just what definition of Islamophobia she did have in mind is not known since her report remains confidential.

The fact is, however, that by distancing itself from his course material and failing to stand up to the malicious bullying and intimidation of Professor Greer, the university has effectively upheld BRISOC's vexatious allegations against him.

On 12th September 2021, the Free Speech Union wrote to the Vice Chancellor of Bristol University to express concern about the university's mishandling of BRISOC's complaints. The letter, available online, raised eight pertinent questions about the actions of the university.[86] The university refused to answer the questions, claiming that there was a requirement for confidentiality. It said that the material relating to Islam in the HRLPS module was still being taught. While claiming that "freedom of expression and academic freedom are at the heart of our University mission" it nevertheless

---

[85] https://www.aljazeera.com/news/2021/2/25/british-law-professor-under-fire-over-islamophobic-content
[86] https://freespeechunion.org/letter-to-the-vice-chancellor-of-bristol-university-about-its-shoddy-treatment-of-professor-steven-greer/

emphasised that "the protections given to academic freedom are a privilege, and with that privilege comes responsibility". This strongly implied that the university believed that Professor Greer had been irresponsible in his exercise of academic freedom.

Professor Greer may have been formally exonerated, but he has been informally discredited. BRISOC's strategy paid off. The university failed to openly support Professor Greer in his exercise of academic freedom and freedom of expression. Instead, it tacitly agreed to BRISOC's demands and BRISOC has received no reprimand or disciplinary action for its conduct. Rather, the university has been at pains to "recognise BRISOC's concerns".[87]

Professor Greer labelled BRISOC's allegations as "a particularly savage example of 'Islamofauxbia'".[88] He defines this as "a false allegation of anti-Muslim prejudice – typically intended to silence the kind of searching reflections upon Islam to which every single… ideology should be exposed". By contrast, the response of the university demonstrates 'Islamophobia-phobia': they were so terrified of being accused of being Islamophobic that they carefully avoided openly supporting Professor Greer when he was subjected to vexatious accusations.

The implications here are momentous. As Toby Young said: "Bristol's treatment of Prof Greer is outrageous. By kowtowing to the Islamic Society, the university has issued a gold-embossed invitation to activists to submit vexatious complaints about its employees."[89] Who will dare to teach about Islam with the slightest critical engagement at Bristol University now? Criticism of Islamic theology or history is now effectively off-limits for universities because of rampant 'Islamophobia-phobia'. No matter how groundless the accusation, guilt is assumed the moment an Islamic Society

---

[87] https://www.bristol.ac.uk/news/2021/october/complaint-outcome.html
[88] Steven Greer. 'Falsely Accused of Islamophobia: My Struggle Against Academic Cancellation.' Academic Press. 2023, pp.168-169.
[89] https://www.dailymail.co.uk/news/article-9980927/University-clears-don-anti-Islam-cancels-course-anyway.html

levels an accusation. In relation to Islam, academic freedom and freedom of expression are effectively lost.

Conclusion

Any attempt to define "Islamophobia" and have that definition adopted by political parties and other organisations is a threat to free speech. Legitimate debate is being shut down by allegations of Islamophobia. Legitimising accusations of Islamophobia not only harms free speech for non-Muslims, but also for Muslims who want to raise questions about their faith, or who simply do not want to restrict debate. Already at least one person has been suspended from a political party for alleged Islamophobia, while an academic has been professionally ruined and seen all his material about Islam cleansed from his university course lest it offend Muslim students. Where will restrictions on free speech end?

The APPG definition, in particular, is not fit for purpose and it is time for politicians and others to recognise that. Political parties that have adopted this definition should abandon it if they care about free speech. The same applies to local councils, universities, and other organisations.

It is encouraging that the government has abandoned its plans to define Islamophobia. However, if Labour comes to power in the next election, this plan is likely to be resurrected.

Anyone who cares about free speech should care about how allegations of Islamophobia are used to restrict the expression of legitimate opinions. In a free society, we must be at liberty to debate and criticise all kinds of beliefs and practices. Legitimising the concept of 'Islamophobia' works against this. We urge the government, politicians, and all who care for our basic freedoms, to recognise this and resist calls to adopt a formal definition of the term.

6

OPEN LETTER: APPG ISLAMOPHOBIA DEFINITION THREATENS CIVIL LIBERTIES

Note: This letter was sent to the then Home Secretary Sajid Javid on 14 May 2018 in advance of a debate in parliament about formally adopting the APPG definition of Islamophobia. The letter was signed by over 40 leading experts from a range of religious backgrounds warning the government against adopting this definition of Islamophobia.

Addressed to Home Secretary Sajid Javid

The APPG on British Muslims' definition of Islamophobia has now been adopted by the Labour Party, the Liberal Democrats Federal board, Plaid Cymru and the Mayor of London, as well as several local councils. All of this is occurring before the Home Affairs Select Committee has been able to assess the evidence for and against the adoption of the definition nationally. Meanwhile the Conservatives are having their own debate about rooting out Islamophobia from the party.

According to the APPG definition, "Islamophobia is rooted in racism and is a type of racism that targets expressions of Muslimness or perceived Muslimness".

With this definition in hand, it is perhaps no surprise that following the horrific attack on a mosque in Christchurch, New Zealand, some placed responsibility for the atrocity on the pens of journalists and academics who have criticised Islamic beliefs and practices, commented on or investigated Islamist extremism.

The undersigned unequivocally, unreservedly and emphatically condemn acts of violence against Muslims, and recognise the urgent need to deal with anti-Muslim hatred. However, we are extremely concerned about the uncritical and hasty adoption of the APPG's definition of Islamophobia.

This vague and expansive definition is being taken on without an adequate scrutiny or proper consideration of its negative consequences for freedom of expression, and academic and journalistic freedom. The definition will also undermine social cohesion – fuelling the very bigotry against Muslims which it is designed to prevent.

We are concerned that allegations of Islamophobia will be, and indeed are already being used, to effectively shield Islamic beliefs and even extremists from criticism, and that formalising this definition will result in it being employed effectively as something of a backdoor blasphemy law.

The accusation of Islamophobia has already been used against those opposing religious and gender segregation in education, the hijab, halal slaughter on the grounds of animal welfare, LGBT rights campaigners opposing Muslim views on homosexuality, ex-Muslims and feminists opposing Islamic views and practices relating to women, as well as those concerned about the issue of grooming gangs. It has been used against journalists who investigate Islamism, Muslims working in counter-extremism, schools and Ofsted for resisting conservative religious pressure and enforcing gender equality.

Evidently abuse, harmful practices, and the activities of groups and individuals which promote ideas contrary to British values, are far more likely to go unreported as a result of fear of being called Islamophobic. This will only increase if the APPG definition is formally adopted in law.

We are concerned that the definition will be used to shut down legitimate criticism and investigation. While the APPG authors have given assurances that it does not wish to infringe free speech, the entire content of the report, the definition itself, and early signs of how it would be used, suggest that it certainly would. Civil liberties should not be treated as an afterthought in the effort to tackle anti-Muslim prejudice.

The conflation of race and religion employed under the confused concept of 'cultural racism' expands the definition beyond anti-Muslim hatred to include 'illegitimate' criticism of the Islamic religion. The concept of Muslimness can effectively be transferred to Muslim practices and beliefs, allowing the report to claim that criticism of Islam is instrumentalised to *hurt* Muslims.

No religion should be given special protection against criticism. Like anti-Sikh, anti-Christian, or anti-Hindu hatred, we believe the term anti-Muslim hatred is more appropriate and less likely to infringe on free speech. A proliferation of 'phobias' is not desirable, as already stated by Sikh and Christian organisations who recognise the importance of free discussion about their beliefs.

Current legislative provisions are sufficient, as the law already protects individuals against attacks and unlawful discrimination on the basis of their religion. Rather than helping, this definition is likely to create a climate of self-censorship whereby people are fearful of criticising Islam and Islamic beliefs. It will therefore effectively shut down open discussions about matters of public interest. It will only aggravate community tensions further and is therefore no long-term solution.

If this definition is adopted, the government will likely turn to self-appointed 'representatives of the community' to define 'Muslimness'. This is clearly open to abuse. The APPG already entirely overlooked Muslims who are often considered to be "insufficiently Muslim" by other Muslims, moderates, liberals, reformers, and the Ahmadiyyah, who often suffer persecution and violence at the hands of other Muslims.

For all these reasons, the APPG definition of Islamophobia is deeply problematic and unfit for purpose. Acceptance of this definition will only serve to aggravate community tensions and to inhibit free speech about matters of fundamental importance. We urge the government, political parties, local councils and other organisations to reject this flawed proposed definition.

Emma Webb, *Civitas*

Hardeep Singh, *Network of Sikh Organisations (NSOUK)*

Lord Singh of Wimbledon
Tim Dieppe, *Christian Concern*
Stephen Evans, *National Secular Society (NSS)*
Sadia Hameed, *Council of Ex-Muslims of Britain (CEMB)*
Prof. Paul Cliteur, *candidate for the Dutch Senate, Professor of Law, University of Leiden*
Brendan O'Neill, *Editor, Spiked*
Maajid Nawaz, *Founder, Quilliam International*
Rt. Rev'd Dr Gavin Ashenden
Pragna Patel, *Director, Southall Black Sisters*
Professor Richard Dawkins
Rahila Gupta, *Author and Journalist*
Peter Whittle, *Founder and Director of New Culture Forum*
Trupti Patel, *President of Hindu Forum of Britain*
Dr Lakshmi Vyas, *President Hindu Forum of Europe*
Harsha Shukla MBE, *President Hindu Council of North UK*
Tarang Shelat, *President Hindu Council of Birmingham*
Ashvin Patel, *Chairman, Hindu Forum (Walsall)*
Ana Gonzalez, *Partner, Wilson Solicitors LLP*
Baron Desai of Clement Danes
Baroness Cox of Queensbury
Lord Alton of Liverpool
Bishop Michael Nazir-Ali
Ade Omooba *MBE, Co-Chair National Church Leaders Forum (NCLF)*
Wilson Chowdhry, *British Pakistani Christian Association*
Ashish Joshi, *Sikh Media Monitoring Group*
Satish K Sharma, *National Council of Hindu Temples*
Rumy Hasan, *Academic and Author*
Amina Lone, *Co-Director, Social Action and Research Foundation*
Peter Tatchell, *Peter Tatchell Foundation*
Seyran Ates, *Imam*
Gina Khan, *One Law for All*
Mohammed Amin MBE

Baroness D'Souza
Michael Mosbacher, *Acting Editor, Standpoint Magazine*
Lisa-Marie Taylor, *CEO FiLiA*
Julie Bindel, *Journalist and Feminist campaigner*
Dr Adrian Hilton, *Academic*
Neil Anderson, *Academic*
Tom Holland, *Historian*
Toby Keynes
Prof. Dr Bassam Tibi, *Professor Emeritus for International Relations, University of Goettingen*
Dr Stephen Law, *Philosopher and Author*

7

WHAT'S WRONG WITH ISLAMIC FINANCE?

Note: This essay was originally published as a Christian Concern booklet in 2018.[1] My own background working in finance led me to take an interest in Islamic finance. At one point I was asked to manage a Sharia fund and had to politely refuse to do so. Here I explain the many issues with Islamic finance and why the government and mainstream financial institutions should not be promoting or using it.

Introduction

In 2014, Britain made history by becoming the first non-Muslim country to issue an Islamic bond.[2] This bond was issued as part of the government's commitment for the UK "to become the western hub of Islamic finance." The British government has been encouraging the growth of Islamic finance for over ten years,[3] and has succeeded in this aim. There are now over 20 banks offering Islamic financial services in the UK – double the number in the US. The global market for Islamic financial services was estimated to be $2tn in 2014, and expected to grow to $3tn by 2018.[4] TheCityUK estimated that there are over 100,000 Islamic-finance retail customers in the UK. The UK is by far the largest provider of Islamic finance courses at both undergraduate and postgraduate level, with offerings in around 70 educational institutions.

---

[1] https://christianconcern.com/resource/whats-wrong-islamic-finance/
[2] "UK Excellence in Islamic Finance," (London: UK Trade and Investment, 2014). https://www.gov.uk/government/uploads/system/uploads/attachment_data/file/367154/UKTI_UK_Excellence_in_Islamic_Finance_Reprint_2014_Spread.pdf
[3] "The UK: Leading Western Centre of Islamic Finance," (London: TheCityUK, 2105). https://www.thecityuk.com/research/the-uk-leading-western-centre-for-islamic-finance/
[4] Ibid.

With so many people seeing this as an attractive growth market, are there any reasons for caution? We think there are many, and this briefing seeks to expose some of the pitfalls and problems with Islamic finance.

What is Islamic finance?

Islamic finance, otherwise known as Sharia-compliant finance, is based on the idea that all forms of interest are prohibited (or *haram*) in Islamic law. In this system, money is viewed as a tool for measuring value rather than an asset with intrinsic value, and therefore charging interest is regarded as exploitative or unjust because it is a charge for the use of money. Instead of interest, some level of risk sharing is used between the borrower and the lender so that an amount similar to interest, but described as profit, is paid to the lender. Various innovative types of transaction are used in order to avoid the use of interest. Islamic finance also prohibits investment in businesses that are *haram* under Sharia law such as pork, alcohol sale or production, pornography, and gambling. This will also include conventional financial businesses because of their use of interest. Compliance with Sharia law is normally monitored by a Sharia advisory board (or Sharia supervisory board), made up of various Islamic scholars.

Problems with Islamic finance

1. The ban on interest is a modern, radical interpretation of the Qur'an.

Muslims throughout history have borrowed and lent money with interest.[5] The idea that interest is banned in the Qur'an is a modern fundamentalist interpretation. As Timur Kuran says, "The alleged antiquity of the doctrine is a myth....even the concept of Islamic economics is a product of the twentieth century."[6] Mahmoud El-Gamal,

---

[5] Patrick Sookhdeo, *Understanding Shari'a Finance: The Muslim Challenge to Western Economics* (Isaac Publishing, 2008), 9-12.
[6] Timur Kuran, *Islam & Mammon* (Princeton University Press, 2006), 83.

a Muslim scholar, writes that "Islamic finance was conceived in the 1970s."[7] Patrick Sookhdeo explains: "The drive for the establishment of an interest-free Islamic economic system was started by Abul A'la Mawdudi (1903-1979), founder of the militant Pakistani Islamist Jama'at-i Islami movement."[8]

The debate on the banning of interest in the Qur'an hinges on two passages. The first is Surah 3:130:

> "O ye who believe! Devour not usury, doubling and quadrupling (the sum lent). Observe your duty to Allah, that ye may be successful."[9]

The Arabic word translated 'usury' here is *Riba*. It is clear in this verse that it is extortionate usury that is meant since the verse talks about 'doubling and quadrupling'. This is why Pickthall translated with 'usury'. The Yousef Ali and Sahih International translations also use 'usury'. As Raquib Zaman says, "this is the only definition of *Riba* available from the Quran."[10] The second passage is Surah 2:275-79:

> "Those who devour usury will not stand except as stand one whom the Evil one by his touch Hath driven to madness. That is because they say: 'Trade is like usury,' but Allah hath permitted trade and forbidden usury. Those who after receiving direction from their Lord, desist, shall be pardoned for the past; their case is for Allah (to judge); but those who repeat (The offence) are companions of the Fire: They will abide therein (for ever). Allah will deprive usury of all blessing, but will give increase for deeds of charity: For He loveth not creatures ungrateful and wicked. ... O ye who believe! Fear Allah, and give up what remains of your demand for usury, if ye are indeed believers. If ye do it not, Take notice of war from Allah and His Messenger. But if ye turn back, ye shall have

---

[7] Mahmoud El-Gamal, *Islamic Finance: Law, Economics, and Practice* (Cambridge University Press, 2009), 137.
[8] Sookhdeo, *Understanding Shari'a Finance: The Muslim Challenge to Western Economics*, 13.
[9] Pickthall translation.
[10] M. Raquibuz Zaman, "Usury (Riba) and the Place of Bank Interest in Islamic Banking and Finance," *International Journal of Banking and Finance* 6, no. 1 (2008): 2.

your capital sums: Deal not unjustly, and ye shall not be dealt with unjustly."[11] This is where some translations have put 'interest' in for *Riba* instead of 'usury' as translated by Pickthall and Yousef Ali.[12] Raquib Zaman shows how all the classical commentators on the Qur'an understood *Riba* as usury.[13] He also shows that there is no support in the Hadith for the meaning 'interest'.[14] Modern Islamists have not drawn on traditional practice or interpretation in order to interpret *Riba* as 'interest'. They have interpreted *Riba* in its strictest possible sense with no actual basis for this interpretation. Now Western financial institutions are promoting this interpretation as if it is the only interpretation, and are therefore agreeing with the modern radical view that Sharia law bans all forms of interest. Not only financial institutions, but the British government itself, states unequivocally: "The taking or receiving of interest (Riba) is strictly prohibited as, under Sharia principles, money is not valuable in itself and no charge should be made for its use."[15] When did the British government become an authority on the meaning of *Riba*? Why have they accepted the modern, strictest possible interpretation? In promoting this understanding of *Riba* they are promoting radical fundamentalist interpretations of the Qur'an.

2. The removal of interest in Islamic finance is deceptive.

Islamic finance products are marketed as being interest-free. In fact, the net result is a product with charges that look a lot like interest. This is not a coincidence. It is a deliberate deception which raises questions about the system. Timur Kuran explains: *"Murabaha,* the most popular lending mechanism of Islamic banks, is simply an ancient ruse. It consists of several interest-free transactions that together amount to interest."[16]

---

[11] Pickthall translation.
[12] Sahih International translates with 'interest'.
[13] Zaman, "Usury (Riba) and the Place of Bank Interest in Islamic Banking and Finance," 2-3.
[14] Ibid., 3-6.
[15] "Uk Excellence in Islamic Finance," 7.
[16] Kuran, *Islam & Mammon,* 15.

Many Muslims have spoken out about this. Kuran cites Khurshid Ahmad from Pakistan as, "a prolific writer who has held influential positions on key government commissions charged with steering the Islamisation of Pakistan's economy." Ahmad has "publicly criticised his country's Islamic banks, saying that '99 percent' of their business is still based on interest."[17] Muhammad Saleem is another Muslim critic of this system. In his book *"Islamic Banking–a $300 Billion Deception"*, he writes:

> "In their murabaha transactions (the dominant mode of financing), the difference between the purchase price and the selling price recognises the time-value of money in the same way that charging interest does. Put more bluntly, Islamic banks charge interest on 95% of their financing transactions, but concealed in Islamic garb. By charging interest in various guises, essentially designed to obfuscate products, Islamic banks engage in deception, duplicity and thus promote dishonesty. The real question is: in the eyes of Allah which is a greater sin, charging interest openly or engaging in dishonest practices."[18]

El-Gamal is another Muslim who criticises this deception. He cites a comment in Fortune magazine: "The result looked a lot like interest, and some argue that murabaha is simply a thinly veiled version of it; the markup [bank's name] charges is very close to the prevailing interest rate. But bank officials argue that God is in the details."[19] He also cites a Reuters report of a sukuk bond issue which is described as "interest free", but with "4 percent annual profit."[20] Elsewhere he argues:

> "Almost all contemporary writings in Islamic Law and/or Islamic finance proclaim that Islamic Law (*Shari'a*) forbids interest. This statement is paradoxical in light of the actual practices of Islamic financial providers over the past three decades. In fact, the bulk of Islamic financial practices formally base rates of return or costs of capital on a benchmark interest rate such as LIBOR, and

---

[17] Ibid., 16-17.
[18] Muhammad Saleem, *Islamic Banking–a $300 Billion Deception* (Xlibris, 2005), 68-69.
[19] El-Gamal, *Islamic Finance: Law, Economics, and Practice*, 2.
[20] Ibid.

would easily be classified by any MBA student as interest-based debt-finance."[21]

Why is the Western world promoting a deceptive form of finance? Islamic finance is interest-bearing finance disguised as interest-free finance.

3. Islamic finance is promoted by and associated with Islamic extremists.

Sheikh Muhammad Taqi Usmani chairs the Sharia Standards Board of the Accounting and Auditing Organisation for Islamic Financial Institutions (AAOIFI), which aims to set up international standards for Sharia finance.[22] He is a Sharia advisor to several banks and has been chair of the HSBC Amanah Sharia Advisory Board, chair of the Sharia Board of the Dow Jones Islamic Index, and chair of the Sharia Board of Citi Islamic Investment Bank.[23]

Usmani's book *Islam and Modernism*[24] has been translated into English, and relevant pages are available online.[25] In this book he responds to a question as to whether Jihad needs to be waged in a country like the UK where Islam can freely be preached. He responds by quoting the Qur'an and stating, "Here killing is to continue until the unbelievers pay Jizyah after they are humbled or overpowered."[26] Jizyah is the subjugation tax imposed on non-Muslims under Islamic rule. He goes on to explain: "If the purpose of killing was only to acquire permission and freedom of preaching Islam it would have been said 'until they allow for preaching Islam.'" He has subsequently been removed from the HSBC and Dow Jones advisory boards, but still sits on several other

---

[21] ""Interest" and the Paradox of Contemporary Islamic Law and Finance," *Fordham International Law Journal* (2003): 1.
[22] http://aaoifi.com/members-2/?lang=en
[23] Hussain Kureshi to Islamic Finance, 18 August, 2013, http://islamicfinancialsystems1.blogspot.co.uk/2013/08/mufti-taqi-usmani.html.
[24] Taqi Usmani, *Islam and Modernism*, trans. Dr. Mohammed Swaleh Siddiqui (New Delhi, India: Adam Publishers and Distributors, 2006).
[25] http://www.saneworks.us/uploads/application/40.pdf
[26] Usmani, *Islam and Modernism*, 131.

advisory boards and is regarded as a leading Islamic authority on Sharia-compliant finance. It stretches credibility to assume that the other Sharia advisors sitting under Taki Usmani's chairmanship of various boards were unaware of his fundamentalist views.

Patrick Sookhdeo, in his book *Understanding Shari'a Finance*, points out several connections with fundamentalist groups that members of Sharia Advisory Boards in the UK have.[27] The McCormick Foundation Report gives detailed profiles of several Sharia Advisory Board members showing their links with extremist groups and in some cases, statements in support of terrorism.[28]

Former Malaysian Prime Minister Mohamed Mahathir told a banking conference in Kuala Lumpur in November 2002 that, "A universal Islamic banking system is a *jihad* worth pursuing, to abolish this slavery [to the West] ... "[29] The enthusiasm of fundamentalists for Sharia finance should be an immediate cause for concern as we think about whether we should be supporting and promoting Islamic finance here in the UK.

4. Islamic finance aims to create a separate, rival financial system.

One has to consider the motivation of radical Muslims in creating and involving themselves in the entirely modern concept of Islamic finance. Their aim is deliberately to create a rival financial system. Islamic finance serves to prevent the integration of Muslims into Western societies. Muslims are told that they are not allowed to use standard financial products. Financial institutions are told that they must create and market separate products for Muslims, distinct from those offered to everyone else. All of this separates Muslims from mainstream economics whilst creating a rival financial system directly influenced by Islamic scholars.

---

[27] Sookhdeo, *Understanding Shari'a Finance: The Muslim Challenge to Western Economics*, 81-88.
[28] "Shariah, Law and 'Financial Jihad': How Should America Respond?," (McCormick Foundation, 2009). http://www.saneworks.us/uploads/application/49.pdf
[29] http://humanevents.com/2005/09/22/financial-jihad/

Timur Kuran puts it this way:

"The real purpose of Islamic economics has not been economic improvement but cultivation of a distinct Islamic identity to resist cultural globalization. It has served the cause of global Islamism, known also as 'Islamic fundamentalism,' by fuelling the illusion that Muslim societies have lived, or can live, by distinct economic rules. In fact, now as in the past, the economic life of Muslims has adhered to the very same principles observed elsewhere."[30]

He further describes the emergence of Islamic economics as, "a weapon of civilizational resistance …" noting that, "Unsurprisingly, the theme of clashing civilisations appears in all early contributions to Islamic economics."[31]

Robert Spencer cites examples where Muslims have successfully refused interest payment to IRS, Mastercard and other creditors.[32] This serves to illustrate the extent to which resistance to Western civilisation is encouraged by Islamic finance. Michael Nazir-Ali questions whether funds provided for Sharia compliant financial products can be obtained from conventional finance. Logically the answer is not, which would then, "require the establishment of free-standing institutions which engaged only in Sharia-compliant activity."[33] A completely 'interest-free' Islamic economy would ultimately be entirely isolated from the rest of the global economy. A rival financial system would be the result. It would be controlled by Muslims and would be very likely to become discriminatory against non-Muslims. Western financial institutions and governments have been incredibly naïve in their encouragement of this subversive system of finance.

---

[30] http://news.usc.edu/20744/Conversation-With-Timur-Kuran/
[31] Kuran, *Islam & Mammon*, 98.
[32] Robert Spencer, *Stealth Jihad: How Radical Islam Is Subverting America without Guns or Bombs* (Washington: Regnery Publishing, 2008), 185-86.
[33] Michael Nazir-Ali, "Islamic Law, Fundamental Freedoms, and Social Cohesion: Retrospect and Prospect," in *Shari'a in the West*, ed. R.J. Ahdar and N. Aroney (Oxford: Oxford University Press, 2010), 83.

5. Islamic finance lends credibility to Sharia law which is illiberal, undemocratic and discriminatory.

Linked to the above creation of a rival financial system is the way in which Islamic finance legitimises Sharia law. The promotion of Sharia finance as a way to enhance the credibility of Sharia law more generally, is a key aim of the Islamists involved. As leading scholar Timur Kuran puts it: "Successful Islamization in one domain lends credibility to Islamization attempts in other domains. So a significant consequence of the economic activities undertaken in the name of Islam is the support they give to the broader Islamist agenda."[34] Once people are comfortable with Sharia finance, they find it harder to criticise Sharia law more generally. Our accommodation of Sharia into the financial world makes it harder to object to accommodating Sharia into family law. Sharia finance has quickly become part of the economy, with jobs and government loans dependent on it. Sharia law is in fact inherently discriminatory in relation to both women and non-Muslims. Sharia finance does not directly discriminate in this way, but lends credibility to a system which does. We should be wary of anything which supports the wider influence of Sharia law in our culture.

6. *Zakat* is paid in some cases – where does it go?

The payment of *zakat* is one of the five pillars of Islam. It is described as charitable giving of 2.5% of profits. Sheikh Yusuf Al-Qaradawi has issued a *fatwa* stating that *zakat* can be used to finance violent Jihad.[35] An internet questioner asked if he can pay *zakat* to UNICEF. He received the answer "No", followed by a list of possible recipients of *zakat* money based on the Qur'an. Point 7 includes: "propagation of Islam, Jihad etc."[36] Indeed, *zakat* is the single largest source of funds for terrorism.[37]

---

[34] Kuran, *Islam & Mammon*, 62.
[35] http://www.freerepublic.com/focus/news/666056/posts
[36] https://uk.answers.yahoo.com/question/index?qid=20100205104923AAh862S
[37] Sookhdeo, *Understanding Shari'a Finance: The Muslim Challenge to Western Economics*, 42.

Brisard, in his report on Terrorism Financing for the Security Council of the United Nations, explains that, using the system of *zakat* "al-Qaeda was able to receive between $300m and $500m" over a decade "from wealthy businessmen and bankers representing 20% of Saudi GNP, through a web of charities and companies acting as fronts, with the notable use of Islamic banking institutions. Most of this financial backbone is still at large and able to support fundamentalist organizations."[38]

A Centre for Security Policy Paper puts it this way:

"Financial jihad through *zakat*, of course, is nothing particularly new and has been carried out for a long time. *Zakat* committees in Gaza have been a prime transfer mechanism of funds for Hamas, for instance, and the radical jihadist madrassas in Pakistan have been partly funded from *zakat* for decades. What's new with Islamic finance is the sheer volume of potential *zakat* collections and a move afoot to centralize both collections and distribution under one central authority that almost certainly will be controlled by committed Islamists. Every bank offering Islamic products appears required to donate 2.5% of revenue generated from them to *zakat* and with some 400 banks in 75 countries and a trillion dollars in Islamic financing currently the potential *zakat* sums are staggering."[39]

Islamic finance then, is increasing the availability of funds for terrorism.

7. Islamic finance is vulnerable to money laundering and fraud due to the lack of transparency.

The additional complexity of Islamic finance lends itself to abuse in various ways. El-Gamal explains:

"The 'degrees of separation' utilised by Islamic bankers to camouflage an interest-bearing loan as commodity or asset trading bear a

---

[38] Jean-Charles Brisard, "Terrorism Financing: Roots and Trends of Saudi Terrorism Financing," (Report prepared for the President of the Security Council, United Nations, 2002), 3.
[39] Alex Alexiev, "Islamic Finance or Financing Islamism?," (Center for Security Policy, 2007), 12-13.

striking resemblance to the 'layering' techniques used in financial crimes. ... Since financial criminals have expertise in utilising similar methods, it would be easy for them to abuse the mechanics of Islamic financial Shari'a arbitrage to reach their criminal ends."[40]

A recent IMF working paper highlights "The complexity of Islamic finance products as a factor increasing exposure to risk" of money laundering.[41] It also states that very little study has been done on the risks of money laundering and terrorist financing from Islamic finance.[42] This risk of money laundering is in addition to the use of *zakat* highlighted above.

8. Islamic finance disadvantages Muslims through increased complexity and transaction costs.

Islamic financial products are more complex than equivalent standard financial products as they must comply with the demands of the fundamentalist view that the Qur'an prohibits interest. This additional complexity results in additional costs. As El Gamal writes: "Islamic finance as it exists today has been shown to reduce economic efficiency by increasing transaction costs, without providing any substantial economic value to its customers."[43] These costs are borne by the customers, thereby disadvantaging them. Inefficiency of Islamic finance is therefore inevitable. El-Gamal explains:

> "Where the substance of contemporary financial practice is in accordance with Islamic law, adherence to pre-modern contract forms (with or without modification) leads most often to avoidable efficiency losses, thus violating one of the main legal objectives that defined classical Islamic jurisprudence."[44]

Muslims using Islamic finance incur increased costs and are thus disadvantaged relative to those using standard financial products.

---

[40] El-Gamal, *Islamic Finance: Law, Economics, and Practice*, 176.
[41] Nadim Kyriakos-Saad et al., "Islamic Finance and Anti-Money Laundering and Combating the Financing of Terrorism (Aml/Cft)," in *IMF Working Paper* (2016), 9.
[42] Ibid., 8.
[43] El-Gamal, *Islamic Finance: Law, Economics, and Practice*, 190.
[44] Ibid., xii.

9. Islamic finance is not supported by most Muslims.

Before the creation of the modern fundamentalist concept of Islamic finance there was no demand for it. Muslims have been happy to use normal financial products for centuries. As El-Gamal says, "In fact, however, Islamic finance has been largely a supply-driven industry, with jurists who participate actively in Shari'a arbitrage helping to expand the industry's customer base through indirect advertisement (at various conferences and publications), as well as religious admonishment that Muslims should avoid conventional finance."[45]

Most Muslims see the problems with Islamic finance and do not want to participate in a fundamentalist, deceptive, disadvantageous system. Timur Kuran cites evidence that, "Where Islamic banks operate alongside conventional banks, their share of Muslim deposits has remained under 20 percent; in some predominantly Muslim countries, the figure is as low as 1 percent."[46] Sookhdeo cites a 2004 survey, which found that 75% of the Muslim population in Britain was indifferent to Sharia finance and that there was no automatic demand for it. 83% of Muslims questioned the necessity of Sharia-compliant Islamic financial products approved by Islamic scholars.[47] In 2013 the Islamic Bank of Britain carried out a survey of attitudes to Islamic finance and found that only 36% of Muslims currently use Sharia-compliant finance, of whom 9% use it exclusively.[48] This seriously undermines the fundamentalists' message that Muslims are strictly prohibited from standard financial products, since the vast majority of Muslims continue to use standard financial products.

---

[45] Ibid., 190.
[46] Kuran, *Islam & Mammon*, 73.
[47] Sookhdeo, *Understanding Shari'a Finance: The Muslim Challenge to Western Economics*, 78-79.
[48] http://www.alrayanbank.co.uk/useful-info-tools/about-us/latest-news/jan-dec-2014/majority-of-non-muslim-uk-consumers-believe-that-islamic-finance-is-relevant-to-all-faiths/

Conclusion

Islamic finance is based on a modern radical interpretation of the Qur'an and is deliberately subversive and deceptive. The idea behind Islamic finance is to create a rival financial system, and to enhance the influence of fundamentalist Islam in the financial world. The extent to which Western financial institutions and governments have not only allowed this system to flourish, but also encouraged and endorsed it as representative of mainstream Islam is remarkable. Their naivety is extraordinary. The only good news is that, in contrast to the banks and the government, most Muslims have not bought into this system. We should be encouraging these moderate Muslims, not joining with fundamentalists in encouraging them to involve themselves in Islamic finance. It is time for the West to wake up to the true nature of Islamic finance and to expose its deceptive roots.

Bibliography

Alexiev, Alex. "Islamic Finance or Financing Islamism?": Center for Security Policy, 2007.

Brisard, Jean-Charles. "Terrorism Financing: Roots and Trends of Saudi Terrorism Financing." Report prepared for the President of the Security Council, United Nations, 2002.

El-Gamal, Mahmoud. ""Interest" and the Paradox of Contemporary Islamic Law and Finance." *Fordham International Law Journal* (December 2003): 1-24.

Islamic Finance: Law, Economics, and Practice. Cambridge University Press, 2009.

Kuran, Timur. *Islam & Mammon*. Princeton University Press, 2006.

Kureshi, Hussain. "Mufti Taqi Usmani." In *Islamic Finance*, 2013.

Kyriakos-Saad, Nadim, Manuel Vasquez, Chady El Khoury, and Arz El Murr. "Islamic Finance and Anti-Money Laundering and Combating the Financing of Terrorism (Aml/Cft)." In *IMF Working Paper*, 2016.

Nazir-Ali, Michael. "Islamic Law, Fundamental Freedoms, and Social Cohesion: Retrospect and Prospect." In *Shari'a in the West*, edited by R.J. Ahdar and N. Aroney, 71-89. Oxford: Oxford University Press, 2010.

Saleem, Muhammad. *Islamic Banking–a $300 Billion Deception*. Xlibris, 2005.

"Shariah, Law and 'Financial Jihad': How Should America Respond?". McCormick Foundation, 2009.

Sookhdeo, Patrick. *Understanding Shari'a Finance: The Muslim Challenge to Western Economics*. Isaac Publishing, 2008.

Spencer, Robert. *Stealth Jihad: How Radical Islam Is Subverting America without Guns or Bombs*. Washington: Regnery Publishing, 2008.

"UK Excellence in Islamic Finance." London: UK Trade and Investment, 2014. https://www.gov.uk/government/uploads/system/uploads/attachment_data/file/367154/UKTI_UK_Excellence_in_Islamic_Finance_Reprint_2014_Spread.pdf

"The UK: Leading Western Centre of Islamic Finance." London: TheCityUK, 2015. https://www.thecityuk.com/research/the-uk-leading-western-centre-for-islamic-finance/

Usmani, Taqi. *Islam and Modernism*. Translated by Dr. Mohammed Swaleh Siddiqui. New Delhi, India: Adam Publishers and Distributors, 2006.

Zaman, M. Raquibuz. "Usury (Riba) and the Place of Bank Interest in Islamic Banking and Finance." *International Journal of Banking and Finance* 6, no. 1 (2008): 1-15.

8

WHAT'S WRONG WITH MULTICULTURALISM?

Note: This article was originally published in the *Affinity Social Issues Bulletin* in March 2018.[1] Here I critique moral relativism which is the foundation for multiculturalism. I argue the case for transcendental, objective moral values from our transcendent God. Multiculturalism is opposed to missionary activity and attempts to morally reform culture. It is therefore opposed to Christianity.

What is 'multiculturalism'?

We need to start by defining our terms. What exactly do we mean by 'multiculturalism'? There is a significant difference between describing something as 'multicultural', and the word 'multiculturalism'. It's that suffix '-ism' that turns the adjective 'multicultural' into the ideology of 'multiculturalism'. Think, for example, of: communism, capitalism, secularism, racism, sexism, nationalism, Marxism, statism, feminism, conservatism, liberalism, Darwinism, fatalism, ecumenism, and vegetarianism. These are all ideologies, as is 'multiculturalism'. A 'multiculturalist' is someone who advocates the ideology of multiculturalism.

The ideology of multiculturalism is based on the idea that all cultures are equally valid. No one culture is better than another. All cultures are worthy of equal respect. As a state-sponsored policy it refers to the policy of expecting people from multiple different cultures to live harmoniously alongside each other without any shared values or customs. Since multiculturalists believe that all cultures

---

[1] https://www.affinity.org.uk/news/424-what-is-wrong-with-multiculturalism/

are equal, they therefore believe that it would be immoral, or even racist, to expect people from radically different cultures to adopt the values, ethics, customs or practices of the mainstream culture. Instead, they argue that we ought to allow them to live their lives according to their own customs, and to respect these practices, no matter how different or conflicting they may be.

The political failure of multiculturalism

The meaning of multiculturalism is demonstrated by showing how politicians have recently used it. It was the German Chancellor Angela Merkel, who was the first major national leader to openly admit the political failure of multiculturalism. In a major 'state of the nation' speech in October 2010 she said:

> "Of course, the tendency had been to say, 'let's adopt the multicultural concept and live happily side by side, and be happy to be living with each other'. But this concept has failed, and failed utterly."[2]

Merkel received a standing ovation and was praised for having the courage to tell a difficult truth in the press. It didn't take long for others to follow. Britain's Prime Minister David Cameron, speaking in February 2011, said:

> "Under the doctrine of state multiculturalism, we have encouraged different cultures to live separate lives, apart from each other and the mainstream. We have failed to provide a vision of society to which they feel they want to belong. We have even tolerated these segregated communities behaving in ways that run counter to our values. So when a white person holds objectionable views – racism, for example – we rightly condemn them. But when equally unacceptable views or practices have come from someone who isn't white, we've been too cautious, frankly even fearful, to stand up to them.

> The failure of some to confront the horrors of forced marriage, the practice where some young girls are bullied and sometimes taken abroad to marry someone they don't want to, is a case in point. This

---

[2] https://www.theguardian.com/world/2010/oct/17/angela-merkel-germany-multiculturalism-failures

hands-off tolerance has only served to reinforce the sense that not enough is shared."[3]

A few days later French President Nicolas Sarkozy joined in, pronouncing multiculturalism to be a 'failure', in a television interview: "The truth is that, in all our democracies, we've been too concerned about the identity of the new arrivals and not enough about the identity of the country receiving them."[4]

It is important to realise that these politicians were not criticising multi-ethnicity. They were stating that the idea of welcoming different cultures, customs and values and treating them all equally, that is, the ideology of multiculturalism, has led to a disjointed segregated society lacking any sense of cohesive identity.

What is culture?

Let's take a step back and examine what culture is. Anthropologists tend to define culture as, "a shared set of values and rules of behaviour that allow a social group to function and perpetuate itself."[5] This is helpful, so far as it goes, but a Christian understanding of culture would seek to broaden and deepen that definition.

First, humans are inescapably religious (Romans 1:25). We all have some ultimate commitment from which we obtain our values and sense of self-worth. Values and rules of behaviour are also inescapably religious. The source of a culture's values and rules is effectively the god of that culture. It is the ultimate authority for that culture. Therefore, all cultures are inescapably religious, whether recognised as such or not. An Islamic culture is a cultural manifestation of Islam. A humanistic culture is a cultural manifestation of humanism, which is another religious worldview. Any culture is

---
[3] https://www.newstatesman.com/blogs/the-staggers/2011/02/terrorism-islam-ideology
[4] https://www.reuters.com/article/us-france-sarkozy-multiculturalism/sarkozy-joins-allies-burying-multiculturalism-idUSTRE71A4UP20110211
[5] Zee, *Choosing Sharia? Multiculturalism, Islamic Fundamentalism & Sharia Councils* (The Hague, Netherlands: Eleven International Publishing, 2016), 5.

necessarily a manifestation of the religion of that society. Hence, Henry van Til loosely defined culture as "religion externalised."[6] Secondly, culture includes more than values and rules of behaviour. Surely it includes works of art, buildings, infrastructure, literature, clothing, food, technology, industry, and much else besides. Culture, more broadly speaking, from a Christian perspective, is what humans make of creation. Genesis 1:28 is often referred to as the 'cultural mandate'. Humanity is instructed to "fill the earth and subdue it." This means that we are to create culture out of creation. God delegated responsibility to humans for creating a social order or culture that glorifies God out of creation. The shortest definition of culture is "what we make of the world."[7] Culture-making is what humans do. All forms of work participate in culture formation. Once again, all this is inescapably religious. Any culture will either be aimed at glorifying the living God or at the worship of some idol(s) or divine substitute from which that society seeks fulfilment and direction.

No neutral cultures

What this Christian understanding of culture makes clear is that there is no such thing as a neutral culture. All cultures proclaim certain values which they understand to be superior to alternative values. Multiculturalists cannot escape from this since they believe that multiculturalism creates superior forms of society. No culture can be religiously or value neutral.

All cultures will have some ultimate commitments that cannot be challenged. A current myth in our society is that 'tolerance' is a helpful ultimate virtue. Confusion arises here because the meaning of 'tolerance' has changed from accepting behaviours that we may continue to object to, to not criticising anyone else's behaviour. True tolerance is not the same as approval. What the new definition

---

[6] Van Til, *The Calvinistic Concept of Culture* (Grand Rapids, Michigan: Baker Publishing Group, 2001), 200.
[7] Crouch, Andy. *Culture Making: Recovering Our Creative Calling* (InterVarsity Press, 2013), 23.

means in practice is that someone who criticises the prevailing morality of society is regarded as 'intolerant', and therefore as someone who is effectively a traitor to this ultimate commitment to be 'tolerant'. Society then becomes highly intolerant of what is seen as 'intolerant' behaviour, whilst claiming to value 'tolerance'! This is why we are starting to see the courts attempting to restrict free speech in this country when people criticise currently accepted sexual ethics.[8] All cultures will have some behaviours that they are intolerant of. Culture is inherently prejudiced and will therefore 'pre-judge' some behaviours as immoral.

This religious nature of culture also enables us to better understand multiculturalism as equivalent to religious pluralism, or state-sponsored polytheism. The multiculturalist tries to say that society can continue without any favoured religion or worldview. This is self-defeating because multiculturalism itself is a favoured worldview. It is also inherently unstable. Different religions and worldviews proclaim different values and ethics which will unavoidably clash. A society with no agreed moral or religious foundation cannot avoid collapsing or fragmenting into a set of isolated subcultures abiding by different values. This is what we are now seeing in the UK with segregation of our society into enclaves dominated by certain religions, most notably Islam in certain areas. Professor Elham Manea aptly described this present reality as "plural monoculturalism."[9]

Cultural Relativism

The foundational doctrine of multiculturalism is the belief that all cultures are equally valid. This leads straight on to cultural relativism, according to which a person's behaviour should be judged relative to their own culture rather than against any other criteria.

---

[8] For example the case of Felix Ngole who was thrown of his university course for supporting Biblical sexual ethics.
Also the case of Richard Page who was dismissed as a magistrate for expressing his belief that children are best raised with a mother and a father. http://www.christianconcern.com/our-issues/employment/employment-tribunal-allows-censorship-of-christian-beliefs

[9] Manea, *Women and Shari'a Law: The Impact of Legal Pluralism in the UK* (London: I. B. Tauris, Limited, 2016), 171.

From a Christian perspective, we can reject outright the idea that all cultures are equal. Clearly a culture aimed at glorifying God is superior to one that glorifies human sexuality or any other idol. Even without this perspective, to say that all cultures are equal makes a mockery of equality. Every culture proclaims certain values and ethical norms which can be in direct conflict with another culture. Therefore, it makes no sense to say that they are all equal. Is a culture that values free speech equal to one that does not? Is a culture that values women's rights equal to one that does not? Is a culture that promotes promiscuity and homosexuality equal to one that does not? What about slavery, racism, polygamy, FGM, etc.? All these are cultural practices, and they are evidently not equal. Of course, to say this is to imply that there is a transcendent source of morality by which all cultures can be judged, which is a truth that contemporary societies seek to reject.

This reality of a transcendent source of morality directly contradicts cultural relativism. A consistent cultural relativist would neither criticise nor seek to curb the practice of slavery, for example, because she sees this practice as culturally relative. She has no moral source to appeal to. As Christians, we recognise the divine origin of moral law as revealed in the Bible, and thus we have legitimate, transcendent grounds to criticise various cultural practices. In fact, we are morally obligated to critique cultures and to proclaim God's laws and moral order to them. This is what the prophets did, not only to Israel, but to the surrounding nations – see Amos 1, for example.

This is why William Carey was able to boldly criticise and campaign against the culturally ingrained, religious practice of Sati in India – the practice of burning widows alive at their husbands' funerals. His campaigns led to the outlawing of the practice.[10] No consistent cultural relativist could consider doing such a thing.

---

[10] http://www.christiantoday.co.in/article/wiliam.carey.played.significant.role.in.abolishing.sati.system/4906.htm

In this way, cultural relativism suffers from what is known as the *Reformer's Dilemma*.[11] If a perspective of cultural relativism is to be adopted, then a person's actions can only be evaluated according to the culture they are from. If that is so, then the greatest crime possible is to try to change the practices of a culture; only a multiculturalist can evaluate cultural change as being immoral. Therefore, the cultural relativist must necessarily condemn people like Gandhi, Martin Luther King Jr., William Wilberforce, William Carey, and many others. Their actions can only be regarded as moral if we accept a transcendent source of morality.

Furthermore, cultural relativism is also undermined by cross-*cultural* actions. What are we to make of a person from culture A having extra-marital sex with someone from culture B, whilst staying in a hotel in culture C? By which culture should the morality of this act be evaluated? How about someone whose biological parents are from cultures A and B, and whose foster parents are from cultures C and D, and who is now living in culture E? By which culture's moral standards is she expected to abide? These are not merely hypothetical examples. Witness the fuss caused by the story about a child with some Christian cultural heritage being cared for by Muslim foster parents who were alleged to be imposing Muslim values on the child last year.[12] The child was actually of mixed cultural heritage, which added to the complexity of the story. The point is that cultural relativism cannot resolve issues like these because it tries to affirm that all the cultures are equally valid even though they clash and conflict in a number of ways. It is the ideology of multiculturalism that has created situations such as this.

Further examples of the absurdities of multiculturalism abound. A court in Ontario ruled that a man was not guilty of raping his wife because he genuinely believed he could have sex with her whenever he wanted.[13] No matter that he broke Canadian law. The judge

---

[11] Moreland, *Kingdom Triangle* (Grand Rapids, Michigan: Zondervan, 2007), 101.
[12] http://www.christianconcern.com/our-concerns/the-multicultural-adoption-case
[13] http://www.dailymail.co.uk/news/article-5001452/Man-NOT-guilty-rape-did-not-know-illegal.html

accepted that he did not know it was against the law to have sex with his wife without her consent. An Australian court granted leave for an Afghan rapist to appeal on the basis that the rapist had "an unclear concept of what constitutes consent in sexual relationships in Australia."[14] A judge in Germany acquitted a Turkish man of a rape that had left the woman incapacitated. The judge argued that in "the mentality of the Turkish cultural circle," what the woman "had experienced as rape" might be considered merely "wild sex."[15] An Iraqi man who raped a 10-year-old boy at a swimming pool in Austria had his conviction overturned after judges found he may have believed the child consented.[16] The victims in all these cases had a valid cultural expectation not to be abused in this way, and a further cultural expectation that their abuser would be punished by the law. Multiculturalism is responsible for such injustices which undermine the fundamental principle of one law for all. The multiculturalist thinks that someone's moral behaviour can only be judged relative to their culture. What this means in practice is that multiculturalists hold people from other cultures to a lower standard of morality, which can be viewed as a form of racism in itself.

Samuel Huntingdon writes: "Multiculturalism is in essence anti-European civilisation. ... It is basically an anti-Western ideology."[17] Western culture was based on Christian values. We have seen that fundamental to multiculturalism is the denial of objective transcendent moral law. Thus, multiculturalism is directly opposed to Christianity, which proclaims that there is one God who is the sole source of objective, transcendent moral law by which all people from all cultures will be judged. Therefore, multiculturalism is fundamentally anti-Christian. It cannot tolerate Christians

---

[14] http://www.frontpagemag.com/point/184298/australian-judge-finds-muslim-cultural-differences-daniel-greenfield
[15] https://pjmedia.com/trending/2017/04/21/german-judge-acquits-turkish-man-of-rape-after-4-hours-of-forced-violent-sex/
[16] http://www.independent.co.uk/news/world/europe/iraqi-refugee-raped-10-year-old-boy-swimming-pool-vienna-austria-sentence-conviction-overturned-a7377491.html
[17] Huntington, *Who are We?: The Challenges to America's National Identity* (Simon & Schuster, 2004). 171

proclaiming that there is a God who "commands all people everywhere to repent" (Acts 17:30).

On cultural identity

Multiculturalism teaches that a person's authentic identity is bound up in their cultural identity, so much so that non-recognition of this cultural identity constitutes psychological harm.[18] The idea that identity is bound up in culture assumes that people never change culture, or convert to another religion. A multiculturalist would take offence at anyone who criticised their original culture – that is seen as a form of treason.

The idea that non-recognition of cultural identity constitutes psychological harm is one of many victim narratives by which contemporary culture is captivated. Why would not being categorised as a member of a particular community constitute harm? Insisting on recognition of different cultural identities is in fact divisive, anti-inclusive, and leads to the fragmentation of society.

Machteld Zee illustrates how this applies in practice.[19]

"Take, for example, 'John'. John is an Iraqi-born Muslim living in Birmingham who disapproves of people who do not follow his religion. In fact, an important part of John's identity is expressed through his dismissive attitude towards non-believers. He wishes not to recognise a non-believer for who that person truly is, preferring to be critical, or even dismissive of Western values. If we were to follow multiculturalist theory, we respect John's true nature. We should not even criticise John for criticising other people's life choices. John has the right to believe whatever he wishes, and we should be respectful and tolerant of his position. So far so good. But now we change John a little bit and this time, he is a white male citizen living in Liverpool. John does not recognise Muslims for who they truly are, in fact he is quite dismissive of Islam. He regularly unfolds his critique of life choices inspired by that religion, stating that Islam is detrimental to individual wellbeing. He questions the

---

[18] Zee, *Choosing Sharia? Multiculturalism, Islamic Fundamentalism & Sharia Councils*, 18-29.
[19] Ibid., 26.

merits of Islam-inspired practices, such as veiling and praying five times a day. Now multiculturalists would label the latter lack of recognition as a form of causing psychological harm, as well as arrogant, condescending, and Eurocentric, possibly even racist and discriminatory. The moral duty of recognising an individual for who he truly is thus a one-way street."

Somehow, as Zee points out, multiculturalists manage to assume that white Euro-Americans are psychologically immune to criticism, even to the extent of being called racist, whilst at the same time assuming that members of minority cultures are dependent on the approval of white Euro-Americans for their sense of self-worth! This inequality is held to be justified because of collective guilt imposed on white Euro-Americans for their alleged past behaviour. This imposed guilt actually requires multiculturalism to be false because it assumes that historically, practices that were culturally bound, were immoral. A true multiculturalist cannot say that past cultural actions were immoral, let alone that present cultures are collectively guilty for those past actions.

It is, in fact, people who should be treated with equal respect and dignity because they are all of equal worth, being created in the image of God. Cultures, however, do not deserve equal respect, because not all cultural beliefs and practices are equally worthy. A person's identity is not intrinsically bound up with their cultural background both because their culture may change, and because they may change their cultural allegiance.

On preservation of culture
One argument put forward by multiculturalists is that minority cultures ought to be preserved. This is an odd argument to make. No one argues for the preservation of Victorian culture. Of course, we should preserve the history and historical information about Victorian culture, but we shouldn't condemn some people to living as though they were in Victorian Britain today. Neither should we insist that indigenous African tribal culture is preserved. Indigenous people often benefit from better education, water supply, healthcare, and many other technologies that their original culture did not have.

They should not be denied these benefits.
Cultures regularly go extinct, largely because people turn away from them. People should have the freedom to do so. Western missionaries have been criticised for changing local cultures by introducing Christianity. But the fact is that cultures change all the time, sometimes for better. The introduction of Christianity will objectively improve any culture with superior morality and religious conviction. Christianity will also tend to improve literacy, education, healthcare, and much else besides. We should all feel morally obligated to seek to change cultures in these various objectively beneficial ways. Multiculturalism is fundamentally opposed to missionary activity and thus opposed to evangelical Christianity.

Our loss of cultural identity

French President Emmanuel Macron famously said, "There's no such thing as French culture."[20] Unpicking his words, he explained: "There is culture in France and it is diverse."[21] This amounts to an admission of no unifying culture. Macron's statement is indicative of a collective loss of cultural identity throughout Western Europe. The British government's commissioned report on integration in our society resulted in an admission that we have basically failed at integration.[22] This is hardly surprising if we lack any sense of collective identity in the first place. The government is now desperately trying to work out what 'British values' are in order to regain some sense of collective identity and shared values. David Cameron was criticised just for wanting migrants to learn English.[23] But surely a common language is the most basic requirement of a cohesive society?

---

[20] https://www.washingtonpost.com/world/europe/emmanuel-macrons-unlikely-path-to-the-french-presidency/2017/05/07/f8943ed8-bdc3-4ed4-8bbb-97a8781ff393_story.html?utm_term=.e486fb213820
[21] https://www.newsroom.co.nz/@future-learning/2017/05/04/24457/macron-french-culture
[22] https://www.gov.uk/government/publications/the-casey-review-a-review-into-opportunity-and-integration
[23] https://www.theguardian.com/politics/2016/jan/18/david-cameron-stigmatising-muslim-women-learn-english-language-policy

Neil MacGregor, former director of the British Museum, claims that modern Britain is the first society to try to operate without shared religious beliefs and rituals at its heart. "In a sense, we are a very unusual society. We are trying to do something that no society has really done. We are trying to live without an agreed narrative of our communal place in the cosmos and in time", MacGregor said.[24] There is truth in this, although it is an exaggeration. No society can hold together without some agreed set of values, and the source of these values is necessarily a religious worldview, whether recognised as such or not. Multiculturalism is an ideology which imposes certain values on society. These values are neither morally nor religiously neutral. What is unusual about multiculturalism is that it expects everyone to accept contradictory values and practices in the same society, and yet to live harmoniously together. This expectation is delusional. No society can accept contradictory values and practices and continue to hold together.

Fundamental freedoms

We now recognise that any society must necessarily adhere to some religious convictions which provide its source of values. Clearly, the best moral framework for any society is the Biblical one. What this framework also provides for is fundamental freedoms such as freedom of religion, freedom of speech, and freedom of conscience. Indeed, it is widely recognised that Christianity formed the moral foundation for the whole concept of human rights.

In any society all these freedoms are limited to some extent, and freedoms naturally come with responsibilities. The laws of the land should be respected, and everyone should be treated equally by them. This is another Biblical principle (Exodus 12:49; Numbers 15:16). Within these constraints, fundamental freedoms should be maintained and protected, with the law also making allowance for freedom of conscience, particularly in controversial areas.

---

[24] http://www.telegraph.co.uk/news/2017/10/11/neil-macgregor-britain-stands-alone-comes-religi1on/

Historically, UK law has allowed conscientious objection during war, and it currently allows conscientious objection to abortion. In general, people should be allowed to object to the production of goods or services on conscientious grounds. Recent cases of bakers and printers being asked to produce goods promoting 'same-sex marriage' have raised the profile of this issue. A principle of 'reasonable accommodation' should be agreed which allows for people to obey their conscience. Such accommodation should not extend to the creation of a *de facto* parallel legal system as we see with Sharia courts in this country, or to discrimination on the basis of sex, race, religion, or to the promotion of hatred for outsiders, for example.

Integration requires a measure of respect for the host culture, including agreement to abide by the laws of the land. Any society also requires not just a common law, but a common language to hold together. Michael Nazir-Ali is quite right to point out that integration does not necessarily mean assimilation, however.[25] Many communities such as Jews, Huguenots, and East Africans have successfully integrated whilst also maintaining something of their own distinctiveness. Others are segregated and are widely understood to have failed to integrate, for which the ideology of multiculturalism must take a large part of the blame.

What is wrong with multiculturalism?

Multiculturalism is an ideology that is fundamentally opposed to Christianity. It refuses to accept a transcendental source of morality and therefore resists accepting the reality of a creator God. It considers missionary activity and attempts to morally reform cultures as immoral. It is damaging to society in that it creates obvious injustices and holds people from different cultures to lower moral standards, which can be regarded as a form of racism. It undermines a fundamental principle of democracy – the principle of one law for all. State sponsored multiculturalism is a form of state endorsed

---

[25] Nazir-Ali, Michael, *Triple Jeopardy for the West: Aggressive Secularism, Radical Islamism and Multiculturalism* (Bloomsbury: London, 2012), xi, 12.

religious pluralism or polytheism. It is unstable and will inevitably result in the collapse or fragmentation of society.

Multiculturalism should be resisted by Christians. Indeed, it has only been able to arise in the context of weakened allegiance to Christianity in this country. Our task, as Paul wrote, is to "demolish arguments and every pretention that sets itself up against the knowledge of God." (2 Corinthians 10:5). Since multiculturalism is opposed to Christianity, it needs to be demolished. This article is an attempt to demonstrate the kinds of arguments Christians can employ to demolish multiculturalism. We, like Paul, are called to proclaim the gospel to people of all cultures (Acts 17). This necessarily involves the proclamation of a creator God who holds all people accountable to his transcendent moral law, regardless of culture. It is the proclamation of this truth that is our primary tool in calling people to reject multiculturalism, and to seek to objectively improve contemporary culture according to God's transcendent righteous moral standards.

9

IS ISLAM A RELIGION OF PEACE?

Note: This article was originally published in the *Affinity Social Issues Bulletin* for November 2018.[1] It featured in the top three Google search results for *Is Islam a religion of peace?* for several years. Consequently, it is by far my most read article.

What makes a religion peaceful?

It is often stated today, in defence of the reputation of Islam against the worst excesses of those who advocate terror, that Islam is a "religion of peace". How should we assess such a statement?

We might ask whether Islam advocates peace. Being a religion of peace could imply that Islam advocates pacifism.[2] But is this really the case? To test this, we need to examine the teaching of Islam in the Qur'an and the Hadith.

Another way would be to ask whether its founder was a person of peace. We would need to look at the life and teaching of Muhammad to make this assessment.

Alternatively, we might ask if the history of Islam has been peaceful. If a religious group has had a long history of peaceful relations with neighbouring groups and religions, this might be grounds to claim it as a peaceful religion. Sadly, the history of Islam is not one of peaceful relations with others. However, it is also the case that so-called "Christian" nations have been far from peaceful

---

[1] https://www.affinity.org.uk/app/uploads/2022/08/bulletin-39-final.pdf
[2] Though the Ahmadiyya sect does teach pacifism, it is not regarded as properly Islamic by the vast majority of Muslims, and they are often heavily persecuted by mainstream Muslims.

themselves, and not just in self-defence. So, this indicator may not necessarily be a reliable guide.

What about if most of the followers of a religion are peaceful and law-abiding? Would this make it a religion of peace? Perhaps. But what if a significant minority claim inspiration from the teaching of their religion to commit acts of war and terrorism? What if this minority has a strong claim to be following the example of the founder of their religion? What if this minority can also point to various religious authorities and examples through history as setting a precedent for their religious understanding?

It is indeed the case that the majority of Muslims are peaceful, law-abiding people. But it is also the case that the majority of Muslims are unfamiliar with the teaching of the Qur'an and the life of Muhammad. They are not usually encouraged to read the Qur'an in a language they can understand. Many Muslims self-identify as such because of culture, birth or relationships. Therefore, if we critique the teaching of their religion, we are not thereby criticising the behaviour or beliefs of every adherent of Islam.

In this article we will start by examining the meaning of "Islam" and "Jihad", and then move on to the teaching of the Qur'an, and the example of Muhammad. We will discuss briefly the teaching of religious leaders and the history of Islam. I will then conclude that Islam cannot be described as a "religion of peace" in terms of its teaching, the example set by its founder, or its history.

The meaning of "Islam"

'Muslims' and 'Islam' are not one and the same. We need to distinguish between the people and the ideology; criticism of Islam is not criticism of all Muslims. To understand what Islam is, we need to examine its teachings from the Qur'an and the example of Muhammad. The fact that most Muslims don't know or agree with all these teachings does not change what the religion actually teaches.

The word 'Islam' does not mean 'peace' as is often assumed. It means 'submission' or 'surrender'. Mark Durie, a linguistics and theology scholar, writes: "In its original meaning, a Muslim was someone who surrendered in warfare."[3] Muhammad's famous phrase *aslim taslam* means "surrender (i.e. submit to Islam) and you will be safe".[4] These words were included by him in letters sent to various rulers offering them peace if they surrendered to Islam. This is important because, far from carrying a peaceful meaning, Islam actually means peace after surrender in warfare or after subjugation.

In fact, Islam was first called a religion of peace only as recently as 1930, in a book published to promote Islam,[5] and as Muslims sought to promote their faith to Western audiences. In other words, for the first 1,300 years of Islamic history, this description was unknown: it occurs nowhere in the texts or traditions of Islam, right until the last century.

The meaning of "Jihad"

The Arabic word *"jihad"* means "struggle" or "strive". It is sometimes ambiguous as to whether it refers to a spiritual or a physical (violent) struggle. The clearest use in a non-violent sense is found in Q 22:78:

> And strive (jahidoo) for Allah with the striving (jihadihi) due to him. He has chosen you and has not placed upon you in the religion any difficulty.

However, there are plenty of clear references to *jihad* as violent struggle, for example, Q 2:216-218:

> Fighting is prescribed for you, and ye dislike it. But it is possible that ye dislike a thing which is good for you, and that ye love a thing which is bad for you... Indeed, those who have believed and those who have emigrated and fought (jihad) in the cause of Allah – those expect the mercy of Allah. And Allah is Forgiving and Merciful.

The claim is sometimes made that there is a distinction between the "greater jihad" and the "lesser jihad". This claim is based on the following Hadith:

---

[3] Durie, "Is Islam a Religion of Peace?" in *Independent Journal Review* (2015). http://www.meforum.org/5715/islam-religion-of-peace
[4] https://en.wikipedia.org/wiki/Aslim_Taslam
[5] Durie, "Is Islam a Religion of Peace?"

Some troops came back from an expedition and went to see the Messenger of Allah sallallahu `alayhi wa-Sallam. He said: "You have come for the best, from the smaller jihad (al-jihad al-asghar) to the greater jihad (al-jihad al-akbar)." Someone said, "What is the greater jihad?" He said: "The servant's struggle against his lust" (mujahadat al-`abdi hawah).

This Hadith is narrated in Al-Bayhaqi in al-Zuhd al-Kabir, though it is noted that "This is a chain that contains weakness."[6] It is dated from the first half of the ninth century and is not related in any of the official canonical Hadith collections.[7] Most significantly, it is contradicted by the Qur'an itself, which says:

> Not equal are those believers who sit (at home) and receive no hurt, and those who strive and fight in the cause of Allah with their goods and their persons. Allah hath granted a grade higher to those who strive and fight with their goods and persons than to those who sit (at home). Unto all (in Faith) hath Allah promised good: But those who strive and fight hath He distinguished above those who sit (at home) by a special reward. (Q 4:95)

Here it is clear that physical fighting is regarded as the greater endeavour. None of the four schools of Sunni jurisprudence, nor the Shi'ite tradition make reference to a "greater jihad". There are numerous references to "jihad" in the most trusted Hadith collections, and with virtually no exceptions they all refer to physical fighting. For example:

> A man came to Allah's Messenger and said, "Instruct me as to such a deed as equals Jihad (in reward)." He replied, "I do not find such a deed." Then he added, "Can you, while the Muslim fighter is in the battle-field, enter your mosque to perform prayers without cease and fast and never break your fast?" The man said, "But who can do that?" Abu-Huraira added, "The Mujahid (i.e. Muslim fighter) is

---

[6] See: http://www.livingislam.org/n/dgjh_e.html, also http://sunnah.org/wp/2011/01/01/documentation-of-the-hadith-of-jihad-al-akbar-greater-jihad/

[7] Cook, *Understanding Jihad* (London: University of California Press, 2005), 35. See the whole chapter for a fuller discussion of the greater jihad concept. See also: https://wikiislam.net/wiki/Lesser_vs_Greater_Jihad, and this online fatwa: https://islamqa.info/en/10455

rewarded even for the footsteps of his horse while it wanders about (for grazing) tied in a long rope." (Bukhari 5:52:44)

Leading scholar David Cook argues that attempts to present *jihad* in purely spiritual terms are completely unsupported by the evidence, and only occur in writings for Western audiences: "Those who write in Arabic or other Muslim majority languages realise that it is pointless to present *jihad* as anything other than militant warfare."[8]

In fact, *jihad* as physical fighting for the spread of Islam is so prominent in the traditional teaching of Islam that it is sometimes referred to as the sixth pillar of Islam. In the earliest Hadith collections, sections on *jihad* immediately follow those on the five pillars.[9] The primary meaning of *jihad* has always been physical fighting. This applies to the Qur'an, the Hadith, Islamic history and classical Islamic hermeneutics.

To conclude, David Cook cites the standard definition of *jihad* given in the new edition of the *Encyclopaedia of Islam:* "In law, according to general doctrine and in historical tradition, the *jihad* consists of military action with the object of the expansion of Islam and, if need be, of its defence."[10]

The teaching of the Qur'an

Confusingly for the ordinary reader, the Qur'anic accounts do not appear in chronological order. The chapters (surahs) appear in order of length, from the longest to the shortest. According to classical Islamic teaching, however, earlier verses (in chronology of revelation rather than position in the Qur'an) are sometimes cancelled by later instructions in a manner somewhat similar to how Christians view the New Testament as cancelling some of the instructions of the Old Testament. This Islamic doctrine is called abrogation, and it is found in the Qur'an:

---

[8] Cook, *Understanding Jihad,* 43.
[9] Qureshi, *Answering Jihad: A Better Way Forward* (Zondervan, 2016), 38.
[10] Cook, *Understanding Jihad,* 2.

> We do not abrogate a verse or cause it to be forgotten except that We bring forth [one] better than it or similar to it. Do you not know that Allah is over all things competent? (Q 2:106)

Or again:

> And when We substitute a verse in place of a verse – and Allah is most knowing of what He sends down – they say, "You, [O Muhammad], are but an inventor [of lies]." But most of them do not know. (Q 16:101)[11]

This doctrine of abrogation enables apparent contradictions in the Qur'an to be resolved – i.e. later verses abrogating earlier ones. Furthermore, Muhammad did not advocate violence earlier in his career, but waited until he had amassed a following large enough to wage war. Earlier verses are thus more peaceful, while later verses urge more violence.

The most famous example of a peaceful verse is Q 2:256:

> There shall be no compulsion in [acceptance of] the religion. The right course has become clear from the wrong. So whoever disbelieves in Taghut and believes in Allah has grasped the most trustworthy handhold with no break in it. And Allah is Hearing and Knowing.

However, this verse, and many others, is regarded as having been abrogated by the "verse of the sword":[12]

> But when the forbidden months are past, then fight and slay the Pagans wherever ye find them, and seize them, beleaguer them, and lie in wait for them in every stratagem (of war); but if they repent, and establish regular prayers and practise regular charity, then open the way for them: for Allah is Oft-forgiving, Most Merciful. (Q 9:5)

---

[11] For more references justifying abrogation see: https://wikiislam.net/wiki/Abrogation_(Naskh)

[12] https://wikiislam.net/wiki/Abrogation_(Naskh) also, http://dev-political-islam.pantheonsite.io/abrogation-and-the-koran/. A list of abrogated verses may be found here: https://wikiislam.net/wiki/List_of_Abrogations_in_the_Qur%27an

In fact, surah 9 is the last chapter to be revealed in the Qur'an and is seen as abrogating earlier instructions. Surah 9 is also the chapter that advocates the most violence, as the following verses demonstrate:

> Fight those who believe not in Allah nor the Last Day, nor hold that forbidden which hath been forbidden by Allah and His Messenger, nor acknowledge the religion of Truth, (even if they are) of the People of the Book, until they pay the Jizya with willing submission, and feel themselves subdued. (Q 9:29)

Here "Jizya" is the Islamic subjugation tax to be paid by Christians or Jews who have accepted the subjugated status of *dhimmi*.

> O Prophet, fight against the disbelievers and the hypocrites and be harsh upon them. And their refuge is Hell, and wretched is the destination. (Q 9:73)

> Allah hath purchased of the believers their persons and their goods; for theirs (in return) is the garden (of Paradise): they fight in His cause, and slay and are slain: a promise binding on Him in truth, through the Law, the Gospel, and the Qur'an: and who is more faithful to his covenant than Allah? (Q 9:111)

> O ye who believe! Fight the unbelievers who gird you about, and let them find firmness in you: and know that Allah is with those who fear Him. (Q 9:123)

Note that these are open-ended commands without qualification. In total, there are well over a hundred verses advocating violence in the Qur'an.[13]

Misquoting the Qur'an

Another verse that is used to argue that the Qur'an does not promote violence is Q 5:32:

> ...if anyone kills a person, it would be as if he killed the whole of mankind; and if anyone saved a life, it would be as if he saved the life of the whole of mankind.

---

[13] For a list of 164 verses see: http://www.answering-islam.org/Quran/Themes/jihad_passages.html

This may be the most misquoted verse in the Qur'an. The whole verse provides the context:

> On that account: We ordained for the Children of Israel that if any one slew a person – unless it be for murder or for spreading mischief in the land – it would be as if he slew the whole people: and if any one saved a life, it would be as if he saved the life of the whole people. Then although there came to them Our messengers with clear signs, yet, even after that, many of them continued to commit excesses in the land. (Q 5:32)

Notice that this command is described as having been ordained for "the Children of Israel" – i.e. the Jews. It is not said to be a command for Muslims today. Even if it were ordained for Muslims today, there is an exception clause that is conveniently left out of the quotation: "...unless it be for murder or for spreading mischief in the land." The question then arises as to what constitutes "mischief" (*fasadin*). The term is very broad. In one passage in the Qur'an, merely disputing Islam is regarded as making mischief (Q 3:60-63). In another passage, rejecting Allah is making mischief (Q 7:103). There is a Hadith that explains that this passage refers to polytheists (Sunan Abu Dawud 38:4359). The classical commentary on the Qur'an, Tafsir Ibn Kathir (2:11) explains:

> "Do not make mischief on the earth", means "Do not commit acts of disobedience on the earth. Their mischief is disobeying Allah, because whoever disobeys Allah on the earth, or commands that Allah be disobeyed, he has committed mischief on the earth."[14]

So, making "mischief" can be seen as any form of disobedience of Allah. This would make any non-Muslim or disobedient Muslim an exception to the instruction not to kill a person.

The very next verse of the Qur'an then goes on to clarify, this time for Muslims and not restricted to Jews, what should be done to those who spread mischief through the land:

---

[14] Qur'an Tafsir Ibn Kathir 2:11 http://www.qtafsir.com/index.php?option=com_content&task=view&id=436

> The punishment of those who wage war against Allah and His Messenger, and strive with might and main for mischief through the land is: execution, or crucifixion, or the cutting off of hands and feet from opposite sides, or exile from the land: that is their disgrace in this world, and a heavy punishment is theirs in the Hereafter. (Q 5:33)

This next verse encourages Muslims to kill or maim those who spread mischief in the land, which as we have seen could refer to any non-Muslim. Not so peaceful after all!

The example of Muhammad

Muhammad's life is held up as "a beautiful pattern (of conduct)" for Muslims (Q 33:21). According to tradition, Muhammad participated in at least twenty-seven military campaigns and deputised in some fifty-nine others.[15] That is a lot of battles! Some of these were defensive, but most were in order to expand territory. As we have seen, he taught that it was a duty of Muslims to fight in physical *jihad*. He himself fought to expand the influence of Islam and encouraged his followers to do the same.

Although Muhammad did not envisage modern terrorism, some of his instructions and actions can be used to justify such. For example, Q 8:12:

> I will cast terror into the hearts of those who disbelieved, so strike [them] upon the necks and strike from them every fingertip.

This Hadith also justifies spreading fear: "I have been made victorious with terror." (Bukhari 4.52.220)

The contrast with Jesus could not be sharper. Jesus said "love your enemies" – a statement found nowhere in the teaching of Islam. Jesus never killed anyone, and criticised Peter for taking up a sword in his defence. Instead of killing and maiming, Jesus healed people and even raised some from the dead.

---

[15] Cook, *Understanding Jihad*, 6.

Teaching of religious leaders

All four principal Sunni schools of Islamic law agree on the importance of *jihad* as warfare, as do Shiites.[16] There is a long history of this teaching because it is very clear in the Qur'an.[17] An online *fatwa* gives ten reasons why *jihad* is prescribed.[18] These include: "to make the people worship Allah alone", "Frightening the kuffaar, humiliating them and putting them to shame", "Acquiring booty" and "Taking [i.e. making] martyrs".

World renowned Islamic scholar, Mufti Taqi Usmani, was a Sharia judge in the Shariat Appellate Bench of the Supreme Court of Pakistan. He has served on the Sharia advisory boards of several financial institutions, including HSBC. In his book 'Islam and Modernism', he responds to a question about whether *jihad* should continue to be waged in a country where Islam can freely be preached. He responds by citing Q 9:29 (cited above) and commenting:

> Here killing should continue until the unbelievers pay the Jizya after they are humbled or overpowered. If the purpose of killing was only to acquire permission and freedom of preaching Islam, it would have been said "until they allow for preaching Islam".[19]

Usmani therefore argues from the text of the Qur'an that "killing should continue" today. There is no question of this being defensive warfare or limited to Muhammad's time.

The historical spread of Islam

Islam is a territorial religion that splits the world into two spheres: *Dar al-Islam,* the house of Islam, and *Dar al-Harb,* the house of war. The primary goal of *jihad* is not to win people over to the faith

---

[16] For references on this see: Bostom ed, *The Legacy of Jihad* (New York: Prometheus, 2008), 27-28. This material is also quoted here: https://islamophobic.wordpress.com/2012/06/03/jihad-according-to-the-four-sunni-schools-of-islamic-jurisprudence-3/
[17] Bostom has translations of over twenty Islamic authorities on the nature of Jihad. *Ibid.*
[18] https://islamqa.info/en/34647
[19] Usmani, *Islam and Modernism* (trans. Siddiqui; New Delhi, India: Adam Publishers and Distributors, 2006), 131. Relevant pages are available online here: http://www.saneworks.us/uploads/application/40.pdf

but to expand *Dar al-Islam,* or the territory of Islam. In the century following the death of Muhammad, Islam conquered territory stretching from the borders of China and India right up to Spain's Atlantic coast.

Writing in 1991, French philosopher and theologian Jacques Ellul observed:

> In a major encyclopaedia, one reads phrases such as: "Islam expanded in the eighth or ninth centuries ..."; This or that country "passed into Muslim hands...". But care is taken not to say how Islam expanded, how countries "passed into [Muslim] hands"... Indeed, it would seem as if events happened by themselves, through a miraculous or amicable operation... Regarding this expansion, little is said about jihad. And yet it all happened through war![20]

It is beyond the scope and space of this article to document the spread of Islam through the centuries and how this has been and continues to be done through violent *jihad*.[21] Suffice to say that force has been used to increase the influence of Islam throughout its history. I will make do with a couple of representative quotes and refer readers to other resources for further study.

Twentieth century Orientalist historian Henri Lammens summarised *jihad* thus:

> The Jehad. The war against the non-Muslims, so frequently recommended in the Medinese suras, almost became, as with the Kharijites, a "sixth pillar of Islam". Islam owes to it her expansion, in which "the mission", properly speaking, has played an insignificant role.[22]

An online *fatwa* responds to the question, "Was Islam spread by the sword?":

> Undoubtedly taking the initiative in fighting has a great effect in spreading Islam and bringing people into the religion of Allah in

---

[20] Jacques Ellul, Foreword to Bat Ye'or, *The Decline of Eastern Christianity under Islam: From Jihad to Dhimmitude,* (Fairleigh Dickinson University Press, 1996), 18 [emphasis and ellipses his].

[21] For extensive documentation see: Bostom, Andrew G. ed. *The Legacy of Jihad.* New York: Prometheus, 2008.

[22] Henri Lammens, *Islam Beliefs and Institutions,* (London 1929), 62.

crowds. Hence the hearts of the enemies of Islam are filled with fear of jihad.[23]

Conclusion: Islam is not a religion of peace

No one can claim that Islam is a religion of peace if by that they mean that it had a peaceful founder, or that its teachings advocate peaceful interaction with people of other religions, or that historically its followers have been violence-free.

In saying that Islam is not a religion of peace, we are not saying that all Muslims are violent people, or even that the majority are such. We are referring to the teaching and history of the religion, not to the behaviour of the majority of people who claim adherence to it. It is important that as a society and as individuals we are clear about this. It is honest and correct to say that most Muslims are peaceful people. But it does not follow from this that Islam is a religion of peace.

---

[23] https://islamqa.info/en/43087

10

IS ISLAM ANTISEMITIC?

In May 2024, I was invited to debate with Reza Aslan on the question, '*Is Islam antisemitic?*'[1]

I was surprised to be asked, since Reza is a professor at the University of California, Riverside, and has written two books which have reached the New York Times bestseller list. After questioning whether I was really the right person, and praying about it and discussing with others, I agreed to the debate. The organisers had clearly seen my earlier article, *Is Islam antisemitic?*[2] and were impressed with my engagement with the texts.

In this chapter, I will demonstrate that Islam, as defined by its texts, is antisemitic. We will look at antisemitism in the Qur'an, in the Hadith, in the Sirah (or biographies of Muhammad), amongst Islamic scholars, and in Islamic history. We will also examine some texts that are cited as examples of apparently philosemitic (or pro-Jewish) texts in Islam. Once we have considered all this evidence, I think you will be convinced that Islam is indeed antisemitic.

Antisemitism defined

Ahead of the debate, I asked that we agree to the Anti-Defamation League (ADL) definition of 'antisemitism'. I didn't want to be arguing with Reza about what was and what wasn't antisemitism. Reza agreed to the ADL definition, which is clear and uncontroversial. This definition says that antisemitism is:

---

[1] See here: https://opentodebate.org/debate/is-islam-antisemitic/ The debate can also be watched on YouTube here: https://www.youtube.com/watch?v=FbNVpJAUlf0, and it is available on mainstream podcast platforms under *Open to Debate*.

[2] https://christianconcern.com/resource/is-islam-antisemitic/ Written in 2021.

"The belief or behaviour hostile toward Jews just because they are Jewish. It may take the form of religious teachings that proclaim the inferiority of Jews, for instance, or political efforts to isolate, oppress, or otherwise injure them. It may also include prejudiced or stereotyped views about Jews."[3]

As I clarified in my opening statement, the question is whether Islam is antisemitic. It is not about Muslims, and whether they are antisemitic. It is about Islam, and Islam is defined by its texts. These texts are the Qur'an, the Hadith, and the Sirah (biographies of Muhammad).

Antisemitism in the Qur'an

There are actually many texts in the Qur'an that are clearly antisemitic. It is worth citing them so that you can see for yourself how antisemitic they are. I will offer very brief comments on each verse. These verses are cited in Qur'anic order for ease of reference.

Q2:61

And [recall] when you said, "O Moses, we can never endure one [kind of] food. So call upon your Lord to bring forth for us from the earth its green herbs and its cucumbers and its garlic and its lentils and its onions." [Moses] said, "Would you exchange what is better for what is less? Go into [any] settlement and indeed, you will have what you have asked." And they were covered with **humiliation and poverty and returned with anger from Allāh** [upon them]. That was because they [repeatedly] disbelieved in the signs of Allāh and killed the prophets without right. That was because they disobeyed and were [habitually] transgressing.

The renowned and highly respected commentator from the middle ages, Ibn Kathir, commented on this verse, indicating that this punishment of humiliation for the Jews "will never cease."[4]

---

[3] https://www.adl.org/antisemitism
[4] http://m.qtafsir.com/Surah-Al-Baqara/Covering-the-Jews-in-Humiliati—-

Q2:65

And you had already known about those who transgressed among you concerning the sabbath, and We said to them, **"Be apes, despised."**

This is one of three verses in the Qur'an in which Muhammad curses the Jews as being apes or pigs (see also Q5:60; Q7:166). Many Muslim commentators take this literally and claim that Jews were physically changed into apes and pigs.[5]

Q2:96

And you will surely find them the **most greedy of people** for life—[even] more than those who associate others with Allāh. One of them wishes that he could be granted life a thousand years, but it would not remove him in the least from the [coming] punishment that he should be granted life. And Allāh is Seeing of what they do.

The verse characterises Jews as being marked by greed.

Q4:47

O you who were given the Scripture, believe in what We have sent down [to Prophet Muḥammad (ﷺ)], confirming that which is with you, before We **obliterate faces** and turn them toward their backs **or curse them** as We cursed the sabbath-breakers.[1] And ever is the matter [i.e., decree] of Allāh accomplished.

Another curse of the Jews.

Q4:51-52

Have you not seen those who were given a portion of the Scripture, who believe in jibt [superstition] and ṭāghūt [false objects of worship] and say about the disbelievers, "These are better guided than the believers as to the way"?

Those are the **ones whom Allāh has cursed**; and he whom Allāh curses—never will you find for him a helper.

Yet another curse of the Jews.

---

[5] https://www.imra.org.il/story.php?id=14285

Q5:13

So for their breaking of the covenant **We cursed them** and made their hearts hardened. **They distort words** from their [proper] places [i.e., usages] and have forgotten a portion of that of which they were reminded. And you will still observe deceit among them, except a few of them. But pardon them and overlook [their misdeeds]. Indeed, Allāh loves the doers of good.

A further curse of the Jews, and an accusation of distorting their scriptures.

Q5:42

[They are] **avid listeners to falsehood, devourers of [what is] unlawful**. So if they come to you, [O Muḥammad], judge between them or turn away from them. And if you turn away from them– never will they harm you at all. And if you judge, judge between them with justice. Indeed, Allāh loves those who act justly.

Characterising Jews as those who listen to falsehoods and devour what is unlawful.

Q5:51

O ye who believe! **take not the Jews and the Christians for your friends and protectors**: They are but friends and protectors to each other. And he amongst you that turns to them (for friendship) is of them. Verily Allah guideth not a people unjust.

A clear command in the Qur'an not to take Jews or Christians as friends.

Q5:60

Say, "Shall I inform you of [what is] worse than that as penalty from Allāh? [It is that of] those whom **Allāh has cursed** and with whom He became angry and made of **them apes and pigs and slaves of ṭāghūt [idols]** Those are worse in position and **further astray from the sound way**."

Cursing of the Jews again.

Q5:64

And the Jews say, "The hand of Allāh is chained." Chained are their hands, and cursed are they for what they say. Rather, both His hands are extended; He spends however He wills. And that which has been revealed to you from your Lord will surely increase many of them in transgression and disbelief. And **We have cast among them animosity and hatred until the Day of Resurrection.** Every time they kindled the fire of war [against you], Allāh extinguished it. And they strive throughout the land **[causing] corruption**, and Allāh does not like **corrupters**.

Here, "And the Jews say, 'the hand of Allāh is chained' " refers to God being bound by his character, which includes, for example, not lying. Muslims, by contrast say that Allah is entirely free and bound by no laws.[6]

Note that the animosity and hatred lasts "until the day of resurrection." This means it is ongoing, to this day. The punishment for 'corruption' is in Q5:33 – crucifixion, or having hands and feet cut off, or being expelled from the land. Linking those two verses provides justification for killing Jews.

Q5:82

You will surely find the **most intense of the people in animosity toward the believers [to be] the Jews** and those who associate others with Allāh; and you will find the nearest of them in affection to the believers those who say, "We are Christians." That is because among them are priests and monks and because they are not arrogant.

Note the future tense "will surely find", indicating that this is ongoing.

Q7:166-167 (the context clearly shows that the reference is to Jews; see Q7:160)

---

[6] See discussion in: Spencer, Robert (2022), *The Critical Qur'an: Explained from Key Islamic Commentaries and Contemporary Historical Research* (Bombardier Books), p90.

So when they were insolent about that which they had been forbidden, We said to them, "**Be apes, despised.**"

And [mention] when your Lord declared that He would surely [continue to] send upon them **until the Day of Resurrection** those who would afflict them with the worst torment. Indeed, your Lord is swift in penalty; but indeed, He is Forgiving and Merciful.

Note again that the verse says that the Jews will be afflicted "until the day of resurrection", which means it is ongoing, and to this day. Note also that this affliction is carried out by people, so this verse justifies afflicting Jews with the worst torment.

Q9:29

Fight against those who do not believe in Allāh or in the Last Day and who do not consider unlawful what Allāh and His Messenger have made unlawful and who do not adopt the religion of truth [i.e., Islām] from those who were given the Scripture–[fight] until they give the jizyah1 willingly while they are humbled.

"... those who were given the Scripture" are Jews and Christians. Muslims are taught that they should fight against Jews and Christians until they pay the *jizyah* tax – a subjugation tax for non-Muslims under Islamic rule. They should be "humbled", or 'subdued' in other translations. Jews and Christians therefore have three options when living under Islamic rule: convert to Islam, be killed, or accept *dhimmi* status and pay the *jizyah* tax and forfeit legal rights.

Q17:4

And We conveyed to the Children of Israel in the Scripture that, "You will surely cause **corruption on the earth twice, and you will surely reach [a degree of] great haughtiness.**"

Remember the punishment for corruption from Q5:33 – crucifixion, the cutting off of hands and feet, or expulsion from the land. Again, in conjunction with 5:33, this justifies killing Jews.

Q60:4

There has already been for you an excellent pattern in Abraham and those with him, when they said to their people, "Indeed, we are disassociated from you and from whatever you worship other than Allāh. We have denied you, and there has appeared between us and you **animosity and hatred forever** until you believe in Allāh alone"–except for the saying of Abraham to his father, "I will surely ask forgiveness for you, but I have not [power to do] for you anything against Allāh. Our Lord, upon You we have relied, and to You we have returned, and to You is the destination.

Abraham's alleged exhortation to hatred of those who didn't believe in Allah is said to be an "excellent example" while his asking for forgiveness for them is not a good example. Note that this 'animosity and hatred' is to last 'forever' – so it continues to this day.

Q62:6

Say, "O you who are Jews, if you claim that you are allies of Allāh, excluding the [other] people, then **wish for death**, if you should be truthful."

So, Jews should 'wish for death'.

I did not cite all these texts in the debate with Reza Aslan. However, Reza made no attempt to claim that the texts I did cite are not antisemitic. The antisemitism in these texts is clear.

Antisemitism in the Daily Prayers

As well as those texts, Q 1:7 is prayed 17 times a day as part of *Salat* – the daily five-times-a-day prayer that devout Muslims observe. I chose not to cite Q1:7 in the debate because it is not self-evidently antisemitic, going by the text alone. However, the evidence from the Hadith and later interpreters that it does refer to the Jews, is overwhelming. Here's what it says:

Q1:6-7

Guide us along the Straight Path, The path of those upon whom You have bestowed favour, not of **those who have earned [Your] anger** or of those who are astray.

Muslim interpreters are virtually unanimous that "those who have earned your anger" are Jews, and "those who are astray" are Christians.[7]

Firstly, there is a Hadith which explicitly states this:

> Allah's Messenger (ﷺ) said, "Say Amen when the Imam says 'Ghairi l-maghdubi `alaihim wala d-daalleen' (not the path of those who earn Your Anger (such as Jews) nor of those who go astray (such as Christians)); all the past sins of the person whose saying (of Amin) coincides with that of the angels, will be forgiven". – Sahih Bukhari 1:12:749[8]

This settles the issue as far as many Muslims are concerned, since Bukhari's Hadiths are regarded as authentic and authoritative.

Here is another Hadith:

> "… that the Prophet (ﷺ) said:' "The Jews are those who Allah is wrath with, and the Christians have strayed.'"–Tirmidhi 5:44:2954[9]

Ibn Abbas (d. 687), the 'father of Qur'anic exegesis' and a companion of Muhammad, said:

> "'Not those against whom You have sent your wrath': other than the religion of the Jews against whom You have been wrathful and have abandoned… 'Nor those who are astray': nor the religion of the Christians, who err away from Islam.' "[10]

Muqatil Ibn Sulayman (d. 767) commented:

> " 'Not those against whom You have sent Your wrath': that is, a religion other than the Jewish one, against which Allah was wrathful. Monkeys and pigs were made from them. 'Nor those who are astray.' Allah is saying: 'And not the religion of the polytheists,' that is, the Christians."[11]

---

[7] See this article for discussion and more sources: https://www.andrewbostom.org/2019/05/qaradawis-ramadan-koran-homily-curse-jews-and-christians-17-times-daily/

[8] https://quranx.com/hadith/Bukhari/USC-MSA/Volume-1/Book-12/Hadith-749/

[9] https://sunnah.com/urn/639380

[10] J. Renard ed. *Windows on the House of Islam: Muslim Sources on Spirituality and Religious Life* (ed.: University of California Press, 1998), 33.

[11] Renard ed. *Windows on the House of Islam: Muslim Sources on Spirituality and Religious Life* (ed.), 30.

The Tafsir (commentary) of Al Qurtubi (d.1273) states:

"The majority say that 'those with anger on them' are the Jews and the 'misguided' are the Christians. That was explained by the Prophet, may Allah bless him and grant him peace, in the hadith of Adi ibn Hatim12 and the story of how he became a Muslim transmitted by Abu Dawud and at-Timirdhi in his Collection [of hadith]. The explanation is also attested to by the Almighty [i.e., elsewhere in the Koran] who says about the Jews, 'They brought down anger from Allah upon themselves' ([Q] 2:61, 3:112) and He [Allah] says, 'Allah is angry with them' ([Q]48:6)" He says about the Christians that they 'were misguided previously and have misguided many others, and are far from the right way.' ([Q]5:77).[13]

The classic Tafsir of Ibn Kathir (d.1373) states:

"These two paths are the paths of the Christians and Jews, a fact that the believer should beware of so that he avoids them. ... the Jews abandoned practicing the religion, while the Christians lost the true knowledge. This is why 'anger' descended upon the Jews, while being described as 'led astray' is more appropriate of the Christians."[14]

The Tafsir of al-Jaylalyayn (Tafsir of the two Jalals) completed in 1505 states:

"not the path of those against whom there is wrath namely the Jews and nor of those who are astray namely the Christians."[15]

A modern encyclopaedia of the Qur'an explains:

Thus the phrase in the daily prescribed prayers 'Guide us to the straight path, to the path of those you have blessed, not of those who incurred [Your] wrath, nor of the misguided' (al-Fatiha, Q1:5-6-7.) The verses mention two groups of people but do not say precisely who they are. **The Prophet** [Muhammad] interpreted [in a canonical Hadith as above] **those who incurred Allah's wrath as the**

---

[12] This is the hadith of Tirmidhi cited above: https://sunnah.com/urn/639380
[13] Tafsīr al-Qurṭubī Vol, Juz' 1: Al-Fātiḥah & Sūrat al-Baqarah 1-141, translated by Aisha Bewley (Diwan Press), 53-54. https://ia803201.us.archive.org/10/items/tafsir-al-qurtubi-4.-Volumes/Tafseer%20Al-Qurtubi/Tafsir%20al-Qurtubi%20Vol.%201.pdf
[14] http://m.qtafsir.com/Surah-Al-Fatiha/The-Faithful-ask-for-and-abide—-
[15] https://tinyurl.com/altafsir

Jews and the misguided as the Christians. The Jews, we are told [i.e., in both the Qur'an, and the Hadith] killed many of their prophets [Q2:91; Q4:155], and through their character and materialistic [Q2:96] tendencies have contributed much to moral corruption, social upheaval and sedition in the world [Q5:33; Q5:64]...[T]hey were readily misled [9:30] and incurred both Allah's wrath and ignominy [Q2:61; Q3:112]. As for the Christians...over time they succumbed to the influence of those who had already deviated from the chosen path. By the time Christianity came to be accepted as the official religion of the Roman Empire, many Christians had long gone astray and had been deprived of their original scripture... **By interpreting the phrase "not of those who incurred [Your] wrath, nor of the misguided" the Prophet identified them and clarified in what way and by what beliefs and deeds a man incurs God's wrath.** This is a warning for the Muslims not to follow in the footsteps of the Jews and Christians."[16]

Sheikh Yousef Al-Qarawadi was president of the European Council for Fatwa and Research and appointed a trustee of the Oxford Centre for Islamic Studies. He stated in 2019:

> "The second type are those who evoked [Allah's] anger. They are those who recognized the truth and nevertheless did not take its path, and even stubbornly opposed it, and were hostile towards the Prophet [Muhammad] after the straight path became clear to them. [They did this] out of reliance on falsity, love of this world, following urges, blind fanaticism, arrogance, or jealousy... and thus they deserve Allah's wrath. **These are the Jews**, for whom the explanation is presented in Surat Al-Maida [5:60, which states]: 'Those whom Allah has cursed and with whom He became angry and **made of them apes and pigs** and slaves of Taghut – these are worse in position and further astray from the sound way'"

> "On this matter, Sheikh Al-Islam ibn Taymiyya [d.1328] compiled his valuable book, The Necessity of the Straight Path in Distinction from the People of Hell. The straight path is a separate way [for the Muslims]; it is not the path of the Jews, who have evoked Allah's anger, nor of the Christians, who have gone astray, and also not of

---

[16] Leaman, Oliver, ed. (2006), *The Qur'an: An Encyclopedia* (Taylor & Francis): 613-614 https://archive.org/details/thequrananencyclopediaed.byoliverleaman_201909/page/n641/mode/2up?q=%22as+the+Jews%22

those who recognize the truth but have not gone in its path... This is the separate path, the path of truth, the path of Allah, the path of the believers."[17]

In a sermon at New Haven, Connecticut Mosque in November 2023, the imam said that Muslims recite the first chapter of the Qur'an 17 times every day in order to be reminded of Allah's anger towards the Jews.[18]

In a sermon in Fort Lauderdale, Florida in April 2024, the imam said: *"[According to the Quran], who are those with whom Allah is upset or angry with? The Jews. Followed by whom? The 'misguided ones,' and those are who? The Christians. Because they always follow them. Don't go too far, right here, in the country where we live, look what the Zionist Christians are doing."*[19]

Thus, the view that this text refers to the Jews is widespread and continues to this day. Many Muslims believe that when they recite their daily prayers they are being reminded of Allah's ongoing anger towards the Jews.

Antisemitism in the Hadith

Apocalyptic Hadith: Kill Jews

The most famous antisemitic Hadith is the so-called apocalyptic Hadith that calls for Jews to be killed.

> "Allah's Messenger said, "The Hour will not be established until you fight with the Jews, and the stone behind which a Jew will be hiding will say. 'O Muslim! There is a Jew hiding behind me, so kill him.'"(Sahih Bukhari 4:52:177; see also Sahih Bukhari 4:52:176; Sahih Muslim 41:6985)[20]

---

[17] https://www.memri.org/reports/ramadan-religious-lesson-muslim-brotherhood-spiritual-leader-sheikh-yousef-al-qaradawi
[18] https://www.memri.org/tv/friday-sermon-new-haven-ct-bow-islam-jews-anger-allah-kill-prophets
[19] https://www.memri.org/reports/fort-lauderdale-florida-friday-sermon-why-are-jews-such-breed-humans-their-talmudic-creed
[20] https://quranx.com/hadith/Bukhari/USC-MSA/Volume-4/Book-52/Hadith-177/ https://quranx.com/hadith/Bukhari/USC-MSA/Volume-4/Book-52/Hadith-176/ https://quranx.com/hadith/Muslim/USC-MSA/Book-41/Hadith-6985/

This Hadith was cited in article seven of Hamas' founding charter.[21]
Two footnotes explained:

> 16. Reference is made to the Day of Judgement. This tradition (Hadith), which is imputed to the Prophet, has been often quoted in Islamic literature, old and modem. The Egyptian troops who launched the assault on the Bar-Lev Line in October 1973, were equipped with "booklets of guidance" which included, inter alia, this same quotation.
>
> 18. Bukhari and Muslim are the authors of the two most authoritative and widely accepted collections of hadith (traditions of the Prophet).

A 2011 poll found that 73% of Palestinians agreed with this Hadith.[22] The Grand Mufti of Jerusalem, Mufti Muhammad Hussein, expressed his agreement with this Hadith in 2012.[23]

Do not greet Jews or Christians

> Do not greet the Jews and the Christians before they greet you and when you meet any one of them on the roads force him to go to the narrowest part of it. (Sahih Muslim 39:16, see also Sunan Abu Dawud 41:5186)[24]

Cursing Jews and Christians

> On his death-bed Allah's Messenger (ﷺ) put a sheet over his face and when he felt hot, he would remove it from his face. When in that state (of putting on and removing the sheet) he said, "May Allah's Curse be on the Jews and the Christians for they **build places of worship at the graves of their prophets**." (By that) he intended to warn (the Muslim) from what they (i.e. Jews and Christians) had done. (Sahih Bukhari 4:56:660)[25]

---

[21] https://irp.fas.org/world/para/docs/880818.htm
[22] https://www.jpost.com/diplomacy-and-politics/6-in-10-palestinians-reject-2-state-solution-survey-finds
[23] https://palwatch.org/page/3447
[24] https://quranx.com/hadith/muslim/in-book/Book-39/Hadith-16/ https://quranx.com/hadith/AbuDawud/USC-MSA/Book-41/Hadith-5186/
[25] https://quranx.com/hadith/Bukhari/DarusSalam/Hadith-3453/

Here Jews and Christians are cursed for building places of worship at the graves of their prophets. It is interesting to note that Muhammad's tomb is now a mosque!

Sins on Jews and Christians

No Muslim would die but Allah would admit in his stead a Jew or a Christian in Hell-Fire. (Sahih Muslim 37:6666)[26]

There would come people amongst the Muslims on the Day of Resurrection with as heavy sins as a mountain, and Allah would forgive them and He would place in their stead the Jews and the Christians. (Sahih Muslim 37:6668)[27]

Jews tormented in their graves

" Allah's Messenger (ﷺ) went out after the sun had set and he heard some sound and said: It is the Jews who are being tormented in their graves. (Sahih Muslim 40:6861)[28]

Antichrist accompanied by 70,00 Jews

The Messenger of Allah (ﷺ) said, "Dajjal (the Antichrist) will be followed by seventy thousand Jews of Isfahan and will be dressed in robes of green coloured satin."(Riyad as-Salihin 1812)[29]

Jews mutated into rats

"A group of Bani Isra'il was lost. I do not know what happened to it, but I think (that it 'underwent **a process of metamorphosis) and assumed the shape of rats.** Don't you see when the milk of the camel is placed before them, these do not drink and when the milk of goat is placed before them, these do drink." (Sahih Muslim 42:7135)[30]

---

[26] https://quranx.com/hadith/Muslim/USC-MSA/Book-37/Hadith-6666/
[27] https://quranx.com/hadith/Muslim/USC-MSA/Book-37/Hadith-6668/
[28] https://quranx.com/hadith/Muslim/USC-MSA/Book-40/Hadith-6861/
[29] https://sunnah.com/riyadussalihin:1812
[30] https://quranx.com/hadith/Muslim/USC-MSA/Book-42/Hadith-7135/

Meat rots because of the Jews

The Prophet (ﷺ) said, "But for the Israelis, meat would not decay and but for Eve, wives would never betray their husbands." (Sahih Bukhari 4:55:547)[31]

Two religions shall not remain together

I will expel the Jews and Christians from the Arabian Peninsula and will not leave any but Muslim. (Sahih Muslim 19:4366)[32]

I will certainly expel the Jews and the Christians from Arabia and I shall leave only Muslims in it. (Sunan Abu Dawud, Hadith 3024)[33]

This is religious-ethnic cleansing.

Jews expelled (641 AD)

'Umar expelled the Jews and the Christians from Hijaz. When Allah's Messenger (ﷺ) had conquered Khaibar, he wanted to **expel the Jews** from it as its land became the property of Allah, His Apostle, and the Muslims. **Allah's Messenger (ﷺ) intended to expel the Jews but they requested him to let them stay there on the condition that they would do the labour and get half of the fruits.** Allah's Messenger (ﷺ) told them, "We will let you stay on thus condition, as long as we wish." So, they (i.e. Jews) kept on living there **until 'Umar forced them to go** towards Taima' and Ariha'. (Sahih Bukhari 3:39:531)[34]

The second caliph, 'Umar, carried out Muhammad's wish by finally expelling the Jews from Arabia in 641 AD.

Don't harm Jews?

In my debate with Reza Aslan, he cited a Hadith which he claimed reports that: *"Muhammad said: 'Anyone who acts violently against Jews or Christians will have me as their accuser at the end of days.'"* Later in the debate he cited this Hadith as: *"Anyone who*

---

[31] https://quranx.com/hadith/Bukhari/USC-MSA/Volume-4/Book-55/Hadith-547/
[32] https://quranx.com/hadith/Muslim/USC-MSA/Book-19/Hadith-4366/
[33] https://quranx.com/hadith/AbuDawud/Hasan/Hadith-3024/
[34] https://quranx.com/hadith/Bukhari/USC-MSA/Volume-3/Book-39/Hadith-531/

harms a Jew has me as their accuser at the end of time." I had not heard of a Hadith which says this and so I didn't challenge it during the debate. In fact, there is no such Hadith to be found in any of the authoritative collections of Hadith. The absence of such a Hadith speaks volumes in terms of showing what little evidence Aslan has to support his case.

There is a disputed Hadith which says: *"Whoever harms a dhimmi, I shall be his foe on the Day of Judgment."* This may be what Reza was inaccurately quoting. An academic article argues that this Hadith should be regarded as authentic, but the conclusion admits that it, *"does not have multiple chains of transmission to back it up, has not been recorded in any of the ṣaḥīḥ works, and has not been transmitted through any of the most highly esteemed isnāds."*[35] In any case, Jews (and Christians) who accepted *dhimmi* status were granted protected status in exchange for paying the *jizya* subjugation tax and being treated as second class citizens. So, even if this Hadith is authentic, it does not support Reza's argument. It does not say that no Jews should be harmed. It merely says that those Jews (and Christians) who have accepted *dhimmi* status should not be harmed.

Antisemitism in the Sirah

The Sirah are the biographies of Muhammad, of which the most well-known is the Life of Muhammad by Ibn Ishaq, as edited by Ibn Hisham.[36] Muhammad is presented in the Qur'an as an example to follow (Q33:32; Q68:4). Devout Muslims will seek to follow the example of Muhammad in numerous ways.

The most famous antisemitic incident in the Sirah is the extermination of the Jewish Qurayza tribe after the Battle of the Trench.

---

[35] Ahmed El-Wakil, ""Whoever Harms a Dhimmī I Shall Be His Foe on the Day of Judgment": An Investigation into an Authentic Prophetic Tradition and Its Origins from the Covenants," *Religions* 10, no. 9 (2019). https://doi.org/10.3390/rel10090516

[36] A.M.I. Hishām, et al., *The life of Muhammad: a translation of Ish*āq's Sīrat rasūl Allāh (trans. A. Guillaume; Oxford: Oxford University Press, 1967), Hereafter: *Life of Muhammad*

Before this incident Muhammad cursed the Jews as 'brothers of monkeys':

> "You brothers of monkeys, has God disgraced you and brought his vengeance upon you?"[37]

Here is the account of the extermination of the Jewish tribe:

> "Then they surrendered, and the apostle confined them in Medina in the quarter of d. al-Harith, a woman of B. al-Najjar. Then the apostle went out to the market of Medina (which is still its market today) and dug trenches in it. Then he sent for them and struck off their heads in those trenches as they were brought out to him in batches. Among them was the enemy of Allah Huyayy b. Akhtab and Ka`b b. Asad their chief. There were 600 or 700 in all, though some put the figure as high as 800 or 900. As they were being taken out in batches to the apostle they asked Ka`b what he thought would be done with them. He replied, "Will you never understand? Don't you see that the summoner never stops and those who are taken away do not return? By Allah it is death!" This went on until the apostle made an end of them."[38]

So, Muhammad ordered the extermination of over 600 Jewish men who had surrendered to him without a battle. A Hadith relates:

> "I was among the captives of Banu Qurayzah. They (the Companions) examined us, and those who had begun to grow hair (pubes) were killed, and those who had not were not killed. I was among those who had not grown hair." (Sunan Abu Dawud, Hadith 4404)[39]

Having pubic hair was thus a death sentence for Jewish males.

Jews threatened to convert

Prior to the extermination of the Banu Qurayzah tribe, Muhammad threatened the Jewish Banu Qaynuqa tribe:

> "O Jews, beware lest God bring upon you the vengeance that He brought upon Quraysh and become Muslims. You know that I am

---
[37] *Life of Muhammad*, 461.
[38] *Life of Muhammad*, 464.
[39] https://quranx.com/hadith/AbuDawud/DarusSalam/Hadith-4404/

a prophet who has been sent – you will find that in your scriptures and God's covenant with you."[40]

Jews terrorised

Muhammad's attacks terrorised the Jews.

"Our attack upon God's enemy cast terror among the Jews, and there was no Jew in Medina who did not fear for his life."[41]

Kill any Jew

Muhammad commanded his followers to kill any Jew that fell into their power.

"The apostle said, **'Kill any Jew that falls into your power.'** Thereupon Muhayyisa b. Mas'ud leapt upon Ibn Sunayna, a Jewish merchant with whom they had social and business relations, and killed him. Huwayyisa was not a Muslim at the time though he was the elder brother. When Muhayyisa killed him Huwayyisa began to beat him, saying, 'You enemy of God, did you kill him when much of the fat on your belly comes from his wealth?' Muhayyisa answered, 'Had the one who ordered me to kill him ordered me to kill you I would have cut your head off.' He said that this was the beginning of Huwayyisa's acceptance of Islam. The other replied, 'By God, if Muhammad had ordered you to kill me would you have killed me?' He said, 'Yes, by God, had he ordered me to cut off your head I would have done so.' He exclaimed, 'By God, a religion which can bring you to this is marvellous!' and he became a Muslim."[42]

Two religions shall not remain

On his deathbed, Muhammad is reported to have said: "*Two religions shall not remain together in the peninsula of the Arabs.*"[43] Sadly, some of his followers have attempted to fulfil this religious-ethnic cleansing wish.

---

[40] *Life of Muhammad*, 363.
[41] *Life of Muhammad*, 368.
[42] *Life of Muhammad*, 369.
[43] *Life of Muhammad*, 525.

Qur'an texts appearing philosemitic

There are some texts in the Qur'an that can appear philosemitic (or favourable to the Jews). When read in context or with interpretation, it is clear that they are not really philosemitic. These texts are discussed here in Qur'anic order.

Q2:47

> O Children of Israel, remember My favour that I have bestowed upon you and that I preferred you over the worlds [i.e., peoples].

The text then continues with various additional *'remember'* items about what Allah had done, only to go on to state:

> And you had already known about those who transgressed among you concerning the sabbath, and We said to them, "Be apes, despised." (Q2:65)

And further:

> How wretched is that for which they sold themselves–that they would disbelieve in what Allāh has revealed through [their] outrage that Allāh would send down His favour upon whom He wills from among His servants. So they returned having [earned] wrath upon wrath. And for the disbelievers is a humiliating punishment. (Q2:90)

> And never will the Jews and the Christians approve of you until you follow their religion. Say, "Indeed, the guidance of Allāh is the [only] guidance." If you were to follow their desires after what has come to you of knowledge, you would have against Allāh no protector or helper. (2:120)

> Those to whom We gave the Scripture know him [i.e., Prophet Muḥammad (ﷺ)] as they know their own sons. But indeed, a party of them conceal the truth while they know [it]. (2:146)

When seen in context, therefore, Q2:47 is not really philosemitic but merely Allah reminding Jews of his previous favour to them. It is critiquing Jews in the light of God's favour to them, not casting them in a positive light.

Q2:62 (=Q5:69)

Indeed, those who believed and those who were Jews or Christians or Sabeans [before Prophet Muḥammad (ﷺ)]–those [among them] who believed in Allāh and the Last Day and did righteousness–will have their reward with their Lord, and no fear will there be concerning them, nor will they grieve.

This is the single Qur'anic text that Reza cited to show that the Qur'an is not antisemitic. This text appears to say that Jews and Christians will be saved in the last day. Many Muslims, however, believe that this text is abrogated by Q3:85 and Q3:19.[44]

And whoever desires other than Islām as religion–never will it be accepted from him, and he, in the Hereafter, will be among the losers. (Q3:85)

Indeed, the religion in the sight of Allāh is Islām. And those who were given the Scripture did not differ except after knowledge had come to them–out of jealous animosity between themselves. And whoever disbelieves in the verses of Allāh, then indeed, Allāh is swift in [taking] account. (Q3:19)

Even if Q2:62 is not regarded as having been abrogated, the text requires Jews or Christians to believe in Allah and the Last Day and to do righteousness. 'To do righteousness' can be interpreted to mean that they accept Islam. Muhammad seemed to believe that Jews or Christians could also be Muslims, and this is what this verse most likely means. Mainstream interpretation of this verse in Islam is certainly not that Jews and Christians will all receive salvation. Also, bear in mind that the previous verse (Q 2:61 cited earlier) is clearly antisemitic.

Q2:122

O Children of Israel, remember My favour which I have bestowed upon you and that I preferred you over the worlds.

---

[44] https://wikiislam.net/wiki/List_of_Abrogations_in_the_Qur%27an#Surah_2 See discussion of abrogation in the chapter: *Is Islam a Religion of Peace?*

It continues:

> And fear a Day when no soul will suffice for another soul at all, and no compensation will be accepted from it, nor will any intercession benefit it, nor will they be aided. (Q2:123)

Q2:256

> There shall be no compulsion in [acceptance of] the religion. The right course has become distinct from the wrong. So whoever disbelieves in ṭāghūt1 and believes in Allāh has grasped the most trustworthy handhold with no break in it. And Allāh is Hearing and Knowing.

This verse is frequently cited by Islamic apologists. However, some scholars believe that it is abrogated by the verse of the sword (Q9:5), while others believe that it has a restricted application to Jews and Christians who are not forced to convert if they accept *dhimmi* status and agree to pay the *jizyah* tax referred to in Q9:29.[45] In any case, it is not obviously philosemitic.

Q3:84

> Say, "We have believed in Allāh and in what was revealed to us and what was revealed to Abraham, Ishmael, Isaac, Jacob, and the Descendants [al-Asbāṭ], and in what was given to Moses and Jesus and to the prophets from their Lord. We make no distinction between any of them, and we are Muslims [submitting] to Him."

This verse is a claim of continuity from the Old Testament to the New Testament and on to the Qur'an. The Qur'an claims that the Old Testament prophets were all Muslims (Noah Muslim Q10:72; Ibrahim Muslim Q3:67, Moses Muslim Q10:84, Isa Muslim Q5:111). Therefore, it is seeking to persuade Jews (and Christians) to follow Muhammad because he claims to be in their tradition. It is not clearly philosemitic. Rather, it implies criticism of the Jews for not accepting Muhammad as a prophet.

---

[45] https://www.answering-islam.org/Responses/Menj/taqiyyah.htm

Q5:5

This day [all] good foods have been made lawful, and the food of those who were given the Scripture is lawful for you and your food is lawful for them. And [lawful in marriage are] chaste women from among the believers and chaste women from among those who were given the Scripture before you, when you have given them their due compensation desiring chastity, not unlawful sexual intercourse or taking [secret] lovers. And whoever denies the faith–his work has become worthless, and he, in the Hereafter, will be among the losers.

According to this verse, Muslim men are permitted to marry Jewish (and Christian) women. However, it does not say that Muslim women are allowed to marry Jewish men. This reflects the belief that men have authority over their wives, and that a non-Muslim cannot be permitted to have authority over a Muslim.

Q5:69

Indeed, those who have believed [in Prophet Muḥammad (ﷺ)] and those [before him (ﷺ)] who were Jews or Sabeans or Christians–those [among them] who believed in Allāh and the Last Day and did righteousness–no fear will there be concerning them, nor will they grieve.

This is the same as Q2:62 above (see comments there) and is repeated here to present the texts in Qur'anic order.

Q12:111

There was certainly in their stories a lesson for those of understanding. Never was it [i.e., the Qur'ān] a narration invented, but a confirmation of what was before it and a detailed explanation of all things and guidance and mercy for a people who believe.

This verse claims that the Qur'an confirms the Scriptures that came before – the Old Testament and the New Testament. Its aim is to persuade Jews (and Christians) to follow Muhammad as a prophet. In no way does it portray Jews or Christians positively.

Q29:46

And do not argue with the People of the Scripture except in a way that is best, except for those who commit injustice among them, and say, "We believe in that which has been revealed to us and revealed to you. And **our God and your God is one**; and we are **Muslims** [in submission] to Him."

This verse claims that Jews (and Christians) worship the same God as the Muslims. But note that it says, "we are Muslims" at the end of the verse. Its aim is to persuade Jews (and Christians) to become Muslims.

Tafsir al-Jalalayn explains this verse:

> And do not dispute with the People of the Scripture unless it be with that — in that manner of disputation bettering the most virtuous way such as calling them to God by reference to His signs and pointing out His arguments; except in the case of those of them who have done wrong by waging war and **refusing to accept to pay the jizya-tax** dispute with these using the sword until such time as they submit or pay the jizya-tax; and say to those who have accepted the imposition upon them of the jizya-tax should they inform you of something stated in their Scriptures 'We believe in that which has been revealed to us and revealed to you — and neither believe nor disbelieve them in that which they tell you — our God and your God is one and the same and to Him we submit' to Him we are obedient.[46]

Q45:16

And We did certainly give the Children of Israel the Scripture and judgement and prophethood, and We provided them with good things and preferred them over the worlds.

It continues:

> And We gave them clear proofs of the matter [of religion]. And they did not differ except after knowledge had come to them – out of jealous animosity between themselves. Indeed, your Lord will judge between them on the Day of Resurrection concerning that over which they used to differ. (Q45:17)

---

[46] https://tinyurl.com/altafsir389

Then We put you, [O Muḥammad], on an ordained way concerning the matter [of religion]; so follow it and do not follow the inclinations of those who do not know. (Q45:19)

So, the conclusion of the passage is that Jews will be judged, followed by an exhortation for Jews to follow Muhammad. It is not so philosemitic within that context.

Other texts that may appear to be philosemitic

The Charter of Medina or 'Sahifa'

The texts in the Sirah that appear most philosemitic in my view are found in what is known as the Charter of Medina. This charter is found in Ibn Ishaq's *Life of Muhammad* and is said to have been established shortly after Muhammad migrated to Mecca in 622 AD. Here are some representative quotes from the charter:

> "To the Jew who follows us belong help and equity."[47]
> "The Jews have their religion, and the Muslims have theirs."[48]
> "The Jew must pay with the believers as long as war lasts."[49]

These quotes seem to provide religious freedom for the Jews and cooperation in warfare with the Jews. Unfortunately, this document has questionable historicity since there is no evidence of it outside of Islamic sources. Even if we accept its historicity, it is clear that Muhammad did not stick to these principles, since within five years there were no Jews remaining in Medina according to Islamic historians![50]

The following timeline will make this clear. When Muhammad migrated to Medina in 622 AD, the population of Medina was around 50% Jewish. This Jewish population was comprised of three tribes: the Banu Qaynuqa, the Banu Al-Nadir, and the Banu Qurayza. The

---

[47] *Life of Muhammad*, 232.
[48] *Life of Muhammad*, 233.
[49] *Life of Muhammad*, 233.
[50] Ayman S. Ibrahim, *A Concise Guide to the Life of Muhammad: Answering Thirty Key Questions* (Baker Publishing Group, 2022), 75.

first two of these tribes were expelled from Medina, and the last was exterminated.

Timeline:

622   Muhammad's migration (or Hijra) to Medina.
622   Charter of Medina[51]
624   Battle of Badr – victory over the Meccan Quraysh tribe (Arabs)[52]
624   Expulsion of **Banu Qaynuqa** on pretext of violating the covenant.[53] Muhammad first threatens them, so being first to breach the covenant. *"O Jews, beware lest God bring upon you the vengeance that He brought upon Quraysh and become Muslims. You know that I am a prophet who has been sent – you will find that in your scriptures and God's covenant with you."*[54] Muhammad intended to exterminate this tribe after they surrendered, but he was persuaded to allow them to leave, and thus be removed from the area.
624   Expulsion of **Banu Al-Nadir** on pretext of treachery.[55] Muhammad claimed that Allah revealed to him that they were plotting to drop a rock from a roof onto his head.
627   Battle of the Trench.[56]
627   Extermination of the **Banu Qurayza** after they were accused of conspiring with Meccans.[57]Gabriel is said to have appeared to Muhammad declaring, "Allah commands you, Muhammad to go to Banu Qurayza. I am about to go to them to shake their stronghold."[58]

---

[51] *Life of Muhammad,* 231-233. See discussion here: https://en.wikipedia.org/wiki/Constitution_of_Medina
[52] *Life of Muhammad,* 289ff.
[53] *Life of Muhammad,* 363-364.
[54] *Life of Muhammad,* 363.
[55] *Life of Muhammad,* 437-445.
[56] *Life of Muhammad,* 450ff.
[57] *Life of Muhammad,* 461ff.
[58] *Life of Muhammad,* 461.

"When Allah's Messenger (ﷺ) returned on the day (of the battle) of Al-Khandaq (i.e. Trench), he put down his arms and took a bath. Then Gabriel whose head was covered with dust, came to him saying, "You have put down your arms! By Allah, I have not put down my arms yet." Allah's Messenger (ﷺ) said, "Where (to go now)?" Gabriel said, "This way," pointing towards the tribe of Bani Quraiza. So Allah's Messenger (ﷺ) went out towards them." (Sahih Bukhari 5:52:68)[59]

628 Surrender of **Jews of Khaybar**.[60] Their property was confiscated. They were then allowed to work it again in exchange for 50% income tax.

Muhammad married a Jew (Safiyah, his 10th wife)

Some Muslims argue that Muhammad could not have been antisemitic because he married a Jew. Safiyah, Muhammad's tenth wife, was indeed a Jew. Her husband was one of the many Jews who were killed in Khaybar. Safiyah was taken captive and claimed by Muhammad as his because of her beauty. Here is the account in the *Life of Muhammad:*

> "When the apostle had conquered al-Qamus the fort of B. Abu'l-Huqayq, Safiya d Huyayy b. Akhtab was brought to him along with another woman. Bilal who was bringing them led them past the Jews who were slain; and when the woman who was with Safiya saw them she shrieked and slapped her face and poured dust on her head. When the apostle saw her he said 'Take this she-devil away from me.' He gave orders that Safiya was to be put behind him and threw his mantle over her, so that the Muslims knew that he had chosen her for himself. I have heard that the apostle said to Bilal when he saw this Jewess behaving this way, "Have you no compassion, Bilal, when you brought two women past their dead husbands?"[61]

---

[59] https://quranx.com/hadith/Bukhari/USC-MSA/Volume-4/Book-52/Hadith-68/
[60] *Life of Muhammad,* 515.
[61] *Life of Muhammad,* 515.

And here is a Hadith relating how she was claimed by Muhammad:

> Then we reached Khaibar; and when Allah enabled him to conquer the Fort (of Khaibar), the beauty of Safiya bint Huyai bin Akhtab was described to him. Her husband had been killed while she was a bride. So Allah's Messenger (ﷺ) selected her for himself and took her along with him till we reached a place called Sa`d-AsSahba,' where her menses were over and he took her for his wife. Haris (a kind of dish) was served on a small leather sheet. Then Allah's Messenger (ﷺ) told me to call those who were around me. So, that was the marriage banquet of Allah's Messenger (ﷺ) and Safiya. (Sahih Bukhari 4:52:143)[62]

Muslim historian Al-Tabari relates that one of Muhammad's followers was concerned for Muhammad's safety when he slept with Safiyah because Muhammad had killed her father, her brother, and her husband.

> Ibn 'Umar [al-Waqidi] – Kathir b. Zayd – al-Walid b. Rabah – Abu Hurayrah: While the Prophet was lying with Safiyah Abu Ayyub stayed the night at his door. When he saw the Prophet in the morning he said "God is the Greatest." He had a sword with him; he said to the Prophet, "O Messenger of God, this young woman had just been married, and you killed her father, her brother and her husband, so I did not trust her (not to harm) you." The Prophet laughed and said "Good".[63]

It is clear from these accounts that this was a forced marriage. Safiyah was taken captive; she had no choice in the matter. One of Muhammad's followers stood outside the tent with a sword when Muhammad slept with her because he was concerned that Safiyah might try to attack Muhammad. This marriage is hardly evidence that Muhammad was not antisemitic.

---

[62] https://quranx.com/Hadith/Bukhari/USC-MSA/Volume-4/Book-52/Hadith-143/
[63] Al-Tabari, *The History of al-Tabari Vol. XXXIX: Biographies of the Prophet's Companions and Their Successors* (trans. E. Landau-Tasseron; vol. 39: State University of New York Press, 1989), 185.

Antisemitism from Islamic Scholars

There are multiple examples of Islamic scholars who have displayed their antisemitism and justified it on the basis of the Qur'an. Here, I have selected some highly influential Islamic scholars of the twentieth and twenty-first centuries.

Muhammad Sayyid Tantawi (d.2010)

Tantawi was appointed grand Mufti of Egypt in 1986, and then Grand Imam of Al-Azhar in 1996, which position he held until his death in 2010. Reza Aslan, in his book, *No God But One,* describes Al-Azhar Mosque and University as *"the closest thing the Muslim world has to a Vatican."*[64] Therefore, the Grand Imam of Al-Azhar Mosque is presumably the closest thing in the Muslim world to the Pope! I quoted Tantawi's examples below in my closing statement in the debate with Reza. They serve to illustrate just how prevalent and ingrained antisemitism is, and how it is justified from the Qur'an.

> [The Qur'an] describes the Jews with their own particular degenerate characteristics, i.e., killing the prophets of God, corrupting his words by putting them in the wrong places, consuming the people's wealth frivolously, refusal to distance themselves from the evil they do, and other ugly characteristics caused by their [...] deep rooted lasciviousness. ... This means that not all Jews are not the same. The good ones become Muslims; the bad ones do not."[65]

> "The Almighty's (Allah's) words [Q5:82], 'You will surely find the most intense of the people in animosity toward the believers to be the Jews"...is a statement that serves, in continuation, to reinforce other verses that preceded it, verses that documented the many despicable characteristics, and crooked and cunning ways of the Jews. The Almighty asserted—through linguistic devices—the content of the message entailed in the statement, and the addressee is the Prophet (Muhammad), and it can also be anyone who is entitled to preach to warn that their (the Jews) condition is no secret to anyone.

---

[64] Reza Aslan, *No god but God: The Origins and Evolution of Islam* (Random House Children's Books, 2012), 137
[65] Tantawi's Al-Azhar University PhD Thesis, cited in: Andrew G. Bostom, *The Legacy of Islamic Antisemitism: From Sacred Texts to Solemn History* (Prometheus Books, 2020), 394

Their enmity is rooted in envy, spite, stubbornness, and pride. Once these vices overcome the soul, it will not be able to find the way to the righteous path and the true religion (Islam)... The first object to His (Allah's) saying 'You will surely find,' is 'the most intense of the people.' The second object is 'the Jews.' Al-Alusi52 said that it is apparently the Jews in general that are meant here. That is to say, those who were in the presence of the Apostle (Muhammad) from the Jews of Medina, and others. This view is supported by the Apostle who said, 'Whenever a Jew is alone with a Muslim, he (the Jew) will strive to kill him (the Muslim).'...It was said that one of the doctrines of the Jews is to cause harm to those who disagree with them in matters of religion by any means possible. Mentioning Jews before those who associate others with Allah is a declaration that they are more intense and far surpass the other group in their animosity (toward Muslims)."[66]

"[T]he Jews always remain maleficent deniers. [T]hey should desist from their negative denial... some Jews went way overboard in denying hostility, so gentle persuasion can do no good with them, so use force with them and treat them in the way you see effective in ridding them of their evil. One may go so far as to ban their religion, their persons, their wealth, and their villages."[67]

Ahmad Al-Tayeb (b.1946)

Ahmad Al-Tayeb is Tantawi's successor as Grand Imam of Al-Azhar Mosque. He said in an interview in 2013:

"A verse in the Koran explains the Muslims' relations with the Jews and the polytheists. The second part of the verse describes the Muslims' relations with the Christians, and the third part of the verse explains why the Christians are the closest and most friendly to the Muslims.

"This is an historical perspective, which has not changed to this day. See how we suffer today from global Zionism and Judaism, whereas our peaceful coexistence with the Christians has withstood

---

[66] Tantawi comment on Q5:82 cited in: Bostom, *The Legacy of Islamic Antisemitism: From Sacred Texts to Solemn History*, ix
[67] Tantawi's Al-Azhar University PhD Thesis (English translation, *Jews in the Koran and Traditions*; completed 1966, published 1968) Cited in: Bostom, *The Legacy of Islamic Antisemitism: From Sacred Texts to Solemn History*, 394

the test of history. Since the inception of Islam 1,400 years ago, we have been suffering from Jewish and Zionist interference in Muslim affairs. This is a cause of great distress for the Muslims.

"The Koran said it and history has proven it: "You shall find the strongest among men in enmity to the believers to be the Jews and the polytheists." [Q 5:82] This is the first part. The second part is: "You shall find the closest in love to the believers to be those who say: 'We are Christians'." The third part explains why the Christians are "the closest in love to the believers," while the Jews and the polytheists are the exact opposite."[68]

Sheikh Atiyyah Saqr (d.2006)

Sheikh Atiyyah Saqr was former head of the Al-Azhar Fatwa Committee. He outlined 20 bad traits of the Jews as described in the Qur'an in an online chat in 2004.[69] These include: fabricating things, loving to listen to lies, hiding the truth, hypocrisy, being gleeful when others are afflicted with calamity, arrogance, rudeness and vulgarity, mercilessness, cowardice, and miserliness.

Sheikh Yousef Al-Qaradawi (d. 2022)

Sheikh Yousef Al-Qaradawi was president of the European Council for Fatwa and Research since its founding in 1997, and was chairman of the International Union of Muslim Scholars. He was also appointed a trustee of the Oxford Centre for Islamic Studies. He said in a sermon in 2009:

> "Oh Allah, take your enemies, the enemies of Islam. Oh Allah, take the Jews, the treacherous aggressors. Oh Allah, take this profligate, cunning, arrogant band of people. Oh Allah, they have spread much tyranny and corruption in the land. Pour Your wrath upon them, oh our God. Lie in wait for them. Oh Allah, You annihilated the people of Thamoud at the hand of a tyrant, and You annihilated the people of 'Aad with a fierce, icy gale. Oh Allah, You annihilated the people Thamoud at the hand of a tyrant, You annihilated the people of

---

[68] https://www.memri.org/tv/sheik-al-azhar-ahmad-al-tayeb-justifies-antisemitism-basis-koran

[69] https://www.memri.org/reports/former-al-azhar-fatwa-committee-head-sets-out-jews-20-bad-traits-described-quran

'Aad with a fierce, icy gale, and You destroyed the Pharaoh and his soldiers – oh Allah, take this oppressive, tyrannical band of people. Oh Allah, take this oppressive, Jewish, Zionist band of people. Oh Allah, do not spare a single one of them. Oh Allah, count their numbers, and kill them, down to the very last one."[70]

He tweeted in 2017:

"The Quran does not devote as much space to the Persians and Romans as it does to the Jews, whose crimes and depraved deeds it exposes. They are the greatest of liars when they speak, the greatest of villains when they quarrel, and the most treacherous of people when they make pacts."[71]

He said in Arabic:

"The Jews are the Ummah's worst enemies! Their hostility to Islam and Muslims was, is, and will remain as long as Muslims and Jews remain on this earth. This issue in which those who have a general understanding of what was, what is, and what has been decided as Allah says (You will find that the people most hostile to those who have believed are the Jews ...) [Q5:82]. So enmity with the Jews is the continuous and permanent belief of Muslims and the testimony of the Holy Qur'an. It is one of the established axioms in the mind and conscience of every Muslim who believes in this book and his belief in this axiom cannot be penetrated or shaken by anything in the world."[72]

In a 2009 interview he said:

"Throughout history, Allah has imposed upon the [Jews] people who would punish them for their corruption. The last punishment was carried out by Hitler. By means of all the things he did to them – even though they exaggerated this issue – he managed to put them

---

[70] https://www.memri.org/reports/sheikh-yousef-al-qaradhawi-al-jazeera-incites-against-jews-arab-regimes-and-us-calls-muslims
[71] https://www.memri.org/reports/sheikh-yousuf-al-qaradawi-calls-resistance-jihad-and-martyrdom-following-trumps-recognition#_edn15
[72] Sam Solomon and E Al Maqdisi, *Al-Yahud* (Pilcrow Press, 2010), 36-37 http://www.khayma.com/internetclinic/yahodman.htm

in their place. This was divine punishment for them. Allah willing, the next time will be at the hand of the believers."[73]

Muhammad Tu'mah Al-Qudah

Muhammad Tu'mah Al-Qudah is a former Jordanian MP. He said on Jordanian TV in October 2019:

> "Today, some Muslims are acting like Jews in their moral values, their behaviour, and their conduct. The Prophet Muhammad warned us against these people. The Quran says: 'You shall find the people strongest in enmity towards the believers to be the Jews and the polytheists.' [Q5:82] Every Muslim should read this verse. Every Muslim should memorize it and carve it onto his mind and his heart. ... [Our] enmity toward the Jews will never end. It will continue until the Antichrist arrives and the Jews are annihilated in the Great Battle, which will take place in the Levant, in our own land, against the Jews. The enmity between us and the Jews will never cease because it is ideological. ... The regimes of the world can sign agreements and peace accords with the Jews, but the people curse the Jews whenever they recite the Al-Fatiha chapter [i.e. Q 1:7] in the Quran."[74]

Salamah Al-Bluwi

Salamah Al-Bluwi is a Jordanian MP. He said in parliament in 2021:

> "What happened and is happening in occupied Palestine constitutes a war crime by the criminal Zionists, the sons of apes and pigs, Allah's curses and curses by the Prophet Muhammad upon them. They must stop their brutal assaults at once. Our conflict with the Jews is of a historical, religious nature. The Jews do not abide by any agreement, contract, or pact."[75]

---

[73] https://www.memri.org/tv/sheik-yousuf-al-qaradhawi-allah-imposed-hitler-upon-jews-punish-them-allah-willing-next-time-will
[74] https://www.memri.org/tv/former-jordanian-mp-tumah-qudah-jews-enemies-islam-terrorism-muslims-acting-like
[75] https://www.memri.org/tv/jordan-parliament-session-discuss-israel-hamas-fighting-annul-agreements-salute-rockets-target-zionists-cowards-wear-diapers-

Ahmed Aboul Gheit

Ahmed Aboul Gheit is Secretary-General of the Arab League. He said in an April 2024 interview:

> "The Jews Have No Conscience Left – It Was Burned in the Holocaust; Israel Does Not Have the Right to Self-Defense Just Like the Nazis Did Not Have It in WWII."[76]

Tareq Al-Suwaidan

Kuwaiti Islamic scholar and Muslim Brotherhood leader Tareq Al-Suwaidan discussed the 7 October 2023 attack on Israel in a November 15, 2023 Al-Minassa podcast episode.[77] He said that all Israelis are soldiers, that they are criminals, and deserve to be killed and expelled for plundering the land. Al-Suwaidan added that Israeli women should be taken captive, because they are soldiers and are not innocent, except for the disabled women. He added that the Jews influence world governments through their control of the media and money in the world. Al-Suwaidan suggested that people read his book *The Jews – Illustrated Encyclopedia*, which claims that 80% of the media outlets in the world are owned by the Jews directly and the rest indirectly.

Muhammad Husayn Tabataba'i (d.1981)

Iranian scholar Muhammad Husayn Tabataba'i in his commentary on Q5:82 said:

> "[T]he enmity of the Jews and polytheists toward the divine religion [Islam] and their sustained arrogance and bigotry, have continued exactly in the same manner even after the Prophet...
>
> These unchanged characteristics in both groups confirm what the Mighty Book [the Koran] had indicated."[78]

---

[76] https://www.memri.org/tv/sec-gen-arab-league-ahmed-aboul-gheit-jews-no-conscience-holocaust-palestine-resistance-not-terrorism

[77] https://www.memri.org/reports/kuwaiti-islamic-scholar-and-muslim-brotherhood-leader-tareq-al-suwaidan-discusses-october-7

[78] Muhammad Husayn Tabataba'i, *Tafsir al-Mizan*, Vol 11, Trans. Said Akhtar Rizvi (Tawheed Institute Australia, 2023), 95 https://almizan.org/vol/11/1-251

Sheikh Abd Al-Rahman Al-Sudayyis

Sheikh Abd Al-Rahman Al-Sudayyis preached at the Al-Haram mosque – the most important mosque in Mecca – in 2002:

> "Read history and you will understand that the Jews of yesterday are the evil fathers of the Jews of today, who are evil offspring, infidels, distorters of [others'] words, calf-worshippers, prophet-murderers, prophecy-deniers… the scum of the human race 'whom Allah cursed and turned into apes and pigs…' These are the Jews, an ongoing continuum of deceit, obstinacy, licentiousness, evil, and corruption…"[79]

Sheikh Muhammad Saleh Al-Munajjid

Sheikh Muhammad Saleh Al-Munajjid is the founder of the popular *fatwa* website IslamQA.[80] He said in a sermon in Al-Damam in 2002:

> "The Jews are defiled creatures and satanic scum. The Jews are the helpers of Satan. The Jews are the cause of the misery of the human race, together with the infidels and the other polytheists. Satan leads them to Hell and to a miserable fate. The Jews are our enemies and hatred of them is in our hearts. Jihad against them is our worship."[81]

Anwar al-Sadat (d.1981)

Whilst serving as the third president of Egypt, Anwar al-Sadat said in a speech in 1972:

> "They are a nation of liars and traitors, contrivers of plots, a people born for deeds of treachery…. they shall return and be as the Quran said of them 'condemned to humiliation and misery.'"[82]

In this context 'return' means to *dhimmitude*.

---

[79] https://www.jewishvirtuallibrary.org/muslim-clerics-jews-are-the-descendants-of-apes-pigs-and-other-animals Cited in: Bostom, *The Legacy of Islamic Antisemitism: From Sacred Texts to Solemn History*, 11
[80] https://islamqa.info/en
[81] https://www.memri.org/reports/friday-sermons-saudi-mosques-review-and-analysis
[82] D.F. Green, *Arab Theologians on Jews and Israel: Extracts from the Proceedings of the Fourth Conference of the Academy of Islamic Research* (Editions de l'Avenir, 1976), 90-91

Sayyid Qutb (d. 1966)

Influential Egyptian Islamic scholar and leading member of the Muslim Brotherhood wrote a book in 1950 titled, *Our Struggle against the Jews*. In this book he says:

> "The Qur'an spoke much about its Jews and elucidated their evil psychology. It is not mere chance that the Qur'an elaborates on this. For there is no other group whose history reveals the sort of merciless, (moral) shirking and ungratefulness for divine guidance as does this one.... Everywhere Jews have been they have committed unprecedented abominations. From such creatures who kill, massacre, and defame prophets one can only expect spilling of human blood and any dirty means which would further their machinations and evilness."[83]

Abdul Sattar El Sayed

Professor Abdul Sattar El Sayed was Mufti of Tursos in Syria when he said in a speech in 1976:

> "We are fortunate enough to have an available document that tells us the truth about the Jews, and reveals their nature, life, and the inherent poison they carry as well as the remedy for such poison. This document is represented in the Holy Qur'an which provides the real description of the Jews, and constitutes the microscope through which we see the pests and poisons that reside in their minds and hearts."[84]

Muhammad Azzah Darwaza (d.1984)

Palestinian politician, historian and educator Muhammad Azzah Darwaza said in a speech in 1976:"It is extremely astonishing to see that the Jews of today are exactly a typical picture of those mentioned in the Holy Qur'an and they have the same bad manners and qualities of their forefathers although their environment, surroundings and positions are different from those of their ancestors.

---

[83] Qutb, Sayyid, *Our Struggle with the Jews*. Cited in: Bostom, *The Legacy of Islamic Antisemitism: From Sacred Texts to Solemn History*, 357. Cited from: Nettler, Ronald L. *Past trials and present tribulations: a Muslim fundamentalist's view of the Jews*, (Oxford 1978).

[84] Green, *Arab Theologians on Jews and Israel: Extracts from the Proceedings of the Fourth Conference of the Academy of Islamic Research*, 41

These bad manners and qualities of the Jews ascertain the Qur'anic statement about their deeply rooted instinct which they inherited from their fathers."[85]

Salah 'Abd al-Fattah al-Khalidi (d.2022)

Muslim scholar and academic lecturer, Salah 'Abd al-Fattah al-Khalidi, wrote in a book published in 1994:

> "The Jews have astonishing attributes. In each Jew is a complex of ethical depravities and behavioural corruptions so astonishing that it is doubtful that this can be found in any other people. These traits have taken permanent root in their character, such as never occurred in any other people. These depravities, corruptions, maleficences, deficiencies, sicknesses, and handicaps have their own special taint, prominent indications, and deep imbeddedness [sic] in the Jews' astoundingly complex personality. These defects reached their furthest development, and then they infiltrated into the very heart and soul of every Jew, to the point that they influence every aspect of the Jew's soul."[86]

A Channel 4 documentary Dispatches programme, *Undercover Mosque,* broadcast in 2007, found DVDs sold in prominent mosques in the UK in which Sheikh Abdul el-Faisal is seen imitating the noise of a pig when referring to Jewish people [per Q5:60] and predicting the mass extermination of the Jews on a "day of judgment."[87]

These examples are sufficient to demonstrate that antisemitism is widely expressed by Islamic scholars to this day, and frequently on the basis of Islamic texts. What about throughout Islam's 1,400-year history?

Antisemitism in Islamic History

The evidence of antisemitism in Islamic history is overwhelming. The texts cited here are provided in chronological order.

---

[85] Green, *Arab Theologians on Jews and Israel: Extracts from the Proceedings of the Fourth Conference of the Academy of Islamic Research*, 33

[86] Sallah Abd al-Fattah al-Khalidi, *Qur'anic Truths regarding the Palestinian Issue* (Muslim Palestine Publications, 1994). Cited in: Bostom, *The Legacy of Islamic Antisemitism: From Sacred Texts to Solemn History*, 431

[87] https://www.jpost.com/international/tv-documentary-exposes-extremism-in-uk-mosques#google_vignette

Decree of Caliph al-Mutawakkil (850AD)

In this decree, we can see clearly what *dhimmi* status actually meant. It was a discriminatory system which gave Jews (and Christians) second-class citizenship, which required distinctive clothing to be worn. They were not allowed to build synagogues or display religious symbols. This was in addition to paying an exorbitant *jizya* subjugation tax. It is not difficult to see how this is very similar to an apartheid system for Jews (and Christians).

"In that year [AH235/850AD), al-Mutawakkil ordered that the Christians and all the rest of the ahl al-dhimma be made to wear honey-coloured taylasans (hoods) and the zunnar belts. They were to ride on saddles with wooden stirrups, and two balls were to be attached to the rear of' their saddles. He required them to attach two buttons on their qalansuwas (conical caps)–those of them that wore this cap. And it was to be of a different colour from the qalansuwa worn by Muslims. He further required them to affix two patches on the exterior of their slaves' garments. The colour of these patches had to be different from that of the garment. One of the patches was to be worn in front of the breast and the other on the back. Each of the patches should measure four fingers in diameter. They too were to be honey-coloured. Whosoever of them wears a turban, its colour was likewise to be honey-coloured. If any of their women went out veiled, they had to be enveloped in a honey-coloured izar (large wrap). He further commanded that their slaves be made to wear the zunnar and be forbidden to wear the mintaqa (Arab military belt).

He gave orders that any of their houses of worship built after the advent of Islam were to be destroyed and that one-tenth of their homes be confiscated. If the place was spacious enough, it was to be converted into a mosque. If it was not suitable for a mosque, it was to be made an open space. He commanded that wooden images of devils be nailed to the doors of their homes to distinguish them from the homes of Muslims.

He forbade their being employed in the government offices or in any official business whereby they might have authority over Muslims. He prohibited their children [from] studying in Muslim schools. Nor was any Muslim permitted to teach them. He forbade them to display crosses on their Palm Sundays, and he prohibited any Jewish chanting in the streets. He gave orders that their graves should be made level with the ground so as not to resemble the graves of Muslims. And he wrote to all his governors regarding this."[88]

al-Jahiz d.869

"Our people [the Muslims] observing thus the occupations of the Jews and the Christians concluded that the religion of the Jews must compare unfavorably as do their professions, and that their unbelief must be the foulest of all, since they are the filthiest of all nations. Why the Christians, ugly as they are, are physically less repulsive than the Jews may be explained by the fact that the Jews, by not intermarrying, have intensified the offensiveness of their features. Exotic elements have not mingled with them; neither have males of alien races had intercourse with their women, nor have their men cohabited with females of a foreign stock. The Jewish race therefore has been denied high mental qualities, sound physique, and superior lactation. The same results obtain when horses, camels, donkeys, and pigeons are inbred."[89]

Note the clear antisemitic attitudes.

Qadi Ahmed b. Talib (d.889)

"A Jew who dresses like the Muslim and fails to wear the clothing that distinguishes him from them will be incarcerated, beaten, and paraded ignominiously through the places inhabited by the Jews and Christians as an example."[90]

In other words, Jews must wear distinctive clothing on pain of incarceration, beating and parading.

---

[88] Ye'or, Bat (2005), *The Dhimmi: Jews and Christians under Islam* (Revised & Enlarged English edn: Fairleigh Dickinson University Press; 7th; tr. from 1980), 185-86.
From: Norman Stillman, *The Jews of Arab Lands: A History and Source Book*, (Jewish Publication Society, 1998), 167-168. https://www.jewishvirtuallibrary.org/decree-of-caliph-al-mutawakkil-850-ce
Original source: Al-Tabari (1989), *The History of Al-Tabari Vol. XXXIV: Incipient Decline* (State University of New York Press), 89-91.

[89] Finkel, Joshua (1927), "A Risāla of Al-Jāḥiẓ", *Journal of the American Oriental Society* 47: 311-34. https://www.jstor.org/stable/593285

[90] Bostom, *The Legacy of Islamic Antisemitism: From Sacred Texts to Solemn History*, 54

Obadiah, the Norman Proselyte (c.1090)

This text is by a Jewish writer who explains how Jews were treated in Baghdad, where he was living at the time. Note how Jews were to be distinguished by the yellow badges they had to wear, and were required to pay a hefty subjugation tax – with any amount owing on death requiring to be paid on their behalf before burial was permitted.

"…Prior to this, the ruler of Baghdad, whose name was al-Muqtadi, had given full authority to his vizier, Abu Shuja, to make a change in policy regarding the Jews living in Baghdad. Now he (Abu Shuja) had already sought on many occasions to destroy them, but the God of Israel had thwarted his intention, and on this occasion too, he protected them from his fury.

He (Abu Shuja) directed that yellow badges should be affixed to the headgear of every Jewish male. In addition to the badge on the head, another of lead, the weight of a silver coin, was to hang round the neck of every Jew. The lead pendant was to be inscribed with the word "dhimmi" indicating that the Jews were tribute bearers. He also imposed that every Jew should wear a distinguishing belt around the waist. Abu Shuja imposed two distinguishing signs upon Jewish women. Each woman had to wear one red shoe and one black shoe. Furthermore, each woman had to have a small copper bell on her neck or on her shoe which would tinkle so that all would know and differentiate between the women of the Jews and of the Muslims. He assigned cruel Muslim men to watch over the Jewish men and cruel Muslim women to oversee the Jewish women, in order to oppress them with every sort of insult, humiliation, and contempt. The Muslims would mock them, and the common rabble, together with their children, would beat Jews throughout all the streets of Baghdad.

The law regarding the tribute which was collected annually by the servants of the ruler of Baghdad is as follows: From every wealthy Jew, they would collect four and a half dinars, from every Jew of the middle class, two and a half, and from the poorest Jews, one and a half. If a Jew died, not having paid the tribute in full, the Muslims would not let him be buried until the remainder is paid, be the amount large or small. If the deceased left nothing of value, the Muslims demanded it from the Jewish community, and they must redeem their dead by paying the outstanding tribute money out of their own funds. If not, the Muslims would seek to burn the body."[91]

Moses Maimonides (d.1204)

Maimonides was a Jewish Rabbi and philosopher, widely regarded as perhaps the greatest Jewish scholar of the Middle Ages. I was surprised that Reza Aslan cited Maimonides as an example of Muslim tolerance towards the Jews. Maimonides' own words show that the experience of his fellow Jews at the hands of Muslims was anything but tolerance. Maimonides is clear that the Jews were heavily persecuted by the Muslims. He viewed it as the worst persecution Jews had ever endured. Here is a section from his 'Letter to the Jews of Yemen':

> "Remember, my co-religionists, that on account of the vast number of our sins, God has hurled us in the midst of this people, the Arabs, who have persecuted us severely, and passed baneful and discriminatory legislation against us, as Scripture has forewarned us, "Our enemies themselves shall judge us" (Deuteronomy 32:31). Never did a nation molest, degrade, debase and hate us as much as they.... Although we were dishonoured by them beyond human endurance, and had to put with their fabrications, yet we behaved like him who is depicted by the inspired writer, "But I am as a deaf man, I hear not, and I am as a dumb man that openeth not his mouth." (Psalms 38:14). Similarly, our sages instructed us to bear the prevarications and preposterousness of Ishmael in silence."... "But the Muslims themselves put no faith in their own arguments, they neither accept nor cite them, because they are manifestly so fallacious. Inasmuch as the Muslims could not find a single proof in the entire Bible nor a reference or possible allusion to their prophet which they could utilize, they were compelled to accuse us saying, "You have altered the text of the Torah, and expunged every trace of the name of Mohammed therefrom." They could find nothing stronger than this

---

[91] Geniza Document, Kaufmann XV in Alexander Scheiber, Fragment from the Chronicle of Obadiah, the Norman Proselyte," Acta Orientalia Hungarica, vol. 4 (1954), pp 278-78. Cited in: Norman Stillman, The Jews of Arab Lands (Philadelphia: Jewish Publication Society, 1979), p 251. https://zionism-israel.com/hdoc/Jews_Baghdad_Eleventh_Century.htm

ignominious argument the falsity of which is easily demonstrated to one and all by the following facts."[92]

Al-Jaubari (d.1222)

"Know that these people are the most cunning creatures, the vilest, most unbelieving and hypocritical. While ostensibly the most humble and miserable, they are in fact the most vicious of men. This the very essence of rascality and accursedness. If they remain alone with a man, they destroy him.... They are the most unbelieving and most perfidious of men. So beware of their company. They have no belief or religion. This is the description of the learned of the Jewish liars."[93]

Blatant antisemitism from this alchemist from Damascus.

Ibn Kathir (d.1373)

"This Ayah [Q2:61] indicates that the Children of Israel were plagued with humiliation, and that this will continue, meaning that it will never cease. They will continue to suffer humiliation at the hands of all who interact with them, along with the disgrace that they feel inwardly." [94]

Ibn Kathir is a highly respected medieval commentator on the Qur'an whose Tafsir (or commentary) continues to be cited.

Al-Maghili d.c.1505 (Algeria)

"Love of the Prophet requires hatred of the Jews."[95]

Al-Maghili was an influential Muslim missionary in Algeria. His writings were widely circulated in Morocco and continued

---

[92] Moses Maimonides, *Epistle to the Jews of Yemen*, 1172 https://en.wikisource.org/wiki/Epistle_to_Yemen/Complete
[93] Moshe Perleman "Notes on the position of Jewish Physicians in Medieval Muslim Countries," *Israel Orient Studies* 2 (1972): 316-317. Cited in: Bostom, *The Legacy of Islamic Antisemitism: From Sacred Texts to Solemn History*, 321
[94] Ibn Kathir, Tafsir on Q2:61 http://m.qtafsir.com/Surah-Al-Baqara/Covering-the-Jews-in-Humiliati—-
[95] Gwarzo, Hassan Ibrahim (1972), *'The Life and Teachings of Al-Maghili, with Particular Reference to the Saharan Jewish Community'* (University of London), 134. https://eprints.soas.ac.uk/33893/

to influence the treatment of Moroccan Jews through to the early twentieth century.[96] Hunwick elaborates further on Al-Maghili's articulation of *dhimmitude:*

> "Any Muslim who befriended a Jew or came to his defence, or opposed the destruction of the synagogue was to be considered an unbeliever. Dhimmis must be considered in a permanent state of abasement. This is why jizya must be paid in a public ceremony in which the Dhimmi at the moment of payment is given a tap on the neck and pushed forward to show him he has thus escaped the sword. This abasement is more important than the sum paid. No religious edifice may be erected by a dhimmi in the land of Islam and if any governor gave permission for one, this permission must be revoked and the building torn down. This is because the manifestation of the dhimmi's religion in the form of a building is a contradiction of the concept of abasement."[97]

Note the insistence that the *dhimmi* be in a state of abasement.

Ahmad Sirhindi d. 1624 (Indian Sufi theologian):

> "Whenever a Jew is killed it is for the benefit of Islam."[98]

Sirhindi was an Indian theologian and mystic who reasserted orthodox Sunnite Islam in India.

Germaine Moüette (1683)

Germain Moüette was a French writer who wrote about what he observed about the degrading treatment of the Jews in Barbary – what is now Morocco.

> "The Jews are very numerous in Barbary, and they are held in no more estimation than elsewhere; on the contrary, if there is any refuse to be thrown out, they are the first employed. They are

---

[96] Bostom, *The Legacy of Islamic Antisemitism: From Sacred Texts to Solemn History*, 691-692

[97] Hunwick, John O. "Al-Mahîlî and the Jews of Tuwât: The Demise of a Community." *Studia Islamica*, no. 61 (1985) 176 https://www.jstor.org/stable/1595412

[98] Friedmann, Yohanan (1966), *'Shaykh Ahmad Sirhindi: An Outline of His Thought and a Study of His Image in the Eyes of Posterity'* (McGill University): 111. [Bostrom p329] https://escholarship.mcgill.ca/concern/theses/5425kf73g Cited in: Bostom, *The Legacy of Islamic Antisemitism: From Sacred Texts to Solemn History*, 329

obliged to work at their crafts for the king, when they are called, for their food alone. They are subject to the blows and injuries of everyone, without daring to say a word even to a child of six who throws stones at them. If they pass before a mosque, no matter what the weather or season might be, they must remove their shoes, not even daring in the royal cities, such as Fez and Marrakesh, to wear them at all, under pain of five hundred lashes and being put into prison, from which they would be released only on payment of a heavy fine.

"They dress in the Arab fashion, but their cloaks and caps are in black in order to be distinguishable.... There is practically never justice for them in these lands."[99]

Note the degrading treatment of the Jews.

American Reverend, Justin Perkins (1836)

"Yesterday an unoffending Jew was publicly beheaded and burned in this city [Urmia, northwest Iran]. The enraged Mohammedans had, for two or three days, thronged the governor's palace by thousands, demanding that the whole Jewish population of the city should be put to death to a man. And to appease the mob, the governor delivered up this individual. He was arraigned under the accusation of having murdered a Mohammedan child. The Mohammedans...cherish the belief, (or profess to cherish it,) that the Jews possess an instinctive thirst for human blood, as well as seek human victims for an annual sacrifice. In this instance, a Mohammedan infant was found dead, before the door of a Jew. The probability is that the child died a natural death and was thus exposed by interested persons, to rouse public indignation against the poor Jews; and so strong is the hatred of the Mohammedans towards the descendants of Israel, that the stratagem proved entirely successful, as is often the case in Mohammedan countries...The hostility cherished by Mohammedans towards the Jews is inconceivably more bitter than their hatred to Christians. The determined aversion which the Jews

---

[99] Germain Moüette, *Historie des conqestes de Mouuley Archy,* (Paris, 1683). Cited in: Norman Stillman, *The Jews of Arab Lands*, 304.

early manifested to the religion of the impostor [Muhammad] is still remembered and strongly resented by his followers."[100]

Note the link with the religion of Muhammad.

French surgeon A.B. Clot (1840)

Clot relates how the Jews were treated by Muslims in Egypt in the nineteenth century.

> "The Israelite race is the one the Muslims hate the most. They think the Jews hate Islam more than any other nation.... Speaking of a fierce enemy, the Muslims say: 'He hates me the way the Jews hate us.' During the past century, the Israelites were often put to death because they were accused rightly or wrongly to have said something disrespectful about the Koran."[101]

J.J. Benjamin II (1859)

Benjamin comments on the state of the Jews in Palestine under Ottoman rule.

> "Deep misery and continual oppression are the right words to describe the condition of the Children of Israel in the land of their fathers.... They are entirely destitute of every legal protection and every means of safety. Instead of the security afforded by the law, which is unknown in these countries, they are solely under the orders of the Scheiks and Pachas, men, whose character and feelings inspire but little confidence from the beginning.... With unheard of rapacity tax upon tax is levied on them. With the exception of Jerusalem, everywhere else the taxes demanded are arbitrary. Whole communities have been impoverished by the exorbitant claims of the Scheiks, who, under the most trifling pretences,

---

[100] Perkins, Justin, *A Residence of Eight Years in Persia*, (Allen Morrill & Wardwell, 1843), 276 https://t.ly/QqHJF

[101] Jacob M. Landau, *Jews in Nineteenth Century Egypt*, (New York University Press, 1969), 152-54 https://archive.org/details/jewsinnineteenth0000unse/page/152/mode/2up Cited in translation in: Bostom, *The Legacy of Islamic Antisemitism: From Sacred Texts to Solemn History*, 39

without any control, oppress the Jews with fresh burdens. It is impossible to enumerate all these oppressions."[102]

Iqraa Television (Saudi Arabia, 2002)

In May 2002, *Iqraa*, the Saudi satellite television station, which, according to its website, seeks "to highlight aspects of Arab Islamic culture that inspire admiration ... to highlight the true, tolerant image of Islam and refute the accusations directed against it," interviewed a three-and-a-half-year-old "real Muslim girl" about Jews, on "The Muslim Women's Magazine" program. The little girl was asked whether she liked Jews; she answered, "No." When asked why not, she said that Jews were "apes and pigs." "Who said this?" the moderator asked. The girl answered, "Our God." "Where did He say this?" "In the Qur'an." At the end of the interview, the moderator said with satisfaction: "No [parents] could wish for Allah to give them a more believing girl than she... May Allah bless her and both her father and mother."[103]

Approvingly broadcasting blatant antisemitism, justified on the basis of what the Qur'an says.

Many more examples could be cited, but the above is a representative sample of evidence of the impact of Islamic antisemitism throughout the centuries of Islamic history. This doesn't prove that Islam, as defined by its texts, is antisemitic, but it does corroborate that thesis. Sadly, there has been plenty of antisemitism in church history as well, but this does not mean that such antisemitism is supported in the Bible.

Contemporary Surveys

Modern surveys show that antisemitic attitudes are more prevalent amongst Muslims than they are amongst the rest of the population.

---

[102] J.J. Benjamin II, Eight Years in Asia and Africa: From 1846 to 1855, (Hanover 1959), 31. https://archive.org/details/eightyearsinasi00benjgoog/page/n55/mode/2up?q=%22deep+misery%22+

[103] https://www.memri.org/reports/what-arab-antisemitism#_edn5

The 2019 ADL survey found that 11% of the UK population harbour antisemitic attitudes. Amongst Muslims, however, it was 54%.[104]

The 2023 ADL Global survey found that 26% of the global population harbour antisemitic attitudes, while amongst Muslims it was 49%.[105] This compares with 24% amongst Christians. Interestingly, the Muslim prevalence of antisemitism in the UK was not indicated in the 2023 survey.

An ICM Survey in 2015 found that 35% British Muslims believe that Jewish people have too much power in Britain.[106]

A Policy Exchange survey in 2016 found that British Muslims were more likely to believe that Jews carried out the 9/11 attacks than to believe that Al-Qaeda was responsible.[107]

The J.L. Partners survey in 2024 found that almost half of British Muslims (46%) thought Jewish people have too much power over UK government policy, compared with 16% of the rest of the population.[108] For male Muslims, this rose to 53%. This was similar for influence over US foreign policy. Four in ten Muslims thought that Jews have too much power over the UK financial system and the UK media industry.

Increased prevalence of antisemitic attitudes amongst Muslims compared to the rest of the population is what one would expect if Islamic texts were antisemitic.

What about the Bible?

Reza Aslan tried to claim that if Islam is antisemitic, according to its texts, then so is the Bible. The one verse he cited to make this claim was the one where the crowd responds to Pilate's decision to crucify Jesus: *"His blood is on us and on our children"* (Matt 27:25).

---

[104] https://global100.adl.org/country/united-kingdom/2019
[105] https://global100.adl.org/map/
[106] https://pollingreport.uk/articles/icm-poll-of-british-muslims-2
[107] https://policyexchange.org.uk/publication/unsettled-belonging-a-survey-of-britains-muslim-communities/
[108] https://henryjacksonsociety.org/wp-content/uploads/2024/04/HJS-Deck-200324-Final.pdf

In the debate, I explained that this verse is not antisemitic since it does not even reference Jews at all, let alone all Jews. It says *"All the people answered, ..."* This verse is therefore merely recording a historical fact that the crowd in front of Pilate at that time said, *"His blood is on us and on our children."* It does not say that they said this because they were Jews or that all Jews said this. It is therefore not antisemitic. The point was made that similar contextualisation could be done with the antisemitic texts I cited from the Qur'an. I responded that this is not possible with those texts since they clearly reference Jews as Jews and in several cases are open-ended saying *"until the Day of Resurrection"* or *"forever"*.

More generally, it is very hard to claim that the Bible is antisemitic since Jesus himself was Jewish, and the Bible is written almost, if not entirely by Jews, and is very largely about Jews. Jesus said: *"I was sent only to the lost sheep of Israel"* (Matt 15:24), and he was mocked and killed as *"King of the Jews"* (Matt 27:37). The Bible clearly explains that God made all nations *"from one man"* (Acts 17:26), and states that *"there is neither Jew nor Greek"* (Gal 3:28). The gospel *"brings salvation to everyone who believes: first to the Jew, then to the Gentile"* (Rom 1:16).

The Apostle Paul was a Jewish Pharisee (Phil 3:5), who said: *"I could wish that I myself were cursed and cut off from Christ for the sake of my people, those of my own race, the people of Israel"* (Rom 9:3-4). That is an extraordinary statement. Paul was willing to give up his salvation for the sake of the Jews. He also wrote *"Brothers and sisters, my heart's desire and prayer to God for the Israelites is that they may be saved"* (Rom 10:1). And further, *"Did God reject his people [the Jews]? By no means!"* (Rom 11:1).

One text in the New Testament is sometimes cited as being antisemitic. It is from Paul's first letter to the Thessalonians:

> "For you, brothers and sisters, became imitators of God's churches in Judea, which are in Christ Jesus: For you suffered the same things from your own countrymen as they did from the Jews, who killed both the Lord Jesus and the prophets, and drove us out, and displease God and oppose all mankind by hindering us from

speaking to the Gentiles that they might be saved—so as always to fill up the measure of their sins. But God's wrath has come upon them at last!" (1 Thessalonians 2:14-16)

At first glance this could appear antisemitic, which would be very surprising given Paul's statements about his love for the Jews cited above. Deeper analysis shows that it is not antisemitic at all. Paul is writing to the Thessalonians that they are suffering persecution from "your own countrymen" – that is, intra-racial persecution. The churches in Judea, which would have been primarily Jewish churches, suffered similar persecution from the Jews – again that was intra-racial persecution. The focus here is not on Jews in general because they are Jews; it is on those Jews who are hindering the progress of the gospel – in particular, hindering them from preaching to the Gentiles. Those who hinder the gospel should indeed be warned about God's wrath, now as then, no matter what their ethnicity.

Paul says that these Jews "killed both the Lord Jesus and the prophets." He means this type of Jews who are actually opposed to God's work in the world. Jews as Jews are not specifically to blame for killing Jesus, any more than all of us as sinners are to blame for that. Elsewhere in Acts, the Bible blames all the people including Herod, Pontius Pilate, the Gentiles and the people of Israel for contributing to the death of Jesus (Acts 2:36; 3:13-17; 4:27-28; 7:52; 13:27-28).

Another text that is sometimes claimed to be antisemitic is one where Jesus is recorded as saying: "*You are of your father the devil, and your will is to do your father's desires*" (John 8:44). It is clear from the context that this is spoken to some Jews who were plotting to kill him (John 8:37, 40). This is not something that Jesus said of Jews as Jews.

Contrary to what Reza claimed, there are no antisemitic texts in the Bible. In fact, there are numerous philosemitic texts. The Bible, therefore, cannot be said to be antisemitic. Nor can it be used to justify antisemitism. As we have seen from the texts cited above, this is in sharp contrast to the Qur'an.

Conclusion

There are plenty of antisemitic texts in the Qur'an. There are also plenty of antisemitic Hadith. There is further clear antisemitism in the Sirah. The alleged philosemitic Islamic texts do not withstand scrutiny. There is clear evidence of antisemitism amongst Islamic scholars and throughout Islamic history. Surveys also show higher prevalence of antisemitic attitudes amongst Muslims than amongst the rest of the population. We can therefore conclude with confidence that Islam, as defined by its texts, is antisemitic.

This conclusion has clear implications for understanding the nature of Islam as a religion and the source of antisemitic attitudes in many societies around the world. It is also very relevant to the contemporary Arab-Israeli conflict. Islamic antisemitism pre-dates the foundation of the State of Israel. It goes right back to Muhammad and the Qur'an. It is clearly taught in Islamic texts, including those cited in daily prayers. It is not too far-fetched to say that antisemitism is integral to Islam and is part of Islamic doctrine, as defined by Islamic texts.

Bibliography

Al-Tabari (1989), *The History of al-Tabari Vol. XXXIX: Biographies of the Prophet's Companions and Their Successors*, (Translated by Ella Landau-Tasseron. Vol. 39. State University of New York Press)

Aslan, Reza (2012), *No god but God: The Origins and Evolution of Islam* (Random House Children's Books)

Benjamin II, J.J. (1959), *Eight Years in Asia and Africa: From 1846 to 1855*, (Hanover)

El-Wakil, Ahmed (2019), *""Whoever Harms a Dhimmī I Shall Be His Foe on the Day of Judgment": An Investigation into an Authentic Prophetic Tradition and Its Origins from the Covenants."* Religions 10, no. 9

Finkel, Joshua (1927), "A Risāla of Al-Jāḥiẓ", *Journal of the American Oriental Society* 47: 311-34

Friedmann, Yohanan (1966), *'Shaykh Ahmad Sirhindi: An Outline of His Thought and a Study of His Image in the Eyes of Posterity'* (McGill University)

Green, D.F. Arab (1976), *Theologians on Jews and Israel: Extracts from the Proceedings of the Fourth Conference of the Academy of Islamic Research*, (Editions de l'Avenir)

Gwarzo, Hassan Ibrahim (1972), *'The Life and Teachings of Al-Maghili, with Particular Reference to the Saharan Jewish Community'* (University of London)

Hishām, A.M.I., I. Ishaq, and M.I. Isḥāq (1967), *The life of Muhammad: a translation of Isḥāq's Sīrat rasūl Allāh*. (Translated by A. Guillaume. Oxford: Oxford University Press)

Ibrahim, Ayman S. (2022), *A Concise Guide to the Life of Muhammad: Answering Thirty Key Questions*, (Baker Publishing Group)

Hunwick, John O. (1985), "Al-Mahîlî and the Jews of Tuwât: The Demise of a Community." *Studia Islamica*, no. 61

Landau, Jacob M. (1969), *Jews in Nineteenth Century Egypt*, (New York University Press)

Moüette, Germain (1863) *Historie des conqestes de Mouuley Archy*, (Paris)

Nettler, Ronald L. (1978), *Past trials and present tribulations: a Muslim fundamentalist's view of the Jews*, (Oxford)

Perleman, Moshe (1972), "Notes on the position of Jewish Physicians in Medieval Muslim Countries," *Israel Orient Studies* 2

Perkins, Justin (1843), *A Residence of Eight Years in Persia*, (Allen Morrill & Wardwell)

Renard, J., ed. (1998), *Windows on the House of Islam: Muslim Sources on Spirituality and Religious Life*. (University of California Press)

Solomon, Sam and E Al Maqdisi (2010) *Al-Yahud*, (Pilcrow Press)

Spencer, Robert (2022), *The Critical Qur'an: Explained from Key Islamic Commentaries and Contemporary Historical Research* (Bombardier Books)

Stillman, Norman (1998), *The Jews of Arab Lands: A History and Source Book*, (Jewish Publication Society)

Ye'or, Bat (2005), *The Dhimmi: Jews and Christians under Islam* (Revised & Enlarged English edn: Fairleigh Dickinson University Press; tr. from 1980)

11

DID PAUL CLAIM THE ATHENIANS WORSHIPPED YAHWEH?

Note: This article was originally published in Affinity's *Foundations Theological Journal*[1] in December 2019. Here I critique the argument that Paul's Areopagus speech in Acts 17 can be used to justify saying that Allah is the same as the God of the Bible.

The same God controversy

Back in 2015, a controversy arose over whether Christians and Muslims worship the same God. Dr Larycia Hawkins, then a professor at Wheaton College in the US, posted a photo of herself wearing a hijab on Facebook with a comment in which she wrote:

> "I stand in human solidarity with my Muslim neighbour because we are formed of the same primordial clay, descendants of the same cradle of humankind …
>
> I stand in religious solidarity with Muslims because they, like me, a Christian, are people of the book. And as Pope Francis stated last week, we worship the same God."[2]

Hawkins was initially suspended by Wheaton College and later, after protracted discussions on both sides, a confidential agreement was reached which included a parting of ways. Along the way there was huge media interest in the issue and whether Muslims and Christians should be described as worshipping the same God.

---

[1] https://www.affinity.org.uk/news/736-the-same-god-did-paul-claim-the-athenians-worshipped-yahweh/
[2] The full post is displayed on Larycia Hawkins' website. <http://www.laryciahawkins.com/> (8 November 2018).

Does Paul's Areopagus address justify referring to Allah as the same God?

The 'same God controversy', has many aspects to it, and too many to discuss in one article.³ Here I want to focus on one particular aspect – the use of Paul's Areopagus address in Acts 17 to defend the assertion that Christians and Muslims worship the same God.

A special issue of the *Occasional Bulletin* of the *Journal of the Evangelical Missiological Society* was devoted to the same God controversy.⁴ Robert Priest guest edited the issue as a past president of the American Society of Missiology and then president of the Evangelical Missiological Society. Priest wrote the introductory article in which he expressed sympathy for Hawkins' statements, arguing that "many American evangelical missionaries and missiologists, and perhaps the Apostle Paul himself would be in danger of dismissal if they taught at Wheaton College." He continued:

> "It is worth noting that Hawkins was using the word 'worship' in the same way the Apostle Paul used the term in Acts 17:23, where Paul referenced an Athenian altar to an unknown god who he said the Athenians 'worship,' and then proceeded to treat this god as the same referent that he wished to tell them about."⁵

The question is, to what extent does Paul's Areopagus address justify referring to Allah as the same as the God of the Bible?

The key verse here which Priest highlights is Acts 17:23. Here Paul is standing in the Areopagus in Athens, and says:

---

3 There are several book length discussions of some of the issues involved. Particularly important are: Sam Solomon, *Not the Same God: Is the Qur'anic Allah the Lord God of the Bible?* (London: Wilberforce Publications, 2016), ; Miroslav Volf, *Allah: A Christian Response* (New York: HarperCollins, 2012),
4 "Special Edition: Wheaton and the Controversy Over Whether Muslims and Christians Worship the Same God," *Occasional Bulletin of the Evangelical Missiological Society* (2016) <https://www.emsweb.org/images/occasional-bulletin/special-editions/OB_SpecialEdition_2016.pdf> This collates a range of perspectives on the 'same God controversy'.
5 Robert J. Priest, "Wheaton and the Controversy Over Whether Muslims and Christians Worship the Same God," *Occasional Bulletin of the Evangelical Missiological Society* Special Edition (2016): 1-3, 31

"For as I passed along and observed the objects of your worship, I found also an altar with this inscription: 'To the unknown god.' What therefore you worship as unknown, this I proclaim to you."

The argument being made is that Paul clearly states that the god the Athenians worship is the same as the God of Israel – the God of the Bible. There is a *prima facie* case here which requires further investigation. I should note that this passage is one of my favourites and the one I wrote my MA dissertation about.[6] My comments here draw extensively on that work.

The arguments of the Areopagus address
First, it is important to recognise that Paul stood accused of preaching about foreign gods (Acts 17:18-20). This is the very charge that Socrates faced in Athens, and which famously resulted in him receiving the death penalty.[7] The parallels of this story with that of Socrates are very strong, and the story of Socrates was well known, so that it is likely that Luke is deliberately setting up Paul as a philosopher to be compared with the great Socrates.[8] The point here is that Paul is on trial for this dangerous charge of introducing a different god to the ones already acknowledged by the Athenians. His listeners do not believe he worships any already recognised god or one that they worship. Nor do they believe that this is what Paul is claiming. Paul's starting point for his discussion with the Athenians was therefore certainly not a claim to be worshipping the same god. Paul's initial approach therefore stands in sharp contrast to that of those contemporary missiologists who want to emphasise sameness. Paul started by emphasising what was different even though he knew this risked him being put on trial for committing what could be a capital offence.

---

[6] Tim Dieppe, "Paul vs. the Pagans: The Apologetic Approach of the Areopagus Address" (Dissertation, Westminster Theological Centre, 2016) Available on www.academia.edu
[7] Plato, *Apology*, 24b-c; Xenophon, *Memorabilia*, 1.1.1
[8] Karl Olav Sandnes, "Paul and Socrates : The Aim of Paul's Areopagus Speech," *Journal for the Study of the New Testament*, no. 50 (1993)

Second, we should note the obvious fact that the inscription on the idol admits ignorance of this god. This is the opening that Paul uses to proclaim the Biblical God. This is quite different from going to a Muslim who is confident about the nature of Allah and saying that we worship the same god. Paul's use of the 'unknown god' here is part of his defence against the charge of preaching a new god.

Third, there is no definite article in the Greek so, although the ESV translates "To the unknown God," it would more naturally be translated, "To an unknown god."[9] The Athenian polytheistic mindset makes it likely that "an unknown god" is the intended meaning of the inscription. Paul is therefore taking a polytheistic inscription and reinterpreting it monotheistically. He uses their admitted ignorance of a god in this inscription as a rhetorical device to proclaim the one true God.

Fourth, Paul takes the masculine 'god' θεὸς and makes it neuter with the phrase "What therefore you worship as unknown, this I proclaim to you."[10] Paul thus depersonalises the idol – "What you worship" not "Who you worship". Paul later personalises his God, creating a further distinction between his personal God and the impersonal gods worshipped by the Athenians.

Fifth, the Greek construction emphasises their ignorance, not their reverence. Conrad Gempf explains: "Paul in effect says ... 'What I proclaim to you is only that which you yourselves, while openly admitting your ignorance, claim to revere.'"[11] Paul is thus agreeing with their ignorance of their object of reverence, which also implies ignorance as to how to worship too. What is more, this 'unknown' (Ἀγνώστῳ) clearly expresses uncertainty as to what god

---

[9] As RSV, NRSV, NIV, NASB. Bruce comments that "the lapidary style would in any case dispense with the article. F. F. Bruce, *The Book of Acts* (The New International Commentary on the New Testament; Grand Rapids, Michigan: Eerdmans, 1992), 335 n. 57
[10] C. K. Barrett, *Acts 15-28* (International Critical Commentary; London: T & T Clark, 2004), 838. As he points out, some texts read with a masculine pronoun, but it is likely that the neuter is original since there was both a grammatical and a theological reason to make the change.
[11] Conrad Gempf, "Paul at Athens," in *Dictionary of Paul and his Letters* (eds. G. F. Hawthorne, et al.; Leicester: IVP, 1993), 52

they are worshipping. Calvin perceptively comments that: "Whosoever doth worship God without any certainty, he worships his own inventions instead of God."[12] In other words, it makes no sense to worship something without having clarity on what it is that you are worshipping. The Athenians' worship was necessarily deficient because of their ignorance. Paul is thus clearly not saying that they are unknowingly worshiping the same god as him.

Sixth, Paul claims later in the speech (v30) that their ignorance is culpable. The Athenians need to repent. The one point of agreement that Paul can find with polytheistic idolatry is an admission of ignorance. He then assumes authority to proclaim the true nature of God to them. This makes it very clear that Paul does not see this worship of an 'unknown god' as worship of Yahweh.

Seventh, the word for 'worship', εὐσεβεῖτε or 'revere', is not the usual word for 'worship' in the New Testament and, as Pardigon points out, "it is never used in relation to Yahweh in either LXX or NT."[13] Jobes notes that this word was used by Philo of pagan sacrificing of children,[14] and suggests that the word had "become tainted by association with pagan religious ritual"[15] so that the New Testament writers avoided its use for worship of God. Worship of Yahweh is therefore in no way being equated with idolatrous, ignorant, polytheistic worship in this verse.[16] Paul carefully avoids using the term that he would use for 'worship' of Yahweh.

Eighth, Paul is very keen in his speech to explain how the key characteristics of his God contrast with the Athenian idols. Paul's Biblical God:
1. Is the single, transcendent creator of the universe:
   "The God who made the world and everything in it."

---

[12] John Calvin, *Commentary on Acts* (trans. H. Beveridge; vol. 2; Edinburgh: Calvin Translation Society, 1844), 155
[13] Flavien O.C. Pardigon, *Paul Against the Idols: A Contextual Reading of the Areopagus Speech* (Eugene: Wipf and Stock Publishers, 2019), 138-39 n55
[14] Philo, *The Special Laws*, 1.312
[15] Karen H. Jobes, "Distinguishing the Meaning of Greek Verbs in the Semantic Domain for Worship," in *Biblical Words and their Meaning: An Introduction to Lexical Semantics* (ed. M. Silva; Michigan: Zondervan, 1994), 208
[16] Pardigon, *Paul Against the Idols: A Contextual Reading of the Areopagus Speech*, 137

2. Is the ruler of all creation:
   "Lord of heaven and earth."
3. Does not dwell in temples:
   "Does not live in temples made by man."
4. Is self-sufficient:
   "Nor is he served by human hands, as though he needed anything."
5. Is life-giving:
   "Since he himself gives to all mankind life and breath and everything."
6. Rules all the nations:
   "And he made from one man every nation of mankind to live on all the face of the earth, having determined allotted periods and the boundaries of their dwelling place."
7. Is to be sought by everyone:
   "That they should seek God, and perhaps feel their way toward him and find him."
8. Is omnipresent:
   "Yet he is actually not far from each one of us"
9. Is the source of all life:
   "For, 'In him we live and move and have our being'"
10. Is the father of all:
    "'For we are indeed his offspring.'"
11. Is not representable by an image or idol:
    "Being then God's offspring, we ought not to think that the divine being is like gold or silver or stone, an image formed by the art and imagination of man."
12. Commands repentance of all people:
    "The times of ignorance God overlooked, but now he commands all people everywhere to repent"
13. Will judge the whole world:
    "Because he has fixed a day on which he will judge the world in righteousness by a man whom he has appointed."

14. Raised an appointed man from the dead:
"And of this he has given assurance to all by raising him from the dead."

This God that Paul is proclaiming is the single transcendent judge of all peoples, and radically different from the gods of the Athenians.

Paul's use of pagan quotations

Points 9 and 10 above are based on quotations from pagan authors that do recognise some similar characteristics between Yahweh and their pagan conceptions of god, and which contribute to Paul's defence against the charge of preaching foreign gods.

The first quote from verse 28, I argue, is from Epimenides.[17] The Cretan philosopher Epimenides (c. 600BC) was well known in the ancient world, and we know that Paul was familiar with his work since Paul quotes him in Titus 1:12, referring to him as a prophet.[18] Epimenides was famously called to Athens to help purify the city to stop a pestilence. Diogenes Laertius recounts the story of Epimenides taking some black and white sheep into the Areopagus and releasing them, ordering the people to mark where each sheep rested and to make a sacrifice there to the local god.[19] Ramsay explains that the Athenians believed themselves to be racked by guilt from the massacre of the adherents of Cylon in 612BC.[20] Each

---

[17] Dieppe, "Paul vs. The Pagans" Appendix 2.
[18] For discussion of the attribution of this quotation see: I. Howard Marshall, *The Pastoral Epistles* (London: T & T Clark, 2004), 198-203; William D. Mounce, *Pastoral Epistles* (Word Biblical Commentary; Dallas, Texas: Word, 2000), 397-399. I am assuming here that Paul wrote Titus which is not uncontroversial. For a discussion of authorship options, see in these commentaries. Clare Rothschild points out that: "Scholars today, however, acknowledge as many connections of style and content between Luke-Acts-Titus as between either of these individual works and Paul's undisputed letters." Clare K. Rothschild, *Paul in Athens: The Popular Religious Context of Acts 17* (WUNT; vol. 341; Tübingen: Mohr Siebeck, 2014), 22. Rothschild then argues that this makes the Epimenides connection more plausible.
[19] Diogenes Laertius, *Lives of the Philosophers,* 1.10.110. Don Richardson narrates the whole story in an entertaining way with some embellishments: Don Richardson, *Eternity in their Hearts* (Ventura, California: Regal Books, 1984), 9-25
[20] Sir William. M. Ramsay, "Epimenides," in *Asianic Elements in Greek Civilization: The Gifford Lectures in the University of Edinburgh, 1915-16* (New Haven: Yale University Press, 1927) <http://www.giffordlectures.org/books/asianic-elements-greek-civilisation/chapter-iii-epimenides> (4 October 2018)

local god may have been known or unknown.²¹ Diogenes then narrates: "Hence even to this day altars may be found in different parts of Attica with no name inscribed upon them, which are memorials of this atonement."²² It is likely that the altar "to an unknown god" which Paul references is a deliberate allusion to the Epimenides story and that this would be recognised by the Athenians.²³ Paul builds on this by quoting from Epimenides in his speech. Paul may be hinting that the god who answered the prayers of Epimenides, who they do not know and are not worshipping properly, is actually the God he is proclaiming. This is another way for him to refute the charge of introducing foreign gods to Athens.

In any case Paul is following Jewish practice, later adopted by the Church Fathers, of appropriating a Stoic quotation without in any way endorsing its original meaning.²⁴ Stoic theology was pantheistic, whereas Jewish theology sees God as transcendent, but also omnipresent. Paul can state that 'we live and move in him' and mean it in a Jewish sense. It is clear by now that Paul's concept of God is clearly different from Stoic ideas.

The second quote, that 'we are his offspring' is reckoned to be "one of the most commonly quoted Stoic lines in antiquity."²⁵ It may be taken from Aratus or Cleanthes, and a related saying is attributed to Epimenides.²⁶ It was a common Greek idea that God or Zeus was the father of humanity.²⁷ This idea is also present in Jewish writings.²⁸ In his speech, Paul attributes this quote to "some of your own

---

[21] Ramsay, "Epimenides,"
[22] Diogenes Laertius, *Lives of the Philosophers*, 1.10.110 (ὅθεν ἔτι καὶ νῦν ἔστιν εὑρεῖν κατὰ τοὺς δήμους τῶν Ἀθηναίωι βωμοὺς ἀνωνύμους, ὑπόμνημα τῆς τότε γενομένης ἐξιλάσεως)
[23] On the historicity of such an altar see Dieppe, "Paul vs. The Pagans" Appendix 3.
[24] Bertil Gärtner, *The Areopagus Speech and Natural Revelation* (ASNU; trans. C. H. King; vol. 21; C.W.K. Gleerup: Uppsala, 1955), 167, 193-95
[25] Craig Keener, *Acts: An Exegetical Commentary: Volume 3: 15:1-23:35* (Grand Rapids, Michigan: Baker Academic, 2014), 2660
[26] Rothschild, *Paul in Athens*, 69-70
[27] Keener, *Acts 15:1-23:35*, 2661-63
[28] Keener, *Acts 15:1-23:35*, 2663

poets." In this way he is again arguing against the charge of introducing a foreign god. He is claiming that some of their conceptions of God are correct. It is true that we are God's offspring. But as he goes on to say, this logically means that this God cannot be represented by idols formed by humans (v29). This true God ought not to be worshipped through idols. So, whilst commending the truth of some statements of some of their philosophers about the nature of God, he uses these same truths to criticise their means of worship.

Some stoic philosophers criticised idolatry, but the wider population took idol worship very seriously.[29] Paul's rejection of idolatry is far more decisive and distinctively Jewish than that of the philosophers.[30] Paul sees idolatry as insulting to God and requiring repentance. Note that Paul includes himself in the injunction with "we ought not" rather than "you ought not", thus identifying himself with their position rather than antagonistically wagging his finger at them.[31]

These quotations were originally referring to Zeus, the king of the Greek gods. Paul takes them as true statements about the true creator God. By this time, it is very clear that Paul is not advocating worship of Zeus, nor is he claiming that worship of Zeus is equivalent to worship of the true God. He is using these quotations to show that his conception of God is not entirely different from their conception, whilst at the same time arguing that there are essential differences requiring repentance on their part.

Paul is not basing his main argument on these quotations; they are merely used to support his points.[32] Paul was not claiming that these pagan authors were divinely inspired in a similar manner to the

---

[29] C. Kavin Rowe, *World Upside Down: Reading Acts in the Greco-Roman Age* (Oxford: Oxford University Press, 2009), 35

[30] Keener, *Acts 15:1-23:35*, 2666. See the multiple Old Testament injunctions against idolatry. E.g. Ps 115:1-8; Is 40:18-20; 44:9-20; 46:5-6. Note especially the reference to "gold and silver" in Ps 115:4 (cf. Is 40:19).

[31] John Span, "The Aeropagus: A study in Continuity and Discontinuity," *St Francis Magazine* 6, no. 3 (2010): 568

[32] Ned B. Stonehouse, *The Areopagus Address* (The Tyndale New Testament Lecture; Cambridge: Tyndale, 1949), 29

Jewish Scriptures, and neither would the Athenians have understood this since they did not believe the philosophers had this kind of inspiration themselves.[33] Paul effectively reinterprets these quotations by redefining God for the Athenians and appropriating them to his God rather than to Zeus.[34] Paul's citations demonstrate a partial recognition of significant truths by these poets, and thus by his audience. It is true that we live and move and have our being in God, or by means of God, but not in quite the way that the Stoics or even Epimenides intended. It is also true that we are God's offspring, but again not in the way that the Stoics thought.

I suggest that the use Paul makes of pagan citations legitimises Christians using quotations from the Qur'an in discussions with Muslims. We can point out things that the Qur'an says that Christians would agree with, without in any way attributing inspiration or authority to the Qur'an. Christians will also want to point out where statements in the Qur'an contradict Christian doctrine to clearly demonstrate that we do not agree with the teaching of the Qur'an and do not view it as inspired.

Conclusion

Paul did not start his discussions in Athens with a claim to be worshipping the same god. Rather, as a result of his preaching, he stood accused of introducing foreign gods to Athens. Nor did he end his speech by claiming they were worshipping the same god after all. He claimed that his transcendent God commanded their repentance. What Paul does do is agree with an admission of ignorance about the nature of God in Athenian culture and proclaim that he is there to explain what this God that they are ignorantly attempting to worship is really like. This is a long way from a claim that the Athenians worship the same god as he does.

There are many other aspects of the same God controversy to discuss. Here, I have focussed on the use of Paul's speech in Athens.

---

[33] Pardigon, *Paul Against the Idols: A Contextual Reading of the Areopagus Speech*, 198
[34] Rowe, *World Upside Down*, 40

I argue that Paul's Areopagus address cannot reasonably be used to justify claiming that Muslims and Christians worship the same God. There may be other reasons which can sometimes justify this claim, but Paul's statements in Acts 17 do not support this approach.

Bibliography

Barrett, C. K. *Acts 15-28*. International Critical Commentary. London: T & T Clark, 2004.

Bruce, F. F. *The Book of Acts*. Revised ed., The New International Commentary on the New Testament. Grand Rapids, Michigan: Eerdmans, 1992.

Calvin, John. *Commentary on Acts*. Translated by Henry Beveridge. Vol. 2. Edinburgh: Calvin Translation Society, 1844.

Dieppe, Tim. "Paul vs. the Pagans: The Apologetic Approach of the Areopagus Address." Dissertation, Westminster Theological Centre, 2016.

Gärtner, Bertil. *The Areopagus Speech and Natural Revelation*. Translated by Carolyn Hannay King. Vol. 21, ASNU. C.W.K. Gleerup: Uppsala, 1955.

Gempf, Conrad. "Paul at Athens," Pages 51-54 in *Dictionary of Paul and his Letters*. Edited by Gerald F. Hawthorne, Ralph P. Martin, and Daniel G. Reid. Leicester: IVP, 1993.

Jobes, Karen H. "Distinguishing the Meaning of Greek Verbs in the Semantic Domain for Worship," Pages 201-211 in *Biblical Words and their Meaning: An Introduction to Lexical Semantics*. Edited by Moisés Silva. Michigan: Zondervan, 1994.

Keener, Craig. *Acts: An Exegetical Commentary: Volume 3: 15:1-23:35*. Grand Rapids, Michigan: Baker Academic, 2014.

Marshall, I. Howard. *The Pastoral Epistles*. London: T & T Clark, 2004.

Mounce, William D. *Pastoral Epistles*. Word Biblical Commentary. Dallas, Texas: Word, 2000.

Pardigon, Flavien O.C. *Paul Against the Idols: A Contextual Reading of the Areopagus Speech*. Eugene: Wipf and Stock Publishers, 2019.

Priest, Robert J. "Wheaton and the Controversy Over Whether Muslims and Christians Worship the Same God." *Occasional Bulletin of the Evangelical Missiological Society* Special Edition, no. (2016): 1-3, 31.

Ramsay, Sir William. M. "Epimenides," in *Asianic Elements in Greek Civilization: The Gifford Lectures in the University of Edinburgh, 1915-16*. New Haven: Yale University Press, 1927.

Richardson, Don. *Eternity in their Hearts*. Revised ed. Ventura, California: Regal Books, 1984.

Rothschild, Clare K. *Paul in Athens: The Popular Religious Context of Acts 17*. Vol. 341, WUNT. Tübingen: Mohr Siebeck, 2014.

Rowe, C. Kavin. *World Upside Down: Reading Acts in the Greco-Roman Age*. Oxford: Oxford University Press, 2009.

Sandnes, Karl Olav. "Paul and Socrates : The Aim of Paul's Areopagus Speech." *Journal for the Study of the New Testament*, no. 50 (1993): 13-26.

Solomon, Sam. *Not the Same God: Is the Qur'anic Allah the Lord God of the Bible?* London: Wilberforce Publications, 2016.

Span, John. "The Aeropagus: A study in Continuity and Discontinuity." *St Francis Magazine* 6, no. 3 (2010): 517-582.

"Special Edition: Wheaton and the Controversy Over Whether Muslims and Christians Worship the Same God." *Occasional Bulletin of the Evangelical Missiological Society*, no. (2016).

Stonehouse, Ned B. *The Areopagus Address.* The Tyndale New Testament Lecture. Cambridge: Tyndale, 1949.

Volf, Miroslav. *Allah: A Christian Response.* New York: HarperCollins, 2012.

12

SOLUTIONS FOR A SEGREGATED SOCIETY

Note: This article was originally published in 2016 following the publication of the Casey Review into opportunity and integration.[1] The review painted a devastating picture of the lack of integration of Muslims into UK society. Here I highlight the key findings of the review and propose ten robust policies that would help to tackle the problems that multiculturalism has landed us with. Not one of these policies has yet been implemented. It remains the case that these policies would go a long way towards tackling the problem of multiculturalism.

The Casey Review and what to do about it

In 2016, former head of the Equalities and Human Rights Commission, Trevor Phillips, warned that, "integration of Muslims will probably be the hardest task we have ever faced."[2] He was commenting on a survey showing the segregation of minority communities in our society. In 2015, the then Prime Minister and Home Secretary commissioned Dame Louise Casey to conduct a review into opportunity and integration in our society. Reports in October 2016 suggested that the Home Office was trying to censor this report,[3] but it has now been published in full.[4]

---

[1] https://christianconcern.com/comment/solutions-for-a-segregated-society-the-casey-review-and-what-to-do-about-it/
[2] https://www.thetimes.co.uk/article/my-sons-living-hell-j72t7fppc
[3] https://christianconcern.com/comment/home-office-censors-report-into-immigration-integration-and-radical-islam/
[4] https://www.gov.uk/government/publications/the-casey-review-a-review-into-opportunity-and-integration

The problem

The report makes for some alarming, if not surprising reading for anyone who has followed discussions about these issues. Perhaps the most striking illustration of the segregation in our society noted in the report is that a survey of pupils at a non-faith secondary school showed that they believed Britain to be between 50% to 90% Asian. That secondary school children in Britain would believe this is extraordinary and shocking, and a powerful demonstration of how segregated some communities are.

In 2013, 50% of ethnic minority students were in schools where ethnic minorities were the majority. In January 2015, there were 511 schools across 43 local authorities with 50% or more pupils from Pakistani or Bangladeshi ethnic backgrounds. The report states that, "Muslims tend to live in highest residential concentrations at ward level." In some wards in 2011, Muslim populations were between 70% and 85%. With this level of segregation, it is unsurprising that secondary school pupils growing up in these areas would assume that Britain is over 50% Asian.

The report points out that the Muslim population in the UK grew by 72% between 2001 and 2011 – a faster growth than any other religious group. This is due to both immigration and higher birth rates. Integration has been "undermined by high levels of transnational marriage" whereby the children of Muslims in the UK marry someone from Pakistan, creating a "'first generation in every generation' phenomenon in which each new generation grows up with a foreign-born parent." A study at Bradford Royal Infirmary found that 80% of babies of Pakistani ethnicity had at least one parent born outside the UK.

The report contains some devastating criticism of current government policy and practice:

> "Too many public institutions, national and local, state and non-state, have gone so far to accommodate diversity and freedom of expression that they have ignored or even condoned regressive, divisive and harmful cultural and religious practices, for fear of being branded racist or Islamophobic."

"At its most serious, it might mean public sector leaders ignoring harm or denying abuse."

"Some public institutions have stepped back and let groups attempt to undermine efforts to prevent terrorism and further alienate the communities we need to engage and protect – whether that is from terrorist radicalisers, perpetrators of violence and hate, criminal gangs or groomers intent on exploiting and abusing vulnerable people."

In relation to Islam in particular, the report highlights evidence of discrimination in Sharia councils that operate in this country. It also discusses the problems arising from unregistered marriages and polygamous 'marriages' that appear to be "more commonplace than might be expected." As the report says in this context:

"We must put a stop to cases where, in the name of religion, women and children are given short shrift, discriminated against and denied the rights that this country provides for everyone."

The report also warns:

"We found a growing sense of grievance among sections of the Muslim population, and a stronger sense of identification with the plight of the 'Ummah', or global Muslim community."

It is very clear then, that a segregated society has emerged from the promotion of multicultural relativism in Britain. Instead of an imagined multicultural utopia, we in fact have a plurality of segregated monocultures. Multiculturalism has failed and damaged our society. Although Islam is not the focus of this report, it is rightly singled out for the segregation it has promoted and established in this country. Everyone agrees that there is a problem here. Dame Louise Casey said: "None of the 800 or more people that we met, nor any of the two hundred plus written submissions to the review, said there wasn't a problem to solve." So, what are the solutions?

Some Solutions

Although Dame Louise Casey is robust in exposing the problems, her policy recommendations are remarkably weak. They amount, in substance, to promoting integration by measuring it and identifying best practice; promoting the proverbial 'British values', but also British laws and history; and considering the introduction of an integration oath for immigrants, and a new oath for holders of public office. These are useful initial steps, but there is much more that can and should be done.

Perhaps I can suggest some more robust responses to the various problems outlined. The problem is big and it will not just go away or be solved by promoting integration and British values, or insisting on oaths being taken. There are, however, several clear and tangible steps that can be taken. Here are ten ideas to start with, in no particular order.

First, adopt Baroness Cox's Bill to curb the operation of Sharia councils, thus protecting the fundamental principle of one law for all.[5]

Second, enforce the registration of religious marriages so as to protect the rights of women and prevent a culture of polygamy arising.[6] (This policy is recommended on page 135 of the report.)

Third, ban the face veil in public to show that oppression and subjugation of women is objectively wrong, and to promote integration. Burqa and niqab face coverings have now been banned in 16 countries around the world including Tunisia, Austria, Denmark, France, Belgium, and Switzerland.[7]

Fourth, tighten up the marriage visa rules so that we reduce the "first generation in every generation" phenomenon.

Fifth, hold police forces accountable for treating all people equally under the law, regardless of their background culture, religion, or ethnicity. This would stop police forces from turning a 'blind eye' to offences committed by ethnic minorities for fear of being branded 'racist', as happened in Rotherham.

Sixth, stop promoting Islamic finance which only serves to promote a radical interpretation of the Qur'an and to hinder integration.

---

[5] https://equalandfree.org/
[6] https://christianconcern.com/comment/women-suffering-on-a-large-scale-due-to-unregistered-religious-marriages/
[7] https://en.wikipedia.org/wiki/Burqa_by_country

Seventh, unashamedly identify this nation as a Christian country whose laws and culture are based around Biblical values which are objectively better for society as a whole, and therefore also promote the teaching of the Bible and Christianity in schools.

Eighth, rather than insisting that all religions should be respected, the government should robustly defend free speech so that people are clearly able to expose the discriminatory nature of Islam and the falsity of its teaching without fear of prosecution for religious harassment.

Ninth, ban foreign funding of Islam in the UK. Islamic countries see funding of mosque building overseas as a way of expanding the influence of their own forms of Islam. This should be stopped.

Tenth, reduce overall levels of immigration. Everyone agrees that integration is not working, so we need to reduce the absolute numbers of immigrants in order to facilitate some progress on integration. Otherwise continued high levels of immigration only exacerbate the problem.

It is only with robust policies like these that we will start to properly deal with the problem. Dame Casey's review is a step forward in acknowledging and describing the extent of the problem we face. What we now need is for more people to agree that robust action is required to tackle it.